Everyday Politics of the World Economy

How do our everyday actions shape and transform the world economy? This volume of original essays argues that current scholarship in international political economy (IPE) is too highly focused on powerful states and large international institutions. The contributors examine specific forms of 'everyday' actions to demonstrate how small-scale actors and their decisions can shape the global economy. They analyse a range of seemingly ordinary or subordinate actors, including peasants, working classes and trade unions, lower-middle and middle classes, female migrant labourers and Eastern diasporas, and examine how they have agency in transforming their political and economic environments. This book offers a novel way of thinking about everyday forms of change across a range of topical issues including globalisation, international finance, trade, taxation, consumerism, labour rights and regimes. It will appeal to students and scholars of politics, international relations, political economy and sociology.

JOHN M. HOBSON is Professor of Politics and International Relations at the University of Sheffield.

LEONARD SEABROOKE is Associate Professor in the International Center for Business and Politics at the Copenhagen Business School and Adjunct Senior Fellow in the Department of International Relations at the Australian National University.

Everyday Politics of the World Economy

Edited by

John M. Hobson

and

Leonard Seabrooke

CAMBRIDGE
UNIVERSITY PRESS

CAMBRIDGE UNIVERSITY PRESS
Cambridge, New York, Melbourne, Madrid, Cape Town, Singapore, São Paulo

Cambridge University Press
The Edinburgh Building, Cambridge CB2 8RU, UK

Published in the United States of America by Cambridge University Press,
New York

www.cambridge.org
Information on this title: www.cambridge.org/9780521701631

First published 2007

Printed in the United Kingdom at the University Press, Cambridge

A catalogue record for this book is available from the British Library

ISBN 978-0-521-87772-5 hardback
ISBN 978-0-521-70163-1 paperback

Contents

Tables

Contributors

MICHELE FORD is Lecturer in the Department of Indonesian Studies at the University of Sydney.

ANDREW HEROD is Professor of Geography at the University of Georgia.

JOHN M. HOBSON is Professor of Politics and International Relations at the University of Sheffield.

PAUL LANGLEY is Senior Lecturer in International Political Economy at Northumbria University.

ADAM DAVID MORTON is Senior Lecturer in the School of Politics and International Relations at the University of Nottingham.

NICOLA PIPER is Senior Lecturer in Geography at Swansea University.

LEONARD SEABROOKE is Associate Professor in the International Center for Business and Politics at the Copenhagen Business School, and Adjunct Senior Fellow in the Department of International Relations, RSPAS, The Australian National University.

J. C. SHARMAN is Associate Professor in the Griffith Asia Institute at Griffith University.

SHOGO SUZUKI is Lecturer in Politics at the University of Manchester.

ARA WILSON is Associate Professor of Women's Studies and Cultural Anthropology at Duke University.

Acknowledgements

A great deal of work has gone into the making of this book. There were four periods of intensive intellectual planning and organisation for the book, some of it in cafés in various places around the world, and much of it over the phone or through document transfers by email. All of the authors in this book were invited for a specific purpose in providing different case studies of 'Everyday IPE', as well as maintaining coherence around the book's key conceptual aims. Following the first submission deadline we wrote extensive comments on the chapters and sent them back for revision. The same process occurred after the second revised submission and most of the chapters in this collection have been revised at least twice. Our thanks go to the contributors to this volume for their patience. We also thank the anonymous readers at Cambridge University Press for their exceptionally insightful, detailed and helpful comments, all of which have made this a much improved book.

Thanks are also due to many colleagues and scholars who offered their thoughts and comments on draft chapters. John thanks colleagues in the Department of Politics at the University of Sheffield for their expert and critical comments on parts of the manuscript – notably Andrew Gamble, Jean Grugel, Graham Harrison, Tony Heron, Tony Payne and Georgina Waylen (as well as his PhD student John Smith). Len thanks colleagues at the Australian National University for their feedback and advice on parts of the manuscript also distributed in seminars, particularly Ben Kerkvliet and Barry Hindess. Len also thanks his colleagues in the Department of International Relations, RSPAS at the Australian National University, where much of the initial work on the book was done, as well as his colleagues in the International Center for Business and Politics at the Copenhagen Business School, where conversations about everyday politics were intermingled with those on institutional change. Special thanks must go in particular to André Broome, Robert Denemark, Colin Hay, Craig Murphy, Ann Tickner, Robert O'Brien and John Ravenhill for their often detailed and always insightful feedback on the project. Our thanks also go to Mary-Louise Hickey for proof-reading the manuscript prior to submission, and to John Haslam at Cambridge University Press for his patience and ever-helpful advice.

Last, but of course, not least, a big thank you to our partners and families – John thanks Cecelia Thomas and Len thanks Anna Carnerup – for allowing us the time to sit around in cafés and chat about the more everyday sources of change in the international political economy.

John M. Hobson and Leonard Seabrooke
Sheffield and Copenhagen

1 Everyday IPE: revealing everyday forms of change in the world economy

John M. Hobson and Leonard Seabrooke

[T]he period of relative calm in the world political economy in the second half of the 1980s was used by many scholars as an opportunity for strengthening the scholastic rigor of IPE without questioning its, often unstated, foundations. Many of us have not been particularly open to rearranging the hierarchy of the substantive issues that IPE studies, nor have we been happy to muck about with the hierarchy of values attached to those issues. (Murphy and Tooze 1991b: 5)

While the general method of analysis is well-established and widely accepted, this hardly means that IPE has exhausted its potential. In fact, it is surprising how narrow is the range of analytical and empirical problems that existing scholarship has tackled in earnest ... It may be that a great deal of theoretical, analytical, and methodological brush needs to be cleared. (Frieden and Martin 2002: 146)

Our everyday actions have important consequences for the constitution and transformation of the local, national, regional and global contexts. How, what and with whom we spend, save, invest, buy and produce in our ordinary lives shapes markets and how states choose to intervene in them. The political, economic and social networks with which we associate ourselves provide us not only with meaning about how we think economic policy is made, but also constitute vehicles for how economic policy, both at home and abroad, should be made.

Surprisingly, however, conventional work in international political economy (IPE) has little to tell us about how our everyday actions transform the world economy. The conventional focus is on hegemony, trade and financial flows and international economic regulatory institutions that exist at the international level (i.e., 'the small number of big and important things'). Such examinations are conducted through reference only to the elites who wield power in the world economy or to the structures that constitute it. Typically, while everyday actors are assumed to exist they, nevertheless, have no role to play in shaping the world economy. It is as if elite actors or international institutions write the script, which everyday actors receive in a passive way. Accordingly, in

1

focusing only on macro-level institutions and processes, so conventional IPE has become detached from the real lives of everyday people. Or as one prominent scholar notes, 'Outlining everyday people in everyday places helps us think of international politics [and economics] existing in places International Relations bypasses through fealty to the relations of only a few international actors of "importance" – great (state) powers and their regimes, decision-makers, economic zones' (Sylvester 1996: 266–7). The thrust of this book is to reveal not simply everyday actors but, more importantly, the manifold ways in which everyday actions can transform the world economy. As we explain later, our central purpose is neither to marginalise the importance of the dominant elites nor to reify the agency of the 'weak', but rather to analyse the ways in which the weak affect and respond to the dominant and how in the process this interactive relationship generates change in the global economy.

'Bringing everyday actions in' in this way enables us to open up new angles for 'doing IPE'. Our task is to produce a sociological framework for IPE – what we call 'everyday IPE' (EIPE) – which can address existing lacunae in what we call 'regulatory IPE' (RIPE). Note that this should not be confused with regulation theory. As shall be explained shortly, we characterise the mainstream as 'regulatory' because the issue of order and the regulation of the world economy occupies centre-stage of the research focus. By contrast, EIPE focuses on transformation in the world economy that has slipped the gaze and purview of RIPE.

This distinction between RIPE and EIPE has clear echoes of the work by Craig Murphy and Roger Tooze in their argument for a more 'heterodox' IPE (Murphy and Tooze 1991a). Crucially, Murphy and Tooze, as have subsequent 'reflectivist' scholars, took their cue from the standard orthodox claim made famous by Robert Keohane (1988: 392): that 'reflectivism' will fail to gain ground until it develops its own coherent research program. They replied by invoking the standard reflectivist claim, that 'there is not *a* unitary reflectivist research program in IPE' (Murphy and Tooze 1991c: 21), and that heterodox IPE is defined by its *pluralism* of research programs. Accepting the *diversity* of research programs rather than trying to reduce them to one is a vital aspect of their thinking – something which subsequently became a mantra for heterodox IPE scholars (e.g., Amin *et al.* 1994; Gills 2001: 236).

But to many conventional IPE scholars, 'heterodoxy' has stood for a bewildering amount of seemingly exotic, if not impenetrable, theoretical discussions with no easy avenue into understanding them, nor a clear empirical pathway to tread in order to undergo IPE research and teaching (see e.g., Krasner 1996). And even for those considering a jump from the grand ship of 'orthodoxy', the alternative may appear to many as akin to an all-too-distant dinghy rocking on tempestuous, murky seas. We, however, avoid what William Connolly calls 'theoretical postponism' – 'the inability to establish secure epistemological grounds for a theory with an obligation to defer infinitely the construction of general theories of global politics' (Connolly 1991: 55). We do require coherence in delineating (not delimiting) what heterodoxy stands for, as well as for generating a manageable empirical 'research agenda' and teaching framework. We seek to achieve this by identifying types of everyday action and key themes that speak to concerns at the heart of both orthodox and heterodox IPE.

Perhaps, ironically, conventional and heterodox IPEs share one thing in common: a commitment to research programs in one way or another. Here we turn away from such a focus. Rather than a 'research program' that delimits what information we consider necessary to contribute knowledge to an existing body of thought, we stress the importance of 'puzzle sets'. These invite us to think comparatively and sociologically, and to include everyday actions and actors as important sources of new information to answer a puzzle. We define a puzzle as an unsolved or counterintuitive problem derived from an understanding of how the world economy works that is to be tested empirically. The problem itself is not pre-defined by theories and approaches within a research program, nor is the use of theories and approaches defined by previous attempts to solve the problem deemed appropriate. Rather, appropriate theories and approaches are established through trial and error as the scholar seeks new information to answer the puzzle. Critically, puzzle sets call upon the scholar to expand the range of information necessary to provide a convincing answer to a puzzle, rather than relying on the confirmation of *a priori* theoretical assumptions through the selection of empirical material. Put simply, this approach rejects the tendency to 'data mine' to confirm a particular theory.

This book brings to light a series of puzzles that are not considered by conventional or heterodox IPE. Examples of these are: 'why has the Organisation for Economic Co-operation and Development's (OECD's) harmful tax practices initiative been so slow in undermining tax havens?' (Sharman), or 'why is everyday finance on property and pensions not considered a source of financial power?' (respectively, Seabrooke and Langley), or 'why are peasants not considered drivers of economic change?' (Morton). Conventional IPE considers such puzzles as beyond the ambit of favoured research programs, while heterodox IPE considers them too heavily focused on 'problem-solving' rather than maintaining a critical distance (Cox 1986). A focus on either 'out-explaining' *within* a research program to rescue it from empirical puzzles or anomalies, or avenues to emancipation that consign such puzzles to obscurity, will necessarily provide us with only partial information of how the world economy works.

One clear pay-off of our framework lies in its ability to reflect about new ways of policy-making to capture real world changes. After all, the aim of the study of IPE is to find out how political and economic change occurs within the world economy, rather than engaging in the numerous intellectual acrobatics that are constantly required when working within a closed research program. Furthermore, increasing standards of social scientific rigour within the orthodox approaches have led to an ever-increasing gap between academic scholarship and work with firm policy implications (Katzenstein *et al.* 1998: 684), while heterodox approaches often have little constructive to say about policy. This is a problem for academics who seek to influence policy, but also for students of IPE who need to relate their intellectual understanding of the discipline to the way things work in their everyday lives. This is an important aspect of EIPE and is considered at more length in the Conclusion.

Our emphasis on 'puzzle-sets' allows us to respond to the call from 'ultra orthodox' scholars, such as Jeffrey Frieden and Lisa Martin, that conventional IPE has become too narrow and leaves much unexplored (cited at the beginning). Moreover, our stress is not simply on any puzzle one may wish to include, but on puzzles that are closely related to our central theme: how everyday actions transform the world economy. In answering such puzzles we are confident that we will reveal not only how everyday actions and actors are important to the world economy, but how their agency provides avenues to emancipation. Often heterodox approaches in IPE use a critical eye to examine the structural impediments faced by non-elites, particularly through discussions of 'hegemony' or 'imperialism', as well as telling us about how new constitutional forces discipline behaviour (Gill 1995). What they often fail to tell us, however, is how the subordinate mediate and at times shape these so-called top-down processes (see also Hobson 2007). We further the call for emancipation by revealing sites of agency, including cases where one would assume there was little or no capacity for voice. In this sense EIPE does not so much furnish a *via media* between conventional and heterodox IPEs, but instead provides a clear 'value added' in offering an alternative approach to studying the world economy while simultaneously providing critical information for the sustenance of both.

Nevertheless we also want to emphasise the point that EIPE does not necessarily have to be realised through a puzzle-set framework. Put differently, it is perfectly possible to develop EIPE through deploying a research program. Our point is simply that a puzzle-set framework enables us to pinpoint many sources of everyday action and change that tend to get obscured within prevailing research programs in the extant heterodox and orthodox schools.

This chapter is divided into two sections. In the first section we examine the mainstream regulatory approach and point to some of its limitations, while in the second we focus on our preferred approach, elucidating its conception of everyday agency and everyday-inspired change.

The organising framework of regulatory IPE: who governs and who benefits?

Standard textbooks often present the triumvirate of traditional theories in table form in order to reveal the differences between the three. Distinguishing differences between the theories is not merely of academic interest since the questions generated within paradigms directly inform policy choices (Katzenstein 1976: 13). In Table 1.1 we (re)present the theories of IPE, juxtaposing regulatory theory from EIPE. We depict three approaches (given that regulatory theory can be sub-divided).

RIPE and EIPE are differentiated in terms of the initial organising questions that lie at their core. The standard regulatory approach – found especially within neoliberal institutionalism, neorealism and, more recently, systemic constructivism – opens with the fundamental question: 'who governs and how is international order regulated?' Certain structures or institutions or particular elites that supply order are then selected as the object of study. This creates a highly parsimonious framework that simplifies the study of the complex world economy into discrete, manageable chunks.

While most IPE scholars take this parsimonious framework for granted, it bears noting that the traditional focus on 'order' is to a large extent a function of the birth of the discipline at a particular time and place, which in turn imbued RIPE with a specific identity (Katzenstein *et al.* 1998: 655–7). RIPE was born in the US during the early 1970s when the world economy was going into recession, with a concern to restore world order and economic growth. In the process mainstream IPE and IR scholars implicitly draw on liberal political theory. So Hobbes finds his approximate manifestation in neorealist hegemonic stability theory (HST), where a dominant hegemonic power takes the form of a benign global leviathan that supplies order and all other states accept this as an unspoken social contract. Conversely, in the absence of a hegemon the world economy devolves into a war of all against all (Kindleberger 1973; Gilpin 1975, 1981, 1987). The Lockean equivalent is that of neoliberal institutionalism, wherein states in the international system, like

Table 1.1. *Juxtaposing aims and approaches in regulatory and everyday IPE*

	Regulatory IPE (neorealism/ neoliberalism/ systemic constructivism)	Regulatory IPE (classical structuralism)	Everyday IPE (sociological)
Organising question	Who governs?	Who benefits?	Who acts and how do their actions enable change?
Unit of analysis	Hegemons/great powers, international regimes, ideational entrepreneurs	Capitalist world economy, structures of rule	Everyday actors interacting with elites and structures
Prime empirical focus	Supply of order and welfare maximisation by elites	Maintenance of the powerful and the unequal distribution of benefits	Social transformative *and* regulatory processes enacted, or informed, by everyday actions
Locus of agency	Top-down	Top-down	Bottom-up
Level of analysis	Systemic	Systemic	Complex/holistic
Ontology	Structuralist	Structuralist	Agential or structurationist
Epistemology	Rationalist/positivist or interpretivist	Rationalist/positivist	Interpretivist/post-positivist and rationalist
Conception of change	Coercion/mimetic conformity/radical uncertainty	Coercion	Defiance/mimetic challenge/ axiorationality

individuals in society, come together and, through an informal social contract, set up a loose set of international institutions or regimes which enable cooperation and long-term welfare maximisation (Keohane 1984). These remain in place only so long as they continue to enhance the interests of states, given that states can choose to opt out of the informal social contract that underpins a particular regime. Most recently – at least in mainstream international politics – the emergence of 'systemic constructivism' has largely taken the form of a Kantian analogy, where international cooperation between states is envisaged as yet more deeply entrenched than that specified by neoliberalism (e.g., Wendt 1999; Finnemore 1996). Indeed systemic constructivists are primarily interested in revealing the positive ways in which states are socialised into deep cooperation within an increasingly tight international society. Thus if the neorealist/neoliberal debate is a synonym for the 'conflict versus cooperation debate', then we envisage systemic constructivism as located on the right-hand side of neoliberalism. It also represents a contemporary form of the neo-functionalist literature on the European Community developed by Ernst Haas and others (Haas 1959; see also Rosamond 2005).

Systemic constructivists have rightly questioned how states create their identities and their self-interests but they have not questioned the regulatory problematique. More importantly, if constructivism is meant to bring sociological analysis into the study of the international political economy (Parsons 2003; Barnett and Finnemore 2004), one wonders where society is beyond the elites. As Colin Hay points out, constructivists require a prominent elite actor to provide an 'ideational focus for the reconstruction of the perceived self-interest of the population at large' (Hay 2004: 210; see also Blyth 2005; Seabrooke 2007c). Their key focus has been on how elite actors – either within international organisations/institutions or within domestic society – provide the function of ideational entrepreneurs in building international cooperation by binding new ideas and/or norms across states. It is, therefore, no coincidence that studies on European monetary union are dominant here (see McNamara 1998; Parsons 2003). Here ideas are understood as weapons wielded by big and powerful actors, who are backed by their own political and material resources in helping to push them through (Parsons 2003: 178, 235). Moreover, within economic constructivism the tendency has been to focus on key ideational entrepreneurs only in times of radical uncertainty – usually associated with periodic economic crises – rather than periods of 'normality' (Seabrooke 2007c).

In a complementary move, a second organising question has also guided the study of IPE: 'Who benefits?' This was initiated by what we call 'classical structuralists', who view the world economy's central dynamic as governed by the structure of capitalism (Frank 1967; Emmanuel 1972; Amin 1973; Wallerstein 1974). By focusing on the capitalist world structure, they argue that the world economy operates in favour of the rich Northern core, which gains through unequal exchange at the expense of the poor Southern periphery. Accordingly, as a wealth of scholars have pointed out, in reifying global structure so they are necessarily unable to provide a picture of bottom-up agency (e.g., Cox 1986; Payne 1998, 2005; Murphy and Nelson 2001; cf. Grugel and Hout 1999a, 1999b). Again, it was no coincidence that dependency/world-systems theory entered IPE at the moment of the discipline's birth in the early 1970s, given that the politics of North-South relations was rapidly becoming important at that time. Moreover, the Organization of the Petroleum Exporting Countries (OPEC) oil shock and calls for a new international economic order (NIEO) by the Group of 77 developing countries (G77) (coupled with its 'failure') consolidated the approach's place in the discipline.

Nevertheless, there are two qualifying points of note here. For while this approach has often been thought of as *the* Marxist theory of IPE it is, of course, striking that of all the critics that this approach has faced, orthodox Marxists have been probably the most vociferous. Robert Brenner, of course, likened dependency theory to a 'neo-Smithian Marxism' which, by focusing only on economic transmissions between core and periphery, obscured the importance of class exploitation within the mode of production (Brenner 1977; also Laclau 1977). This opened the way forward for analyses where agents – in this case classes – were reinstated at the centre, thus entering the ground of EIPE. Moreover, with its criticism of dependency theory as overly structuralist, Gramscianism provides another strong Marxist potential for contributing to an EIPE (e.g., Cox 1986, 1987; Augelli and Murphy 1988; Payne 2005). However, as Robert O'Brien (2000) has stressed, it is surprising how some of its chief spokespersons have at times reified the power of a transnational ruling class at the expense of exploring the agency of the dominated (e.g., Gill 1990; Van der Pijl 1998). Nevertheless, Gramscianism does offer a potential space for subaltern agents, not least through its emphasis on the importance of counter-hegemonic blocs. And notably, in this volume, Adam Morton produces one such version that returns the focus squarely onto 'subaltern' agency.

Second, we have labelled traditional world-systems theory/dependency theory as 'classical structuralism' in order to differentiate it from a more recent departure that can be called 'neo-classical world system theory' (see Hobson 2000: 141–2), or 'world system history' (Denemark *et al.* 2000). This is a new approach that extends its classical predecessor in new directions, not least by arguing that a world system has been around for several millennia. And one of its strengths is not only to reconsider agency but above all to break with Eurocentrism – see the contributions in the three pioneering edited volumes (Chase-Dunn and Hall 1991; Frank and Gills 1996; Denemark *et al* 2000). Notable too is that these authors have often developed their approach and its variants in contradistinction to classical structuralism – see Wallerstein (1996) and Amin (1996) for their replies. Accordingly, we do not include this recent approach within the regulatory framework.

Finally, it might be assumed that rational choice and public choice perspectives provide an alternative approach and converge with EIPE insofar as they focus on individual agents and bottom-up processes (e.g., Frey 1986). But we argue that they fit squarely within the regulatory framework insofar as they seek to provide a 'better' account of the sources of regulation and order. Furthermore, while a focus on individual choice is certainly part of EIPE, nevertheless, we envisage such choices as being informed by historically and socially contingent identities and interests. By contrast, rational choice theorists posit a self-maximising individual often obscured from time and place or social context. Even the more sensitive rational choice analyses that see actors' values as important require them to be understood as 'deep core beliefs' that are culturally fixed and path dependent (e.g., North 1990; North and Thomas 1973). Such a depiction of social life masks many of the forms of transformation in and of the world economy that we seek to reveal. And finally, perhaps the most fundamental of differences between rational choice and EIPE is that for the former, individuals often 'bandwagon' with the dominant or seek to dominate others. This can blind us to revealing everyday contestations to the exercise of power by elites.

It is undisputed that neorealism, neoliberalism and classical structuralism are accepted as the defining core of IPE (though systemic constructivism is now emerging as a fourth candidate, or as a replacement for classical structuralism – see e.g., Gilpin 2001). The 'common sense' of what constitutes the core is so ingrained that it provides us with clear avenues to study the key topics of IPE, such as American hegemony, international regimes, globalisation, and North/South relations (cf. Murphy and Tooze 1991b, 1991c; Payne 2005). These ways of studying the key topics of IPE have undoubtedly provided dozens of important insights that are indispensable for the discipline. However, we question the extent to which these approaches to IPE reveal new sites of information that can assist us in better understanding the dominant topics. For example, how can we understand the 'hegemony' or 'imperialism' of great powers in the world economy without revealing their domestic sources and the challenges to their identity and power that are issued by everyday actors (Langley, Seabrooke and Suzuki, this volume)? Equally, how can we understand the globalisation of markets without attempting to reveal how formal and informal sub-national organisations seek to shape the form that globalisation takes (Herod, Ford and Piper, Morton and Sharman, this volume)? Moreover, how can we understand regimes in the world economy only by focusing on formal institutions without recognising the many informal regimes that are created by everyday actors? To do so puts policy design ahead of real world implementation. Or finally, how can we hope to understand the genesis or spread of market capitalism and the diffusion of globalisation if we view these processes through a framework that sees them as primarily a European or American invention, when Eastern agents have played such important roles here (Hobson and Wilson, this volume)? These questions ask us to reveal information at the local and transnational levels that tell us how the actions of the key players in IPE are contested by everyday actions. They also ask us to discover information about how everyday actions inform the dominant processes of the world economy, as well as point out moments of their transformation. In both cases, the constraints of power are unmasked, thereby providing a more complete picture of how the world economy works.

The key problem with delimiting what information we want to tell us about the world economy is that it leads to a number of distortions. Key among these is a pervasive problem of 'selecting winners' and 'deselecting' all others on the grounds that they are 'losers'. As a number of scholars point out, standard IPE courses devote much time to analysing the actions of US hegemony-as-winner and whose interests are equated with the universal, the assumption being that we can learn most, if not all, of what we need to know through such a focus (Tooze 1988; Murphy and Tooze 1991a; Wæver 1998; Holsti 1985; Crawford and Jarvis 2001; Nossal 2001). Notwithstanding the bluntness of the formulation, Stephen Krasner's words at the 1990 American Political Science Association conference provide an important example: 'Sure people in Luxembourg have good ideas. But who gives a damn? Luxembourg ain't hegemonic' (cited in Higgott 1991: 99). And this was echoed by Kenneth Waltz who tells us that '[i]t would be as ridiculous to construct a theory of international politics based on Malaysia and Costa Rica as it would be to construct an economic theory of oligopolistic competition based on the minor firms in a sector of an economy' (Waltz 1979: 72). Indeed this bias, both in terms of IPE teaching and research, can be found in many text books (e.g., Blake and Walters 1976; Gilpin 1987, 2001; Spero 1992; Lairson and Skidmore 1993; Balaam and Veseth 1996; Cohn 2000), though by no means all (Schwartz 1994; Peterson 2003; O'Brien and Williams 2004).

The standard text books reel off an almost identical series of topics and issues, often in virtually the same order and all of which are situated within a winner/loser dichotomy. They typically begin in 1944 with the Bretton Woods agreement and the rise of US hegemony as the principal guarantors of world order and global welfare maximisation. The next chapter might look at international monetary management and the regulation of the fixed exchange rate system by the International Monetary Fund (IMF). And the next chapter usually recounts the story of the IMF alongside the General Agreement on Tariffs and Trade (GATT) to account for the spread of free trade and the concomitant growth of world trade. North-South issues are usually dealt with, though consistent with the privileged focus on the powerful North, the story is one of 'southern failure'. Thus the calls for a NIEO in the 1970s on the back of the successful economic coup that was delivered by oil cartel power end with the failure of non-oil cartel power, thereby ensuring that prime focus should remain upon the North. We then receive a deepening of the story of 'Third World failure' and 'Northern hegemony' with a strong focus on the Third World debt crisis and the various Northern 'plans' and IMF structural adjustment programs that were imposed on the 'failing' economies of the Southern debtors. Finally, while there is often a chapter on Japan and the East Asian newly industrialising countries (NICs), this focus weakened with Japan's recession after 1991 and was terminated with the 1997 East Asian financial crisis, thereby returning the focus back on to the US-as-winner. None of this is to say that these topics are unworthy of consideration – merely that they obscure the many other 'bottom-up' constitutive processes that inform the world economy.

Not surprisingly the elite suppliers of order – viewed as power-makers – constitute only a very small minority of the world's population. For neo-realists it is the actions of the US hegemonic state that are focused upon; for neoliberals it is the actions of state-created international regimes/ institutions; for systemic constructivists it is the actions of ideational elites or individuals; and for classical structuralists it is often state elites and the transnational capitalist class. It is as if the study of the world economy can be gleaned by examining the actions of ten per cent of the world at most, while the other ninety per cent are but power-takers whose actions are inconsequential for the making of the world economy. And it is to assume that this ten per cent are responsible for 'the big and important things' (read 'the only significant things worthy of study') that go on in the world economy. That this top ten per cent should corner the market for scholarly attention is justified on the grounds that they devise the rules and distribute the benefits owing to the fact that they are the winners. Of course, understanding the processes of power and distribution is important and we in no way wish to dismiss this. But such an exclusive focus means that 'doing IPE' becomes a circular process of selecting 'winners' while deselecting the 'insignificant' majority, who are cast in the role of losers or passive beneficiaries/victims and, therefore, have no impact either in effecting change or making their own economic destinies. In a recent book this has been aptly characterised through an 'iceberg metaphor', where the top ten per cent are likened to the iceberg's exposed tip, while the other ninety per cent are invisible, being hidden below the waterline (Tétreault and Lipschutz 2005: 167). Moreover, regulatory theory's focus on the 'big things' means that IPE happens 'out there' at several steps removed from the lives of everyday people (George 1994). Indeed we ask: are we really to believe that the ninety per cent of the world's population who are conventionally ignored have *no* input into shaping their own lives, if not others around and beyond them?

It seems that IPE has reached an impasse – a view that others are increasingly sharing. Indeed a range of scholars are now developing various approaches which rethink IPE so as to move out of the impasse, some of which overlap with our theme on everyday agency. Most prominent here is the work on extending IPE beyond the core economies, which in turn requires new conceptualisations beyond the assumptions held by the orthodoxy (Neuman 1998; Chan 1999; Dunn and Shaw 2001; A. B. Tickner 2002, 2003; Phillips 2005). And an emergent stream of scholars are seeking to bring small 'everyday' agents into IPE (Amoore 2002; A. B. Tickner 2003; Davies and Neimann 2002; Davies 2005; Tétreault and Lipschutz 2005; Watson 2005). In this book we extend these analyses to show how everyday actors shape not only the 'big and important things' (i.e., affecting the governance of the global economy) but also shape the 'many small but important things' (i.e., effecting change in the local, national, regional, international and global contexts).

The sociology of everyday IPE: who acts and with what consequences?

Instead of asking 'who governs and who benefits and how is international order maintained?', we begin with the sociological question: 'who acts and how do their actions constitute and transform the world economy in its multiple spatial dimensions?' In the process we necessarily bring back into focus the actions of the bottom ninety per cent. Reminiscent of the claims for a 'new IPE', we agree that regulatory theory is rendered problematic 'because it derives from a political interest in the question "How to keep order?" at a time when the politically more salient question is "How to achieve change?"' (Murphy and Tooze 1991c: 13). Asking 'who acts?' rather than 'who governs?' or 'who benefits?' enables us to reveal new sites of agency wherein the sources of change lie.

Asking 'who acts?' demands that we be open to how agency can be exercised by social actors conventionally considered as 'power-takers' rather than 'power-makers'. This question also demands that when looking at the powerful actors, we problematise and elucidate the practices of their behaviour and the bottom-up social principles that guide and inform their actions. In particular we are not calling for a kind of intellectual division of labour in which regulatory theory monopolises the top ten per cent while EIPE focuses on the bottom ninety per cent. Rather, we suggest that our approach can reveal the bottom-up processes and every-day actions which both effect change in the local, national, regional or global structural contexts, and/or inform the actions of the top ten per cent. Nevertheless, we emphasise here the point that it would be wrong to assume that we see all developments in the world economy as but the product of bottom-up processes given that dominant elites also play an important role (see also Nederveen Pieterse 1990). Rather, our claim here is simply that dominant elites do not play the *exclusive* role. And as we noted above, we can paradoxically learn a great deal more about the power as well as the limits of the legitimacy and authority of dominant elites by examining everyday contests to their power.

One core concept that we stress in this volume is *legitimacy*. This concept reminds us that those who govern are obliged to make claims to the rightfulness and fairness of their actions, and that those who are governed have some capacity to reject or confer these claims, either through their voice or through their actions (Beetham 1991; Seabrooke 2006a: Ch. 2). Legitimacy is crucial to giving everyday actors a voice because it reminds us, at its most basic level, that even the subordinate have some capacity to change their political, economic and social envi-ronment. Legitimacy, after all, is not about how those in power, our 'ten per cent elites', command or proclaim the legitimacy of their policies while the ninety per cent (i.e., the rest of us) are conceived of as 'dopes blindly following the institutionalized scripts and cues around them' (Campbell 1998: 383). More often than not rejections of legitimacy claims are made not through open explicit protest, but through more subtle everyday forms of resistance that provide impulses to the dominant to change their ways (Kerkvliet 2005).

One key reason why an actor may want to reject a claim to legitimacy by those who seek to govern is that it conflicts with their identity. RIPE places little importance on identity, and tends to views an actor's prefer-ences as aligned with their material self-interest. Even the systemic constructivists who discuss how identities are diffused by actors or norm-entrepreneurs view it as the internalisation of an obligation rather than as a source for agency from everyday actors (Seabrooke and Sending 2006). Accordingly, to have a strong conception of legitimacy, EIPE also requires a strong conception of identity. In particular, we stress the agency not just of everyday Western actors but also of Eastern actors and identities in the world economy, where the latter have for too long been obscured by a focus on a world that is thought to emanate from, and reflect the discourse of, the West (Hobson 2004, 2007; Hobson, Suzuki and Wilson, this volume). Identities, for us, are important in our eco-nomic, social and political choices. They are also malleable. While many critical scholars place identity centre-stage, nevertheless their studies are often top-down and elite-focused. Accordingly, they miss the point that often identities are created among the broader public within an everyday context; for an excellent discussion see Hopf (2002). In sum, understanding the creation, maintenance and fall of identities at the everyday level is important to understanding political, economic and social change not only at the local level but also at the international, regional and global levels.

None of this is to say that everyday actors can behave entirely as they please or that they always succeed in getting what they want. Nor do we wish structures of power and repression out of existence. By definition agents who are peripheral act within structurally repressive 'confines'. But while at certain times the subordinate are indeed victims, nevertheless at other times they attain agency. Indeed no agent is either entirely powerless or purely 'confined' within a structural straitjacket for there is always a space, however small, for the expression of agency. Thus we are *not* suggesting that everyday action is limitless in terms of what it can achieve. But we are saying that many of these small, unexplored sites turn out to be far more significant than has been conventionally assumed. Moreover, we would add the point that structures are a product of everyday actions (as much as vice versa).

When discussing everyday agency, the reader might well assume that this implies resistance on the part of the subordinate. But as we shall explain shortly, while resistance is indeed important – especially in the context of power contestation/legitimacy – our approach must not be seen as one that simply reveals how 'the weak get one over on the strong'. Nor must it be assumed that we can demonstrate the pertinence of everyday actions only when these subvert, or 'trump the power of', the dominant. Indeed, everyday actions do not have to 'win' to be meaningful. We also insist that everyday actions need not be strategic in the sense discussed by the literature on social movements and 'contentious politics' (McAdam *et al.* 2001; Davis *et al.* 2005).

In this light the literature on 'everyday politics' is particularly important (Scott 1976, 1985, 1990; de Certeau 1984; Lefebvre 1991b; Kerkvliet 1977, 1990, 2005). Here agency is generally expressed through subtle forms of defiance, which is conducted at the local level and is effected by everyday people in the form of verbal taunts, subversive stories, rumour, 'sly civility' and so on. As Kerkvliet's work demonstrates, everyday politics is more subtle and more common than the more grandiose and dramatic forms of overt resistance that we often associate subordinate agency with. For example, in his study of collectivised agriculture in Vietnam, Kerkvliet illustrates how everyday acts such as cheating on rice stocks, local stories and ignoring national government policies developed in small incremental ways. But crucially, these aggregated into affecting national policy change with regard to collective agriculture, not because of a national ideological change but because the system had become so compromised that it could no longer be legitimately sustained. Thus while there were no overt protests or riots, economic policy was transformed nonetheless (Kerkvliet 2005). In other, complementary, veins, work on everyday politics is broadening out across a variety of disciplines including: sociology (Sallaz 2007; cf. Goffman 1959) social psychology (Wagner and Hayes 2005); politics (Bang and Sørensen 2001; Ginsborg 2005); and international relations (Amoore 2002; A. B. Tickner 2003; Tétreault and Lipschutz 2005; Darby 2004). Importantly, many of our chapters lift the analysis of everyday action from the meso level into the national, regional and global contexts in order to consider how this impacts on change beyond the local or national levels. This, then, begs the question as to how we conceptualise the ways in which everyday actions promote change in the various spatial realms.

As mentioned at the beginning, a central purpose of EIPE is neither to marginalise the importance of the dominant, nor to reify the agency of the weak. Rather, it is to analyse the interactive relationship between the two; one that in many ways constitutes a dialogical, negotiative relationship. This can, of course, take the form of resistance by the weak, but ultimately we are interested in how the weak can influence the agendas of the elites (though the opposite also holds), and how elite agendas often depend upon everyday actors. It is therefore a two-way street that privileges neither but recognises the agency of both. This, of course, takes us beyond the either/or framework of RIPE and of much heterodox IPE. Instead, it takes us into the realm of co-constitutive interactive social relations.

Accordingly, we are interested in revealing the manifold ways in which everyday actors shape their own lives and others around and beyond them whether or not they are resisting power. Thus we need to recognise that everyday actions are ultimately significant to the extent to which they *constitute* the global economy in its multiple spatial dimensions. And, of course, all this implies that everyday actors must not be viewed as passive beneficiaries of the actions of hegemons, international regimes, ideational entrepreneurs (neorealism, neoliberalism and systemic constructivism respectively), or as passive victims of the capitalist world economy (classical structuralism). How then can we conceptualise everyday agency as well as everyday actor-inspired change?

Everyday actions are defined as *acts by those who are subordinate within a broader power relationship but, whether through negotiation, resistance or non-resistance, either incrementally or suddenly, shape, constitute and transform the*

Table 1.2. *Juxtaposing types of change in regulatory and everyday IPE*

Regulatory IPE ('top-down' change)	Everyday IPE ('bottom-up' change)
Coercion	Defiance
Mimetic conformity	Mimetic challenge and hybridised mimicry
Radical uncertainty	Axiorationality

⌊*political and economic environment around and beyond them.* ⌉This broad definition of everyday actions allows us to include a range of agents from individuals to meso-level groupings (e.g., peasants, migrant labourers, trade unions, small investors, low-income groups), and mega-scale aggregations (e.g., peripheral states and peoples). And it is, of course, here where we encounter a contentious issue, since we include governments within Caribbean and South Pacific tax havens in this volume (Sharman). We acknowledge that a tax haven is not a typical everyday actor. But we have stretched the term in this case because tax havens are peripheral within the world economy on the one hand, and engage in everyday actions (specifically 'mimetic challenge') on the other.

To clarify our purpose, in Table 1.2 we juxtapose the three dominant forms of viewing change in RIPE with their counterparts in EIPE. In the left-side column we envisage that 'coercion', 'mimetic conformity' and 'radical uncertainty/crisis' are the typical ways of explaining change in RIPE. Coercion is often found as an explanation for change in neorealism – where 'might makes right' – and also in the exploitative North-South relationship highlighted by classical structuralism. What we have termed 'mimetic conformity' is a common neoliberal institutionalist explanation for why states play the game according to a bounded rationality. Through bounded rationality actors learn that conformity is in their long-term self-interest and therefore persist in embracing the dominant structures in question. Finally, radical uncertainty/crisis has been embraced by systemic constructivists as an explanation and locale for the transformative power of ideas carried by elites (for a critique see Widmaier *et al.* 2007). Most notably, all three types of change are 'top-down'.

By contrast, in the right-hand column, we propose 'defiance', 'mimetic challenge' or 'hybridised mimicry' and 'axiorationality' as three conceptions of bottom-up change within EIPE. Overt defiance is commonly stressed by those who seek to understand how everyday actors repel elite coercion through their *overt resistance* activities. Mimetic challenge – or 'symbolic ju-jitsu' (Scott 1990) – is a common type of *covert resistance* strategy. Change here is generated when everyday actors adopt the discourse and/or characteristics of the dominant to cloak their resistance-challenges to the legitimacy of the dominant. Here agents appeal to the normative discourse of the dominant in order to push through their own subversive agenda (e.g., the strategies of colonial resistance movements during decolonisation). The key strategy here involves revealing how elite actions contradict their own self-referential discourses of appropriate behaviour. In such a way, they become 'rhetorically entrapped' or, put more simply, they become hoist by their own discursive petard (Schimmelfennig 2001). In delegitimising the policies of the dominant, the way is opened towards ending them. Thus revealing such strategies moves us beyond the coloniser/colonised or the elite/marginalised dichotomies, entailing a dialogic or negotiative relationship, as noted earlier.

A complementary concept here is that of 'hybridised mimicry', to adapt Bhabha's concept of 'mimicry' (Bhabha 1994). This entails when agents appear to adopt dominant discourses, but filter them through their own cultural lenses so as to produce something new and hybridised within the 'receptor societies'. Again, this entails a series of negotiative strategies that are deployed by everyday actors. This is most clearly in operation when 'non-Western' agents filter Western ideas or practices through their own cultural lenses so as to produce a synthesis, while retaining the autonomy of indigenous cultural practices. This process has also been characterised as 'vernacularization' (Appadurai 1996: 110–12) or 'inflections' (Ahluwalia 2001: 124–30).

Finally, axiorationality provides a contrast with systemic constructivism's emphasis on temporary moments of radical uncertainty/crisis. Rather, 'axiorationality' is habit-informed, reason-guided behaviour within which an actor still retains a concept of interest. Axiorational behaviour is neither aimed at purely instrumental goals nor purely value-oriented goals. Rather, axiorational behaviour is where an actor uses reason to reflect upon conventions and norms, as well as the interests they inform, and then chooses to act in ways which are in accordance with broader intersubjective understandings of what is socially legitimate. It helps to understand axiorationality by contrasting it with rationalist understandings. The common materialist critique of constructivism in political economy asserts that actors operate rationally according to predefined interests (i.e., prior to social interaction). In addition, Marxists insist that rational behaviour is socially prescribed but that this is based on the exigencies of the mode of production. Our claim, rather, is that actors often behave in economically rational ways, but that this is in part defined by norms and identities that prevail at any one point in time.

Importantly, axiorational behaviour is the most common form of every-day activity, but also allows us to see how actors innovate by selecting new behavioural conventions that meet with their welfare-enhancing interests (not just economic, but also social well-being). Actors do not, therefore, simply act according to a rationalist 'logic of consequence' or internalise a constructivist 'logic of appropriateness' (Sending 2002), but have the agency to change their everyday actions. Incrementally the selection of new conventions by a host of actors will then inform new social norms (Seabrooke 2006a: Ch. 2; Boudon 2001). Such actions take place during 'normal' times rather than during periods of radical uncertainty. And because such actions are not subsumed under the category of resistance, it is often the case that the actors concerned may not know that they are contributing to change in the local, national, regional or global contexts. Thus axiorational agency is something that goes on much of the time rather than in selected moments of uncertainty and periodic economic crisis – *pace* systemic constructivism (see Seabrooke 2007c).

Here it is helpful to draw upon the arguments of the component chapters in order to illustrate the three different forms of everyday agency as they impact upon change in the local, national, regional and global contexts. First to defiance agency, which is expressed through overt resistance. Adam Morton produces an 'everyday Gramscian' approach to reintroduce the theme of subaltern peasant agency in the context of Mexico. In resisting the neoliberalism of the North American Free Trade Agreement (NAFTA), globalisation and the shift in Mexican political economy towards neoliberalism, he focuses on the wars of 'manoeuvre' and 'position' undertaken by the Zapatista Army of National Liberation (EZLN). Entering the public stage in 1994 (having previously been involved in various forms of peasant associations stemming back to the 1970s) he reveals how the EZLN focused mainly on the 'war of position'. He reveals how its actions mobilised national defiance in manifold ways. Moreover, he also suggests that the EZLN's defiance has stimulated global resistance movements to global capital (e.g., the Make Poverty History movement, the International Finance Facility, and others). In the process he reveals how the spatial realms – the local, national and trans-national – are fused together not least through the defiance agency of Mexican peasant resistance.

Andrew Herod develops the theme of defiance agency in the context of the US labour movement, and reveals how such agency constructs the global geography of capitalism. Critical of the focus on the capital-centrism of some Marxist approaches, he rejects viewing labour as a passive victim of capitalist globalisation. Drawing on Bruno Latour's 'network' conception, he views each spatial realm as rope-like or capillary-like, thereby suggesting that each is inextricably linked rather than separate. In turn this helps reconceptualise workers' praxis. For in traditional or conventional accounts, each realm exists prior to workers' interaction, such that workers are thought to be confined to the national realm. Accordingly, workers are thought to suffer from spatial impotence, always facing the superior 'trumping' power of capital that is allegedly derived from its unique spatial-global organisation. But by resisting capital, workers' movements come to construct the geography of global capitalism in ways that would ordinarily be obscured by top-down capital-centric analyses.

Similarly, Michele Ford and Nicola Piper discuss how Filipino workers in Japan are able to organise themselves, partly by linking onto transnational advocacy networks (TANs), to improve their lot. However, in this case they are not making a direct challenge to those who stand in a superordinate relationship but seek to gain position and influence through more subtle forms of everyday politics. Ford and Piper demonstrate that collective action through informal groups provided a support network to resist employer attempts to downgrade conditions and pay. Such collective action occurred prior to TAN involvement, with TANs providing an external legitimating discourse that permitted Filipino migrant workers to expand their capacity to organise and resist at the regional level.

Two of our authors focus principally upon the process of 'mimetic challenge' as a covert strategy of resistance (though Ara Wilson also introduces this theme as a part of her approach). J. C. Sharman reveals how the discursive/normative aspects of international regimes are autonomous sites of cultural contestation wherein peripheral states can not only resist the strong but can even push through their interests against those of the majority of the wealthy Northern states. This also brings into powerful focus the issue of a regime's legitimacy. His chapter focuses on how tiny 'non-European' offshore tax havens have challenged and battled the OECD's harmful tax practices regime. This story is not simply one of another Third World cartel from the Global South that can be picked apart by powerful states in the Global North. Nor is it an example of how peripheral states band together through cartel power to achieve their ends (as in the conventional framework for understanding North-South relations). Rather, the culture of regimes has a certain autonomy from the powerful states, even if they originally constructed the relevant discourse. By playing on the 'double-edged' nature of regime discourse, so these 'weak' tax havens are able to rhetorically challenge the Western states on their own discursive grounds in order to maintain their economic interests *against* those of the wealthy OECD. Thus, as a result of their mimetic challenge strategies, the OECD has been unable to crack down on so-called 'unfair' tax competition (see also Sharman 2006). In short, to paraphrase the Krasner quote from above, it is clear that Samoa or Vanuatu (or Luxembourg) *have* agency 'even though they ain't hegemonic'.

Shogo Suzuki provides an account of how peripheral states can, through mimetic challenge, use the ideational resources of a dominant state to legitimate everyday actions that help transform the economic environment. He examines the Chinese international tribute system and reveals how the 'vassal states' exercised their agency in order to transform the system. In particular he illustrates how Japan was able to call upon the legitimacy of the tribute system to create a miniature version of the system around its neighbours. This 'mimetic challenge' was expressed through everyday actions, such as the adoption of different calendars, that was in direct opposition to Chinese hegemony but was justified to Chinese authorities as an inculcation of legitimate social practices. As a consequence Chinese authorities permitted the Japanese-led system to flourish even though it undermined China's authority.

Ara Wilson focuses on 'hybridised mimicry' to understand the creation of Asian modernity. She reveals how Asian diasporas and Thai producers frequently imitate Western practices but filter them through indigenous cultural frameworks to produce economic meaning that is transformed into an Asian context. In this way Asian modernisation is produced through hybrid or creolised forms of Western and Asian cultural-meaning and production systems. To provide just one example: the choice of the name Central Department Store appears to be an acculturation of English but is in fact a synthesis of Western and Chinese influences. The store's name reflects an admiration for the system of Chinese government called 'Tong Iang' (Central), as much as it does the recognition that English is the global lingua franca of modernity. The term reflects the notion of Chinese 'centralisation' which conveys the importance of large-scale, vertically hierarchical organisations upon which the business is based. Nevertheless, as we explain below, Wilson places more emphasis on the third type of everyday agency.

Turning now to the third type of agency – axiorationality – we emphasise the point that it is qualitatively different to the first two forms. For unlike overt defiance and mimetic challenge, axiorationality is not a form of resistance. Axiorational agency, which occurs as everyday agents go about their everyday business, can be seen to inform the policies of great power political economy (Seabrooke), or macro-shifts in international finance (Langley), or the rise of Oriental globalisation (Hobson) or the creation of Asian modernity (Wilson). Leonard Seabrooke's chapter seeks to understand everyday domestic influences on the foreign financial policies of leading Western 'hegemonic' states – England in the late-nineteenth century and the United States after 1945. He discusses how access to everyday social wants such as credit, property and lower tax burdens for lower income groupings inform the domestic character of financial systems, which in turn inform a state's capacity to transform the international financial order (see also Seabrooke 2006a). His key point is that the extent to which a state can work within legitimate social practices (according to the 'moral economy' of lower income groupings) informs a state's foreign financial policy. Contestations to the legitimacy of a state's financial system do not take place only, or even primarily, in times of radical uncertainty and crisis, but instead through everyday incremental actions. Seabrooke contends that it is vital to recognise that while dominant actors claim legitimacy for their actions, active legitimation requires consent from the subordinate within the relationship. And without sufficient legitimacy a hegemon's financial power is ultimately undermined (see also Seabrooke 2001).

In a move complementary to Seabrooke's chapter, Paul Langley shifts the focus away from the 'top end of town' and towards the agency of small everyday investors in the US and the UK. He reveals how their actions are increasingly transforming the global financial system through the shift from 'defined benefit' to 'defined contribution' pension systems. Langley demonstrates that risk in pension systems has been redistributed to the individual, whereby everyday investment choices now have a greater potential impact than in any other world financial order due to the volume of individual investors. This process of individualisation has emerged from the 1980s Anglo-American discourses of 'shareholder society', 'popular capitalism' and, most recently, 'the ownership society' proclaimed by the new Bush administration. This individualisation requires increasingly stringent self-governance in the sense that investment becomes a 'technology of the self'. Langley sees this process as one of inculcating a new 'neo-liberal morality' whereby personal freedom is directly tied to skill in financial investment and enterprise as an everyday activity for ordinary investors, and extends to full-time 'day traders' through to workers in formal financial institutions.

John Hobson's chapter reveals how the everyday, axiorational practices of Eastern agents led to the creation of an Eastern-led global economy after the sixth century. Moreover, 'Oriental globalisation' was maintained and reproduced by Eastern agents in all manner of ways right down to the early nineteenth century. In this Oriental *longue global durée*, the everyday practices of Eastern agents were not geared towards resisting external Western structures of dominance (which did not exist in Asia at that time), nor were such agents interested in subduing or dominating the West. Moreover, a key part of the argument involves revealing the ways in which everyday Eastern practices – technological, institutional, ideational and commercial – had a cumulative impact insofar as they enabled the 'rise of the West' and the creation of modernity, thereby returning a strong sense of agency to the East in the making of the modern world.

Ara Wilson carries this non-Eurocentric argument into the present. Her argument similarly deconstructs the myth of exclusive Western agency in the making of the modern world by showing how the axiorational practices of everyday Eastern agents led to the creation of Asian modernity (in the context of Thailand). She produces a detailed account of the Chirathivat family – a Chinese family which emigrated to Thailand – and reveals how the everyday practices of the family's men and women generated one of the most important retail outlets that rode the crest of the wave of Thai modernisation.

Finally, it should be noted that we have chosen to divide up the chapters according to three key themes of IPE rather than to a specific form of everyday agency. The themes are important in revealing blind spots within conventional IPE literature, as well as locating new topics for discussion. The three themes are: 'Regimes as cultural weapons of the weak', 'Global economic change from below', and 'Bringing Eastern agents in'. The first theme brings to light the importance of 'bottom-up' formal and informal regimes, which provides an alternative framework to RIPE's focus on 'top-down' formal international regimes. This theme also highlights how peripheral actors can use everyday actions to constrain the power of the dominant. Our second theme discusses how seemingly everyday actions have important consequences for the transformation of domestic political economies, and through them, the world economy. Here economic change is not directed by the state and/or by international regimes, but occurs through incremental changes in social economic norms, or in defiance of dominant structures. Finally, our third theme seeks to redress the predominant focus accorded to Western elites and structures. Of course, there is plenty of discussion in the conventional, and even in the critical, literature on processes that occur in the 'non-Western' world. But these are almost always conducted or interpreted through Eurocentric concepts and ideas (see Hobson 2007). By contrast, this section contributes an alternative frame of reference for rethinking the role played by Eastern agents in the world economy. We rejoin these three themes in the Conclusion, specifically in our discussion of how puzzle sets can further expand EIPE.

Conclusion

This volume seeks to highlight how everyday actions can transform the world economy. In the process we not only answer the call made by

Murphy and Tooze for a more 'heterodox' IPE made some fifteen years ago, but also respond to the recent call made by the North American 'ultra-orthodoxy' through Frieden and Martin. The time is ripe for the transformation of the discipline. In our view 'heterodox' IPE is more than ready to move beyond deconstructing the discipline to reconstructing it around problem-driven 'puzzle sets' that encourage methodological dynamism alongside critical reflection of what is being asked (and for a full discussion of research puzzles see Chapter 11). 'Orthodox' IPE is also looking for a greater diversity of answers and may be more open than some think to asking different questions and embracing different perspectives to obtain them. In moving beyond the intellectual straitjacket of RIPE and the confines of heterodox theory by exploring EIPE, we reveal hitherto unexplored sites of agency by discovering how everyday actions have an impact for the majority of peoples and, therefore, the world economy. Such findings, in turn, challenge our own assumptions, explanations and understandings about the multiple sources of transformation in the local, national, regional and global contexts.

Part I

Regimes as cultural weapons of the weak

2   The agency of labour in global change: reimagining the spaces and scales of trade union praxis within a global economy

Andrew Herod

In this chapter I explore how we might rethink labour's agency in the global economy. Specifically, I consider how three features of theorising about the nature of global capitalism have intersected to shape the way in which regulatory international political economy (RIPE) literature has historically considered workers and their organisations. The first feature of much RIPE literature is its capital-centric nature, which has presented a theoretical approach in which capital is viewed implicitly as *the* agent of global economic change, while labour is seen largely as little more than a passive victim of capitalist economic forces. The second feature is that the central focus of RIPE has been the interactions within the international arena of nation-states, to the general exclusion of other social actors such as labour organisations. The third is that RIPE has commonly theorised the geographical scales at which social life is typically seen to exist – scales such as 'the local', 'the regional', 'the national' and 'the global' – in areal terms, that is to say as little more than spatial 'containers' of social life. In such a view, social actors like unions are viewed as constituted ontologically *within* the confines of these various spatial units (e.g., *within* localities, regions, nation-states, or the global economy), rather than as being constituted, say, *along a continuum* of spatial scales (what I mean by this distinction will become clearer below). In combination, RIPE's approaches to understanding the making of the geography of the global economy and to theorising how it is spatially scaled have (at least) four important implications for our attempts to comprehend unions and their activities in an apparently globalising world.

First, adopting an approach which views geographical scales in areal terms incorporates within it particular understandings of how the world is scaled, that is to say how scales such as 'the local' and 'the global' relate to one another. Second, the national scale has clearly been privileged in RIPE as a scale of activity for unions and for analysing their activities – the ways in which unions and their members are conceived of as political and economic actors is through the lens of the nation-state. Thus, there is little recognition either that unions might have sets of interests which they pursue in the international realm which are separate and/or different from those of whichever government controls any particular nation-state's organs of political power, or that unions may bypass the nation-state altogether and develop international contacts at the sub-national level with workers overseas – perhaps on a plant-to-plant or region-to-region basis. Rather, the nation-state is viewed both as a receptacle for labour and as the portal through which 'domestic' actors such as unions envision and engage with the broader 'international realm'.

Third, and relatedly, given that in much globalisation discourse 'the global' is thought of as being superior to, and inherently more powerful than, other scales such as 'the national' or 'the local', unions – because they are generally viewed as contained within the spatial boundaries of the nation-state – are invariably portrayed as being subject to 'larger-scale' and 'higher-level' global forces but are not viewed as capable themselves of acting globally or of shaping global forces and institutions (such as those of 'globalisation'). In such a discursive formation, 'the global' – which is taken implicitly to be the scale of capitalist organisation – is embodied as the supernal scale of social existence to which all other scales of social organisation are subordinate, and unions are represented as capable of operating only at some 'sub-global' scale. Rhetorically, of course, such a representation plays into the 'TINA' ('there is no alternative') discourse concerning globalisation in which, it is argued, capital may always use its imagined global scale of organisation to 'trump' activities at other spatial scales, such that there is little point in anti-capitalist actors challenging capital's hegemony. Fourth, in conceiving of unions in such a way RIPE has been inclined to have a fairly limited view of how the emerging geography of global capitalism is made. As a result of RIPE's focus upon the interactions of nation-states and how global flows of capital impact these, unions' roles as moulders of the geography of capitalism have been ignored in two ways. First, regional variations at the sub-national scale in terms of things like union response to national-level or international-level public policy or economic transformations have tended to be overlooked. Thus while geographical variations in unions' political and economic agendas and praxis are recognised at the national level (as in proclamations such as 'Italian unions do it this way while Canadian ones do it that way'), sensitivity to sub-national geographical variations in union praxis has tended to be more limited, even though such spatial variations can have significant impacts upon, for instance, global flows of capital investment. It is, rather, national-level labour institutions which have captured most of

RIPE's attention. And second, by default the geography of global capitalism has been seen to be the product of capital's praxis: workers and their organisations are conceived of as, effectively, spatially impotent.

In this chapter I seek to advance what the editors term an everyday international political economy (EIPE) approach by showing how unions and workers can, in fact, have global agency and that, through their praxis, they can have real impacts on how the nascent geography of global capitalism is unfolding. Specifically, I argue that in addition to capital and nation-states, labour also constitutes an important agent that provides defiance to, and can enact, global economic change. Put another way, I wish to challenge the conceptions of globalisation which argue – implicitly or explicitly – that capital is the sole agent capable of operating globally and so of shaping the geography of global capitalism. The chapter is organised into two main sections. First, I explore some recent work concerning how we conceptualise the spatial scales at which social life is organised, for such conceptualisations have important implications for how we think of unions as geographical actors capable of shaping processes of globalisation through their defiance agency. Second, I outline an argument for how the making of geography is central to how capitalism as an economic system perpetuates itself, and how struggles over the making of this geography are fundamental elements of the capital-labour relationship. To illustrate my argument I provide some real world examples of workers and their organisations having significant impacts upon the unfolding geography of the global economy. Finally, I ponder what such matters might mean for furthering an EIPE approach.

Theorising scales of political praxis

Within studies of the international political economy, as in much of the social sciences and humanities, the geographical scales that we use to make sense of the world have usually been taken to be self-evident conceptual devices for dividing up the Earth into manageable and relatively distinct spatial units for purposes of understanding various political and economic processes. In such an approach, scales like 'the local' or 'the regional' are viewed more or less as spatial vessels for social life and processes. For instance, national boundaries (which mark the spatial extent of 'the national' scale) serve to partition the surface of the globe into different absolute spaces – the boundary between, say, France and Germany distinguishes those spaces that contain 'things French' from those that contain 'things German'. However, such scalar representations bring with them particular sets of conceptual baggage for understanding how political and economic processes and practices are structured spatially. For example, within such an understanding of scale the world is typically seen as a series of hierarchically ordered units of space which build from 'the local' on up through 'the regional' and 'the national' to 'the global'. In this view, 'the regional' scale and 'the national' scale are usually seen as discrete areal units that sit somewhere between 'the local' and 'the global' within a spatial taxonomy of social life, with 'the local' scale being contained within 'the national' scale, which is itself contained within 'the global' scale. Certainly, this is not to say that scalar boundaries are regarded as incapable of being transgressed – local processes may be argued to 'spill beyond' the local, for example. But it is to say that the boundaries of 'the local' or 'the regional' or of other scales perform the role primarily of circumscribing particular expanses of geographical space. (As an aside, it should be pointed out that even at the moment of arguing that processes may 'spill beyond' the limits of the 'local', 'regional', or even 'national' scale, such a rhetorical construction merely reaffirms an episte-mological stance that views those scales as areal containers of social life, ones whose boundaries have been breached by the process in question. Ontologically, then, the scales which contain social life are seen to exist *a priori* to those processes which are spilling over their spatial rims, much like a cup must exist before it can be filled to overflowing with liquid.)

Viewing scales in such areal terms has significant implications for theorising processes of globalisation and workers' places in the world. In particular, conceptualising scales as areal units for circumscribing and containing social processes and practices brings with it questions con-cerning how different scales are seen to be connected to one another. There are (at least) three different ways in which what are arguably the four most-commonly discussed spatial scales – these being 'the local', 'the regional', 'the national' and 'the global' – are represented discursively as relating to each other. First, such scales have frequently been represented as forming a 'scalar ladder' in which there is a strict progression from 'the local' (which is usually seen to be the bottom rung on the ladder) up through the regional and national scales until one reaches 'the global' scale of social life. (Significantly, the English word 'scale' is actually derived from the Latin *scala*, meaning 'a ladder'.) In such a representation each scale/rung on the ladder is viewed as discrete and as connected to the other scales within a particular scalar order – 'the regional' and 'the national' scales are conceived of as being above 'the local' scale but below 'the global' scale, for instance (e.g., see Castree *et al.* 2004: xix). A second image popularly used to describe the scaling of our world is that of scale as a series of concentric rings, with 'the local' at the centre and other scales encompassing it, such that 'the global' is represented by the outermost ring and contains all others (e.g., Knox and Marston 2004: 6).

As with the ladder metaphor, in this representation each scale is viewed as a separate and discrete entity. However, rather than 'the global' being *above* all other scales, in this case it is seen to *contain* all other scales, while 'the local' is not below all other scales but is, instead, contained within them. The shift from the ladder to the concentric ring metaphor, then, involves a shift in orientation from a vertical to a horizontal plane and a shift in language from a description of scales as being above or below one another to their encompassing or being contained within each other.

A third common metaphor is that of the nested hierarchy of scales which are perhaps best represented by the famous Russian *matryoshka* nesting dolls. In this metaphor each scale is again seen as a discrete entity, yet the picture can only be understood as a whole when each separate scale is fitted in the correct order inside the scale which is immediately 'larger' than itself (e.g., Christaller 1966; Lösch 1954). Although this metaphor shares some similarities with the other two – 'the global' scale/ outside doll quite literally contains all other scales (as with the rings metaphor) and is the 'largest' scale of all – there are some differences. Hence, whereas it is possible to conceive, perhaps, of missing a rung or two in the ladder metaphor – implying that one may be able to pass over, say, 'the national' rung in climbing from 'the local' to 'the global' – this is less so with the *matryoshka* doll metaphor, which implies much more forcefully than the other metaphors that there is a tightly connected and strict hierarchy in which one scale fits snugly inside of another (see Herod 2003a for more on such metaphors).

Although these three metaphors – versions of which are fairly common in RIPE – have some significant differences with regard to expressing the scaled nature of our world, the one similarity which they share is that they all conceive of spatial scales as discrete and bounded areal units of absolute space. However, as Bruno Latour has argued, one can also view the scales of social life not as hierarchies of areal units but, instead, as rope-like or capillary-like, with scales such as 'the local' and 'the global' conceived of not as discrete spatial entities but as connected in much the same way as the two ends of a piece of string. Thus, he argues (Latour 1996: 370), the world's complexity cannot be captured by 'notions of levels, layers, territories, [and] spheres', and should not be thought of as being made up of discrete levels (i.e., scales) of bounded spaces that fit together neatly. Instead, Latour maintains, we need to think about the world as being 'fibrous, thread-like, wiry, stringy, ropy, [and] capillary'. In Latour's view, then, it is impossible to distinguish where the local ends and the global (or one of the other scales) begins. Rather than being smaller or larger areal units, 'the local' and 'the global' instead 'offer points of view on networks that are by nature neither local nor global, but are more or less long and more or less connected' (Latour 1993: 122). Drawing upon Latour's imagery, we might think of scale as more akin to a spider's web or as a set of earthworm burrows or tree roots which are intertwined through different strata of soil. For Latour, 'the global' and 'the local' are not so much opposite ends of a scalar spectrum but are, rather, a terminology for contrasting shorter and less-connected networks with longer and more-connected networks.

So what does all of this have to do with workers' international activities? Simply put, such conceptualisations of how our world is scaled have quite significant implications for how we view the possibilities for workers' praxis. For example, if we take the view that scales are areal containers of discrete absolute spaces then the activities of workers come to be viewed as taking place at separate and distinct spatial resolutions (e.g., 'within' the nation-state), while the only way to expand the geographical scale of their political praxis is for them to 'jump' from one scale to another scale of spatial organisation, such as that of 'the global' – a process which might be seen as climbing to a 'higher' scale or as expanding to a 'wider' scale, depending upon whether one imagines the world as scaled like a ladder or a series of larger or smaller rings. Framing the issue of workers' praxis in this manner, however, has at least two important consequences. First, talk of how workers might 'jump scales' so as to move from, say, 'the national' to 'the global' scale of activity suggests that such scales are already pre-made and that actors need simply to vault themselves from one to the other. Such a representation, paradoxically, conceptually denies actors the social agency to construct the geography of global capitalism in different and varied ways, for it suggests that the global scale of capitalist organisation is something that simply exists waiting to be discovered and used, rather than something that had to be made and is constantly remade through the actions of diverse social actors – firms, unions, environmental groups, nation-states, non-governmental organisations and the like. Put another way, there is no room conceptually for imagining that such social actors might construct global capitalism – or perhaps even alternatives to it – in ways that defy and differ from its present formulation.

Second, conceiving of geographical scales as containers of social life allows political actors to represent such scales as spatial enclosures which may be used to contain social action by opponents, such that the only way to break out of this geographical constraint is to jump to a higher spatial scale of economic and political organisation – something which, in the rhetorics of neoliberalism, capital is usually seen as inherently more capable of doing than labour. The ability to frame a particular dispute in such a manner can be a central aspect of exercising political power.

Hence, capitalists' ability to convince workers that they are doomed to only ever be able to engage in praxis which is constrained within, say, 'the national' scale because they can never successfully jump to a higher (that is to say 'global') scale of organisation can be a powerful psychological weapon in matters of class struggle. On the other hand, a Latourian view of how the world is scaled may allow workers to view their situation and praxis as simultaneously 'local' and 'global', a view which changes dramatically the dynamics of political struggle and what is thought to be possible. Given that in Latour's formulation the world is seen as interconnected in such a manner that it becomes impossible to say where one scale ends and another begins – much as it is impossible to describe where one part of a spider's web or an earthworm's burrow ends and another begins – a dispute at any particular location (such as a factory) is always a multi-scaled event, at once 'local' and 'global' (and 'regional' and 'national' too). To 'act locally', then, is concurrently to be connected into and affect broader 'global' processes, while 'acting globally' is always grounded in particular 'local' places.

What is important for theorising workers' praxis in a 'global economy' in all of this, of course, is that conceptualising scale and political praxis in Latourian terms may make it much harder – if not impossible – for capitalists to argue that workers are confined within or to particular scales: if everything is networked scalarly, with 'the local' and 'the global' simply serving to distinguish between shorter and less-connected networks and longer and more-connected networks (which are themselves part of a planetary interconnectivity), then no scale serves to constrain social actors to existence within particular spatial resolutions of praxis. Furthermore, if Latour's approach is adopted, then it quickly becomes apparent that what we have come to call the 'global economy' is, in fact, simultaneously constituted 'locally' (and 'regionally' and 'nationally' and at myriad other scales). Indeed, one might even go so far as to suggest that from this perspective the *global* economy' is imaginary, nothing more than a planetary collectivity of *local* practices in which the idea of globalness serves primarily as a powerful disciplining tool (similarly, on 'governmentality' see Paul Langley's contribution to this volume). Certainly, this is not to say that belief in the existence of a *global* economy' does not have very real and powerful impacts upon political and economic behaviour. But it does mean that if the existence of the *global* economy' is merely the result of looking at the nature of contemporary capitalism from a particular perspective – seeing the economy as organised as a coherent 'global' whole rather than as something which is 'multi-local', for example – and that the *global* economy' exists as nothing more than a discursive device for disciplining social thought and behaviour, such that, upon closer inspection, everything 'global' disintegrates into a myriad of things 'local' (and 'national' and 'regional', etc.), then Latour's conceptualisation has important implications for thinking about workers' activities in response to 'globalisation'. Responding to capitalist firms which are conceived as being organised 'multi-locally' is a very different matter to responding to firms which are thought of as being organised 'globally'.

In considering such issues of scale, though, I do not want to suggest that Latour's formulation is necessarily a 'better' representation in some absolute sense of how the world is actually scaled – there may be distinct advantages to thinking of the world as scaled through a series of discrete areal units, such as allowing us to imagine how workers might confine anti-union practices to some 'local' scale. Rather, my point is that different conceptualisations have different implications for thinking about political practice and that, instead of accepting scales as some kind of taken-for-granted, 'natural' way of dividing the world up into manageable bits, thinking about scales in disparate manners can help us envision the possibilities for praxis in different ways. Thus, changing our scalar metaphors does not change how the world itself is, in fact, scaled but it does change our point of engagement with it – which has significant implications for praxis. Such a discussion of metaphors and representations of scale is particularly important, I would argue, when considering workers' praxis in the face of globalisation because of the way in which what are often taken to be the two scalar extremes of social life – 'the local' and 'the global' – are frequently placed in binary opposition to each other, especially given that 'the global' is generally accorded greater potency than is 'the local'.

In this latter regard, Gibson-Graham (2002) has outlined at least six ways in which 'the global' and 'the local' are often seen to relate to one another. First, 'the global' and 'the local' are often seen not as things in and of themselves but, instead, as interpretive frames for analysing situations – what is considered to be the reality of a situation from a 'global perspective' may appear to be quite different when considered from a 'local perspective'. Second, 'the global' and 'the local' are frequently viewed as each deriving meaning from what they are not and serve as each other's opposite, such that 'the global' and 'the local' only make sense when contrasted with each other. Third, as we have seen, 'the local' and 'the global' may be understood as discrete areal domains at the extremities of some scalar hierarchy or, instead, as part of a spatial terminology for contrasting shorter and less-connected networks with longer and more-connected networks. Fourth, 'the global' may be understood really to be 'local', such that 'the global' does not really exist and if you scratch anything 'global' you will find locality (multi-national firms, for instance, can be seen as actually being 'multi-local' rather than 'global'). Fifth, 'the local' is conceived of as 'global', such that 'the local' is simply where 'global' forces touch down on the Earth's surface; 'the local', then, is not a place but is instead an entry point to the world of 'global' flows which encircle the planet. Sixth, 'the global' and the 'local' are conceptualised not as locations but as processes wherein globalisation and localisation are simultaneously at work to produce all spaces as hybrids, as 'glocal' sites of both differentiation and integration; in such a representation 'the local' and 'the global' are not fixed entities but are always in the process of being remade – 'local' initiatives can be broadcast to the world and adopted in multiple places, while 'global' processes always involve localisation (thus McDonald's customises globally its products to particular local tastes, serving beer in France, pineapple fritters in Hawaii and vegetarian 'hamburgers' in India).

Gibson-Graham's outline of how 'the local' and 'the global' are frequently represented as relating to one another, then, has significant implications for how we think about workers' praxis in an apparently globalising world, particularly if, as is often the case, either 'the global' or 'the local' is thought of as being inherently more powerful – or far-reaching or adaptive to particular situations – than the other. Thus, certain representations of how the world is scaled reinforce rhetorics of neoliberalism (such as the TINA discourse), while others open new vistas for understanding how workers may play roles in shaping the geography of global capitalism. Hence, whereas much neoliberal discourse tends to present 'the global' as the scale of social life from which there is no escape, the scale that defines the 'reality' of contemporary capitalism, the acme of scalar organisation, conceptualising current developments not as processes of 'globalisation' but as processes, say, of 'multi-localisation' or of 'glocalisation' transforms how workers and their organisations are seen to interact with the wider world. This has far-reaching consequences for how workers' praxis is theorised in the world economy. In particular, it reworks the relationship between entities such as unions and the nation-state – if social praxis is viewed as simultaneously 'local' and 'global', or as 'glocal', then how can workers' praxis be seen to be contained within the nation-state? – and opens a conceptual entry point for considering how workers (rather than just firms or nation-states) engage in shaping the emergent geography of global capitalism.

Workers as shapers of the geography of global capitalism

Typically, the geography of the global economy has been seen to be the result of the actions of two major sets of social institutions, these being nation-states and transnational corporations (TNCs). Furthermore, social theory aimed at understanding how the geography of global capitalism is made has tended to have a rather unsophisticated conception of space, generally viewing space as simply a stage upon which historical actors play out the drama of class conflict. This approach to theorising the social relations of capitalism has a history stretching back at least to the mid-nineteenth century and the writings of such quintessentially modernist writers as Karl Marx, who tended to emphasise social transformation over time and who did not particularly recognise that space and the ability to manipulate spatial relations between places can be a source of power and an object of social struggle (for more on the historicism of social theory and the failure to develop much of a 'geographical imagination', see Soja 1989). Put another way, transformations in the spatial relations of global capitalism tend to be seen in much RIPE as contingent matters, merely the geographical reflection of other economic and political processes rather than as a central element to what we have come to call 'globalisation'. In contrast, I want to argue here that recognising that the spatiality of global capitalism – that is to say the way in which the global economy is organised geographically – makes a difference to how capitalism as a system works is an important aspect of theorising contemporary 'globalisation'. This argument draws upon the work of a number of social theorists and critical human geographers who have explored how what French Marxist Henri Lefebvre (1991a) called the 'production of space' has been central to the operation of capitalism as an economic system (see also Amoore 2002).

Central to these arguments about space and capitalism is the proposition that the way in which capitalism is structured geographically is central to its ability to function. Thus, for Lefebvre (1976, 1991a) capital's ability to shape the geography of capitalism in particular ways is a central, rather than contingent, aspect of capitalism's social relations: capitalists, Lefebvre maintains, must ensure that landscapes are made in such a way as to ensure that the accumulation and realisation of surplus capital can take place, which may necessitate making investments in certain locations and in certain types of physical infrastructure. Similar ideas have been explored by a number of Marxist geographers, most particularly David Harvey, Neil Smith and Doreen Massey. Harvey (1973, 1982), for example, has argued that capitalists must create what he calls a 'spatial fix' in the landscape, by which he means that they must create particular geographies of their own organisation and of capitalism more broadly if accumulation is to proceed. For his part, Smith (1990) has shown how contradictory spatial tendencies within capital have fueled the uneven geographical development of capitalism, while Massey (1995) has shown how the economic landscape of capitalism is a product of the differential layering of rounds of capital investment over time and their interaction with extant patterns of investment, such that the spatial organisation of capitalism systematically structures the social relations of accumulation and vice versa. (For a more in-depth discussion of these ideas and arguments, see Herod 2001, particularly: 1–49.)

However, while these authors have made substantial intellectual advances concerning how the spatiality of global capitalism is made, their approaches have had a propensity to be somewhat capital-centric – that is to say they have focused upon the actions of capital for their explanatory power. Such capital-centrism has tended to reinforce neo-liberal views that the restructuring of the global economy through 'globalisation' is by the hand of capital and that workers are merely the passive bearers of the geographical transformations wrought by capital. Yet, as I have argued elsewhere (see Herod 1995, 2001, 2002, 2003b, 2003c), it is important to recognise that workers also play roles in shaping the global geography of capitalism, whether by design or inadvertently, and that the geography of capitalism is actively struggled over rather than being simply the outcome of the working out of capital's internal contradictions. Acknowledging that workers, too, have a vested interest in shaping how the geography of capitalism is made allows us to view contemporary processes of 'globalisation' and the restructuring of capitalism's global geography not in some TINA fashion but, instead, as contested. Workers may therefore employ defiance agency to shape globalisation and its processes. Drawing upon the earlier discussion of scale, it becomes evident, depending upon how one views the scaled relationships between different places, that there are multiple ways in which workers may impact globally the geography of capitalism, from implementing trans-spatial solidarity actions to engaging in putatively 'local' struggles – which, if we follow Latour, are simultaneously 'global' (and 'regional' and 'national') in nature, though in ways different from those actions that are specifically designed to be trans-spatial in character.

Here, then, I want to outline three case studies of how workers and unions have employed strategies of defiance to shape the geography of global capitalism (for more details on each of these cases see, respectively, Herod 2001: 161–96, 1995 and 2000).

Engineering spaces of anti-communism

Fidel Castro's seizure of power in Cuba in 1959 greatly concerned both the US State Department and the American Federation of Labor–Congress of Industrial Organizations (AFL–CIO). Fearing that Castroism might spread through the labour movements of Latin America and the Caribbean, in the early 1960s the AFL–CIO began to devise ways of undermining anti-American and pro-Communist sympathies. US union leaders determined that the deliberate spatial engineering of Latin American and Caribbean workers' neighbourhoods and living spaces would be an effective way to promote pro-US attitudes among the region's workers and to undermine the appeal of Communist unions. Using both its own members' pension funds and federal government monies, during the 1960s and 1970s the AFL–CIO, through its regional organisation the American Institute for Free Labor Development (AIFLD), financed the construction of low-cost, owner-occupied housing for workers in unions that were either anti-Communist or threatened with take-over by Communist elements. This was part of a strategy to influence the political and economic geography of the region by showing workers that 'free trade unions can produce results, while the Communists produce only slogans' (AIFLD 1964: iv). Effectively, the AFL–CIO wished to shape the global terrain of the cold war through the deliberate spatial manipulation of the built environments in numerous small towns and cities across Latin America and the Caribbean, to the extent that by 1967 the AFL–CIO President, George Meany, could claim that AIFLD was the 'largest builder of worker-sponsored, low-cost housing' in the region (AIFLD 1967).

The first major housing project involving AIFLD was dedicated in Mexico City in 1964. The 96-building, 3,100-apartment 'John F. Kennedy Housing Project' at *Colonia Balbuena* was financed, in part, by US union pension funds and housed primarily members of Mexico's Graphic Arts Workers' Union. Other housing projects were established across the region, including in Argentina, Brazil, Colombia, the Dominican Republic, Guyana, Honduras and Uruguay. AIFLD also provided funds and expertise to construct schools, vocational training centres and sanitation and irrigation projects in rural communities. Significantly, these projects were usually chosen according to AIFLD's geopolitical concerns, with local partner unions and workers selected on the basis of the specific sector of the economy in which they worked – communications workers, transport and port workers and local government workers were particularly favoured – or whether they were located in key regions of various countries. The goal of such programs was, simply, to improve workers' local living conditions and to transform their neighbourhoods in the hope that this transformation in the local geographies of workers' lives would limit the appeal of Communist ideology. By the time AIFLD's housing program ended in the late 1970s, the Institute had been involved in building more than 18,000 housing units in fourteen nations, together with numerous other projects. Although

AIFLD's activities undeniably had certain benefits for US capital – such as helping to undermine militant anti-US unionism – it is important to recognise that the Institute's policies were an integral part of its own virulent anti-Communism. (On housing and US capitalism see also Len Seabrooke's contribution to this volume.) Certainly, it might be argued that AIFLD was merely acting on behalf of US capital, thereby negating the claim of labour's agency in shaping the geography of globalisation, but this misses the point that unions do not always or necessarily act in progressive ways, no matter how much we might wish that they did. AIFLD's actions may very well have dovetailed with US corporate interests, but fundamentally they were driven by the Institute's own anti-Communist agenda for Latin America and the Caribbean. In defying Communism through such spatial engineering, then, AIFLD played an important role in shaping the political and economic geography of globalisation with respect to the region.

Developing global solidarity

In November 1990 some 1,700 members of United Steelworkers of America (USWA), Local Union 5668, were locked out of their aluminium smelting plant in Ravenswood, West Virginia, in a dispute over health and safety and pensions. Initially, the dispute was played out locally between managers and union workers. However, within a few months the union had learned that the plant – which had recently been bought by a consortium of investors – was part of a multi-billion dollar corporation with headquarters in Switzerland and was owned, ultimately, by an international financier, Marc Rich. Rich, it turned out, was a fugitive from US justice. Upon learning of this connection, workers and union officials, both locally and in Pittsburgh, Pennsylvania (where the USWA has its national headquarters), began to initiate contacts with workers in countries where Rich had business interests or where he wished to expand his operations. Working through a number of international trade union organisations such as the International Metalworkers' Federation, USWA members and operatives consequently outlined a strategy for bringing pressure to bear on Rich, whom they saw as the person ultimately behind events in Ravenswood. Their research revealed that Rich had interests in Switzerland, Britain, France, Finland, the Netherlands, Spain, Czechoslovakia, Romania, Bulgaria, Russia, Israel, Venezuela, Hong Kong and Australia, among other places.

By mid-summer 1991 the USWA had established an office in Paris to co-ordinate anti-Rich activities and was busy making connections with European unions. The Steelworkers sent a delegation to Switzerland to meet with Swiss parliamentarians sympathetic to their cause and also arranged, through the Dutch bankworkers' union, a meeting with representatives of the Nederlandsche Middenstandsbank which had helped finance Rich's recent purchase of the plant in Ravenswood. This meeting allowed the union to alert the bank's officers to a number of legal challenges to Rich that were pending in the United States, an action which resulted in the bank withdrawing some additional funding it had promised him. Through their European contacts the USWA also met with representatives of the Czech metalworkers' union OS KOVO who, in turn, met with the Czech President, Vaclav Havel. This was important, because Rich was negotiating to buy a government aluminium smelter in the Czech Republic. As a result of OS KOVO's intervention, Havel personally rejected Rich from the bidding process. Elsewhere in Europe trade unionists rallied to the aid of the Ravenswood workers. Some 20,000 came out to protest Rich's proposed acquisition of the famous Athénée Palace Hotel in Bucharest, a rally which was instrumental in leading the government to prevent Rich from purchasing the hotel. Events in support of the Ravenswood workers were also staged in several other Eastern European countries, including Bulgaria and Russia.

Whilst Rich's plans to expand his operations in Europe were being hindered, in Latin America he was finding that his efforts to enlarge his holdings in bauxite, oil and other commodities were also being stymied by the USWA. In particular, the union contacted the former Jamaican Prime Minister, Michael Manley, who had worked with the USWA as a young man when he had been an organiser in the country's bauxite mines and who had made Rich's ownership of Jamaican bauxite mines an issue in his own 1989 election campaign. Manley, in turn, contacted the Venezuelan government, as Rich had a deal pending in that country. Manley's intervention subsequently led the Venezuelan President, Carlos Andres Perez, to dismiss Rich as one of three final bidders for the purchase of an aluminium smelter. Following this, the USWA briefed representatives of the International Confederation of Free Trade Unions, who resolved to disrupt Rich's operations throughout Latin America and the Caribbean.

Combined with a North American boycott of products using aluminium made by non-union replacement workers at the Ravenswood facility, international actions in twenty-eight countries on five continents harassed Rich and his operations to such an extent that in April 1992 – a year and a half after the lock-out began – he moved to settle the dispute. After a reshuffling of the Board of Directors of the Ravenswood smelter, Rich instructed his deputies to begin negotiations with Local Union 5668 representatives. Eventually, an agreement was reached in which the unionised workers were allowed back into the plant, their replacements were dismissed, and the union secured a strong successorship clause and wage and pension increases. Through their abilities to network trans-nationally, then, USWA members not only succeeded in ensuring that locked-out workers in Ravenswood were able to regain access to their plant but also had a significant impact on the unfolding organisational geography of Rich's global investments, limiting his plans to expand into Eastern Europe and Latin America.

'Local' action, 'non-local' consequences

On 5 June 1998, some 3,400 members of United Auto Workers (UAW), Local Union 659, in Flint, Michigan, went on strike over plans by the General Motors corporation (GM) to change work rules and reduce the number of job classifications at their plant. Within a week a second Flint plant – this one a wholly-owned parts supplier – had also struck. As a result of GM's adoption of 'just-in-time' inventory management practices, the consequences of these two disputes quickly spread throughout the company's North American operations and beyond. By mid-June virtually all of GM's North American vehicle assembly operations had been closed due to lack of parts, while at its height (23 July) the dispute resulted in the laying off of 193,517 workers at 27 of GM's 29 North American assembly plants and at some 117 components supplier plants owned by GM subsidiaries. Ultimately, the dispute would lead GM to post an estimated $2.3 billion after-tax loss in the second and third quarters of 1998 and to lose production of some 500,000 vehicles.

Significantly, this dispute between GM and its workers was not part of a deliberate strategy of trans-spatial solidarity in which workers in one community went on strike in support of their fellow workers elsewhere. Rather, the dispute's geography was the result of a cascade effect as various plants began to run out of parts. Thus, as assembly plants which relied on the components produced in Flint could not get them, they had to send workers home. In turn, this meant that those assembly plants were no longer using components from other plants, so these plants' workers were sent home, with the result that additional assembly plants could not then get the components these workers had been producing. In all, the consequences of the strikes in just two plants in Flint quickly spread throughout the network of assembly plants and components suppliers, such that GM's corporate structure could be traced by observing the temporal order in which plants began to send workers home. Of course, this cascade also had geographical implications, as communities in different parts of North America were affected according to their closeness to Flint, with closeness measured not in terms of absolute spatial measures of distance (i.e., miles) but in terms of their relative connections to Flint in organisational terms – thus, those communities with assembly plants which relied upon the Flint plants directly were affected before those which were supplied by different plants. Significantly, GM's corporate structure meant that some two dozen components plants in Mexico were some of the first impacted, much earlier than many plants within the United States – a situation which, in some ways, made the dispute 'international' before it was 'national' in scale. After several weeks GM settled the issues which had caused the disputes at the two Flint plants and agreed to a number of concessions, including increasing capital investment in Flint.

The GM–UAW dispute, then, allows us to draw some important lessons. One is that the control of time was an important element in the relationship between management and workers – GM's reliance upon timely delivery of components made the company vulnerable to disruptions in its supply chain, while the UAW also only had a limited amount of time available to it to secure its goals before the company was able to reorganise its supply chains and secure alternative sources of components. But perhaps more important is the fact that the dispute highlights how action at a small number of strategic points in GM's corporate structure allowed autoworkers to cripple the company's North American operations within only a few days. UAW workers in Flint were able to use the highly integrated nature of GM's continental (Canada-US-Mexico) 'just-in-time' organisation to underpin their own defiance agency to force GM to settle a local dispute involving just two plants in a single community. Put another way, they were able to spread far beyond Flint the consequences of a dispute over local work rules in these two plants and to force the company to consider the impacts on its continental corporate structure of the actions of local management in Flint. Furthermore, the highly integrated nature of GM's North American production network meant that it was difficult to tell whether this was, in fact, a 'national' or even 'international' dispute on the part of the UAW (given its spread to Canada, Mexico and even Singapore, where a supplier plant was impacted) or whether it was simply a 'local' dispute which had 'national' and 'international' consequences. Regardless, this significant act of defiance has important implications for considering the geographical scale of workers' actions and the relationship between their 'local' and 'global' praxis.

Conclusion: so what does this all mean for IPE?

What I have tried to do in this chapter is to explore a number of issues which relate to the ways in which we think about how the geography of global capitalism is made and the role of workers and their organisations in this. As I hope the three case studies outlined above indicate, despite what neoliberal rhetoric may have to say about the global as being the domain of capital, unions can, in fact, have defiance agency in influencing processes of globalisation. Clearly, then, when thinking about how the geography of the global economy is being reconstituted, it is important to understand how unions and other labour organisations can act beyond the territorial confines of the countries within which they are constituted. Such a recognition is important, for it allows us to challenge the theoretical and political position which sees globalisation as a phenomenon created only by capital and which views workers' actions as confined to sub-global levels of praxis. Plainly, workers and their organisations can and do play important roles in shaping how processes of globalisation play out.

Perhaps more significant, though, is that attempts to understand the place of labour in the global economy rely crucially upon how we understand the material and discursive construction of geographical scale. Thus, viewing scale in terms of a delineator of different absolute spaces will result in a different understanding of unions' relationships to entities such as the nation-state than will viewing scale in terms of, say, a network of capillary-like connectedness. Equally, if all social action must be grounded spatially somewhere (as it must), on what basis do we determine that a dispute in a particular place is a 'local' one rather than either a simultaneously 'local' and 'global' dispute or, alternatively, a 'global' dispute which is manifested 'locally'? Such a question is not to argue for a hollow relativism in which everything is multi-scaled and therefore geographical scale as a concept is meaningless. Rather, it is to argue that the discourses we use to describe and analyse our world are powerful disciplining tools which shape how we see things and which affect how we choose to engage with the world. Whether we view a particular action as inherently 'local' or as tied into a broader spatial network of interconnections and consequences is the result of how we frame particular issues analytically and politically (see also Jason Sharman's chapter in this volume). Such discursive framing has immensely important implications for how we view unions' roles in, and responses to, globalisation – and therefore everyday sources of transformation in the world economy. Indeed, the scalar framework which we adopt when analysing unions' practices is paramount for how we understand unions' place within international relations.

In coming back to the issue of how to push an EIPE approach forward, then, engaging with concepts such as the role of workers in shaping the geography of global capitalism through their desire to construct spatial fixes which help them to pursue their economic and political goals (even if these are for reactionary purposes, as with efforts to undermine radical unionism in Latin America and the Caribbean), together with interrogating the concept of geographical scale and how we talk of the scaling of social praxis, forces us to re-evaluate the relationship between unions and the nation-state. Whereas RIPE has tended to view unions as constituted *within* the bounds of the nation-state, this is clearly a problematical stance to take conceptually for it unduly privileges the nation-state as a spatial container of social life. Thus, even when adopting a view in which different geographical scales are seen as delineators of various absolute spaces, the activities of workers such as those from Ravenswood show that they are capable of acting beyond the spatial bounds of the nation-state to impact how globalisation is playing out (restricting the expansion of Marc Rich's investments into Eastern Europe and the Caribbean, for example). Equally, adopting a Latourian view suggests that, in a world in which everything is linked to everything else to a greater or lesser degree, social praxis cannot be conceptually envisioned as confined to within particular areal units ('the local', 'the national', etc.) because 'local' practices occurring within particular nation-states are also simultaneously 'global' (and 'national' and 'regional'). Hence, in the case of the GM dispute, the quick spread to Mexico of the effects of the closures of the two Flint plants illustrated that there existed a closer linkage between Flint and components plants overseas than there did between Flint and many other communities within the United States – that the 'local' was, in many ways, more closely linked with the 'international'/'global' scale while 'the national' scale of organisation was initially bypassed, an outcome which has important conceptual and political implications. Furthering an EIPE approach, then, requires us to think about the ways in which the world is scaled and how the geography of global capitalism is a contested social product.

3   The agency of peripheral actors: small state tax havens and international regimes as weapons of the weak

J. C. Sharman

In the last decade core states acting through international organisations have attempted to set global standards to combat financial crime, shore up the stability of the global financial architecture and especially regulate 'harmful' international tax competition, targeting in each case small state tax havens. In response the small states in the sights of multilateral regulatory initiatives have successfully employed 'weapons of the weak', particularly 'rhetorical action', in subverting and reversing core states' rhetorical justifications for the inter-related campaigns. Through normative appeals, argument and rhetoric based on deeply held beliefs concerning the virtues of competition and principles such as inclusive, non-discriminatory standard setting, small states have undermined the legitimacy of core state proposals. These global regulatory campaigns came to be perceived as employing coercive methods and embodying double standards in pursuit of anti-competitive goals. With reference to the Organisation for Economic Co-operation and Development (OECD) harmful tax competition campaign in particular, this chapter examines how a coalition of the world's richest and most powerful states has been defeated by an unlikely clutch of small island states and mediaeval hold-overs through what the editors refer to as a 'mimetic challenge'.

In discussing international organisations, norms and power politics, the chapter deals with central issues for the field of international relations, including how political factors shape the global economy, as well as governance and authority relationships in the international system generally. Yet this chapter diverges from mainstream scholarship in being centred on the actions of a group of forty-one small state tax havens[1] targeted by core states via the OECD, thus turning the spotlight on small, peripheral actors which have traditionally been marginalised by the dominant regulatory framework. More than just curios, small tax havens in the Caribbean, the Pacific and Europe have been crucial in shaping an emerging international tax regime, overturning key policies favoured by core states and delegated to exclusive international organisations. Thus this chapter returns to the subject of core–periphery conflicts in international political economy that has been partially eclipsed with the decline of the dependency theory approach.

More concretely, it is argued that small states, using 'rhetorical action' (Schimmelfennig 2001), were able to defeat these various financial initiatives largely due to the double-edged nature of regime discourse. Having so closely identified themselves with the virtues of competition, core states, and even more so international economic institutions, could not be seen to violate these precepts without losing legitimacy. Furthermore, the nature of international organisations makes them poorly suited to building or changing international regimes via coercive strategies. In analysing how small states' tactics could be so successful, the chapter takes a distinct line from the 'neo-neo' consensus. However, it also challenges some constructivist international relations scholarship. In importing concepts like 'norm entrepreneurs' and 'framing' from sociology, constructivist scholars must be careful to avoid the voluntarist excesses of the social movement theorists that coined these terms. The need for caution is all the more apparent as these terms are being renounced by their creators. Conversely, the chapter also argues against the view that dominant norms must serve the interests of the powerful. Instead it is argued that a more dialogic conception of discursive politics is needed, in which the principles of the strong can be used for the ends of the weak via a mimetic challenge. The following section presents the background of the 'top-down' regulation in building an international tax regime, before explaining how these measures were defeated by tax haven states in the periphery. The argument then moves on to discuss competing sociological inspirations for constructivist international relations theory while the conclusion draws out the policy and normative implications of the material presented.

Global financial reform and 'top-down' regulation from 1998

In 1998, spurred by general anxieties about economic globalisation and the recent experience of financial crises in developing markets, the United States and the European Union decided to embark on an ambitious program of reform for the global financial order. Existing international organisations were entrusted with new functions and new bodies were set up to carry out various initiatives under the general umbrella of the Group of 7 industrialised countries (G7). A new Financial Stability Forum (FSF) was set up to counter the problem of financial contagion across borders. The Financial Action Task Force (FATF), operative since 1990 in countering money laundering, was given new powers. Most significantly, however, the OECD's Committee on Fiscal Affairs was entrusted with a new initiative to combat 'harmful tax competition'. The United States and the European Union, although beginning from different premises, arrived at the same conclusion: that their fiscal sovereignty was threatened by increased competition for internationally mobile capital. It was feared that without preventative action, a 'race to the bottom' would ensue, with states engaging in a bidding war of tax cuts, endangering overall revenue, skewing the tax burden away from mobile capital towards immobile labour and ultimately undermining democratic accountability. Radaelli describes the 'doomsday' scenario present in Europe as follows:

If EU countries do not act together, a political time bomb will bring the disintegration of the welfare state. Capital income taxes will spiral down to zero, corporations will move profits to special tax regimes, and governments will be left with the sole option of asking for more revenue from low skilled labour. (Radaelli 1999: 670)

As such, concerns about tax competition and, more broadly, financial stability and crime, reflect general anxieties about the difficulty of maintaining national economic sovereignty in the face of the global economy.

Although these new initiatives targeted different aspects of the global financial system, they shared a common diagnosis and solution. Above all, the FSF, FATF and OECD believed that a few dozen small, underregulated jurisdictions were the source of these overlapping problems. These tax havens not only attracted large sums of money away from OECD economies, but also served to exert pressure on others to follow their lead in cutting tax rates and lowering regulatory standards to attract foreign investment. Tax havens were seen as engaging in 'unfair' competition, aiding OECD country nationals in avoiding or evading tax, and turning a blind eye to criminal activity such as money laundering (OECD 1998; Wechsler 2001). G7 countries, and particularly the Clinton administration, decided that because of the importance of the issues at stake, and because of the new realities created by globalisation, a novel strategy was required. A deliberate decision was taken to avoid working through the World Trade Organisation, the United Nations or other bodies with open membership and equal voting rights. These features were seen as a recipe for drawn-out negotiations, messy compromises and lowest common denominator solutions. Instead the G7, and particularly the US and EU, favoured an approach whereby they would work towards designing a new international tax regime, and then impose key aspects on the rest of the world. The method by which these new standards were to be spread colloquially became known as 'naming and shaming'. The OECD, FATF and FSF would assess non-member jurisdictions against the new standards and blacklist those which fell short. The former Special Advisor to the US Treasury Secretary explained the logic as follows:

> The Clinton administration realised that any new approach had to focus on stemming the proliferation of underregulated jurisdictions and tackling those jurisdictions that were already established ... Furthermore, any strategy had to be global and multilateral, since unilateral actions would only drive dirty money to the world's other major financial centres. Yet Washington could not afford to take the 'bottom-up' approach of seeking a global consensus before taking action; if the debate were brought to the UN General Assembly, for example, nations with underregulated financial regimes would easily outvote those with a commitment to strong international standards ... The three efforts [OECD, FATF and FSF] each followed a 'top-down' approach in which nations would establish international standards and evaluative criteria before engaging with those who lacked the commitment. (Wechsler 2001: 49)

In mid-2000 these organisations each released overlapping blacklists, comprised almost exclusively of micro-state, non-member jurisdictions (see endnote 1), which were judged to be under-regulated. The blacklists were coupled with threats that unless the new regulations on collecting more financial and tax information and sharing this information with foreign authorities were enacted, further measures would be taken.

Small states' victories

The G7 governments and the international organisations entrusted with imposing new global regulations on tax, finance and banking were confident of their ability to overcome any opposition and the ultimate success of the regulatory projects. This optimism is hardly surprising given that most of the forty-one jurisdictions judged as under-regulated by the OECD were very small (almost all with under a million people, a majority with under 100,000), usually poor, aid-dependent and generally extremely vulnerable to coercion. Yet since 2001 the various 'top-down' initiatives have either failed or been modified to become more consensual, inclusive 'bottom-up' exercises. Materialist approaches like realism have difficulty explaining this result, taking into account the huge difference in resources between the G7 states and the micro-state tax havens like Liechtenstein and the Bahamas. Instead this chapter argues that regime discourse, and particularly the valorisation of market competition, provided tax havens with an opportunity to trip up core states and the OECD with the very same principles these actors had helped to establish. A mimetic challenge could therefore be established and executed by the tax havens. More generally, the nature of international organisations means that they are just not very good at using coercion to establish new global rules and standards (see the following section). The confrontational 'top-down' approach provided more haste but less speed relative to the more traditional 'bottom-up' method. Before developing these points further, it is important to outline briefly progress of the OECD Harmful Tax Competition initiative.

As noted earlier, from the mid-1990s OECD governments were concerned by the spectre of a 'race to the bottom' in taxes. Tax havens were seen as catalysing this development, by allowing firms and wealthy individuals to avoid or evade tax. Individuals and firms could transfer their assets to offshore trusts, manipulate transfer-pricing rules, or negotiate with tax haven governments for 'designer' tax regimes (Palan 2003). These concessions offered by tax havens to attract investment were most often 'ring-fenced', in that they were available only to foreign investors, domestic investors being ineligible. Such concessions were explicitly directed at attracting foreign investment, passing the revenue cost of tax competition onto other countries while protecting tax havens' domestic tax base. The OECD declared that ring-fenced tax concessions were no longer acceptable in attracting financial services (but allowed continuing ring-fenced tax concessions often used by OECD countries in attracting physical plants). Small state tax havens are crucially dependent on ring-fencing, with next to no domestic investment and few other attractions for foreign companies, and thus perceived that they would be driven out of the market for financial services if they adopted the new standards. Indeed, many tax haven governments alleged that this was just what the OECD wanted, especially those states with large financial centres (Such as London, New York and Tokyo) that stood to gain from removing the competition. Tax havens were also incensed by the 'top-down' approach employed, which they characterised as a neo-colonial exercise in bullying and hypocrisy, directly at odds with the sovereign prerogative of states to make their own laws.

From 2000 the OECD was persistently criticised for demanding that small, poor states adopt standards that two of the OECD's own members, Switzerland and Luxembourg, which engaged in many of the same practices as the targeted states, had rejected. Others objected that as a 'rich countries' club', the OECD was in no legal or moral position to dictate the tax and banking codes of non-member sovereign states, particularly as there had been no effort to compensate the developing states affected. Small states secured a key victory in persuading the United States to defect from the OECD campaign in May 2001. The Washington-based ambassadors of Caribbean nations like Antigua and Barbuda and Barbados managed to channel their arguments through conservative American lobby groups and think tanks, which were incensed by the prospect of a 'global tax police' run from Paris on behalf of 'socialist' European welfare states. Taking turns to represent the public face of the opposition, Caribbean representatives and think tankers mobilised a coalition from across the political spectrum against the Harmful Tax Competition initiative. This stretched from Republican stalwarts to the Democrats' Congressional Black Caucus. After a period of initial indecision, the Bush administration became convinced by the rhetoric of the tax havens and their supporters (Sharman 2006).

Small states were able to appropriate and reverse the OECD's own rhetoric regarding competition and the 'level playing field' to highlight the shortcomings of the campaign. From the standpoint of dominant liberal economic beliefs, tax competition may well constitute a healthy discipline over governments in forestalling illiberal economic policy (Helleiner 1999). The OECD has acted as one of the primary vehicles of these beliefs. Porter and Webb (2004, 11) refer to the organisation's economic 'liberalising vocation' as its fundamental purpose. In line with this vocation, one OECD official remarked with reference to the tax competition campaign: 'As an economist, how can you ever say anything bad about competition?' (*Economist*, 21 September 2000). From the other side, one representative of Pacific tax havens echoed the same point: '*Harmful* tax competition? You're the OECD, you love competition' (author's interview, Suva, Fiji, November 2004). The success of this line of attack can be gauged by the OECD's confused and defensive reaction, dropping the formula 'harmful tax competition' and replacing it with 'harmful tax practices', and then charging that tax havens actually undermined tax competition. The extent to which the OECD convinced itself in executing this U-turn is an open question, but it did not convince tax havens or third parties (Gilligan 2004; Webb 2004).

Embarrassed by widely publicised accusations of anti-competitive behaviour and discriminatory standards, by early 2001 the OECD had noticeably softened its stance on sanctions and agreed to negotiate the content of the new regulatory package. Although the campaign was not officially abandoned, the central plank of abolishing ring-fenced concessions was dropped and the 'top-down' approach compromised by removing the threat of sanctions and agreeing to dialogue. Tax havens, now referred to by the OECD as 'participating partners', managed to extract a further important concession in early 2002 when they gained agreement that they would reform only after all thirty OECD members had taken equivalent measures. As Switzerland and Luxembourg have consistently refused to make any of the necessary reforms relating to information sharing, this concession effectively means that tax havens are under no obligation to adopt new standards.

While the FSF and particularly FATF campaigns have met with more success, there has been a similar tendency to dilute or abandon the 'top-down' coercive approach. In November 2002 the FATF agreed to discontinue its annual naming and shaming exercise. Similarly, despite an early commitment to blacklisting and sanctioning, the FSF has ceded its functions to the International Monetary Fund (IMF) which emphasises dialogue, consensus, capacity building and technical assistance. The IMF Offshore Audit exercise specifically rejects blacklists and sanctions, and only makes findings public with the consent of jurisdictions audited. Why has the top-down approach to imposing new global standards for finance and tax brought such meagre results, even when applied to such vulnerable states?

Explaining small states' victories: regimes and international organisations

Above all, this section argues that the nature of international institutions often at the heart of regimes such as the OECD and FATF provides opportunities for small states to increase their influence on the process of global standard-setting by holding such bodies, and through them large states, accountable to basic and widely accepted principles of justice and fairness in international politics. This sheds light not only on the experience of attempts at reforming global financial regulation from 1998, but also broader questions of power and influence in international relations.

Four characteristics of international organisations in particular are important for small states seeking to influence these institutions, and through them regimes, by the use of mimetic challenges (for an expanded account, see Sharman 2006). Firstly, while often state creations to foster or uphold regimes, international organisations are to a significant degree autonomous from their member states and put a high priority on their own institutional survival and success. Secondly, these organisations are poorly equipped to employ coercion and monitor unwilling compliance in building, maintaining and policing regimes, even in the limiting case of the international financial institutions with conditional lending. Instead the means employed to establish and sustain regimes by international organisations, moral and reasoned suasion, are crucially dependent on their institutional reputation and legitimacy. Attempts to foster voluntary compliance with and 'ownership' of specific regulations and more diffuse regimes reflects not so much a normative stand as a pragmatic acceptance that international regimes are unlikely to be effective in the face of resistance from even small and developing states. Thirdly, international organisations can be held accountable or shamed in public debate when they act at variance with central regime norms such as the importance of competition. As such international organisations are sensitive to the kind of 'political ju-jitsu' or 'accountability politics' often practiced by non-government organisations, whereby they can be pressured into conforming with widely shared conceptions of appropriate behaviour as well as specific earlier public commitments, whether or not these earlier commitments were sincere or merely expedient. Fourthly, bodies such as the FSF, FATF and even the OECD operate in an environment of 'institutional Darwinism', i.e., of many close competitors operating to sustain any given regime, and member states who put increasing emphasis on getting 'value for money', creating pressures to adapt and survive. International institutions that fail to live up to members' expectations or attract too much bad publicity may find themselves marginalised and starved of funds. The ruthlessness of US administrations when dealing with international organisations that have fallen foul of domestic political priorities makes this fact particularly salient.

Although founded, funded and in the last instance controlled by member states, these international organisations have a significant degree of autonomy (Barnett and Finnemore 2004). If they were instruments of states pure and simple there would be no self-interest in maintaining their institutional survival, or promoting their public profile as goals in and of themselves. In fact, however, international institutions such as the OECD and FATF put a premium on organisational survival and success above and beyond the immediate interests of their constituent member states. As such this autonomy and self-interest gives a point of entry for critics. International organisations are concerned with their public profiles and hence vulnerable to bad publicity. For example, although the failure of the Multilateral Agreement on Investment owed a great deal to intra-OECD disagreements, the associated negative publicity for this particular initiative was both consequential and damaging to the OECD as a whole (Henderson 1999). Negative publicity can lead to indirect pressure as politicians fear the electoral repercussions of activist protests and campaigns, and more directly as international organisations worry about their ability to successfully reach specified goals and maintain their budgets (see below). Less tangibly but more importantly such bodies depend on their reputation for embodying the techniques of international best practice and more broadly on their authority as principled participants in international relations.

Because institutions like the OECD, FATF and FSF generally rely on such forms of moral and reasoned suasion as benchmarking, black- or whitelisting, peer review and peer pressure, each of which is in turn reliant on institutional standing and reputation, damage to their public image very directly translates into reduced effectiveness, and greatly hinders their ability to meet important institutional goals. A paper by the OECD secretariat on the importance of these methods notes that mutual trust between the parties involved is key to the success of the exercise, and that 'there is a strong linkage between the credibility of the process and its capacity to influence' (Pagani 2002, 13). Relatedly, the standards agreed on by various specialised bodies often rely on voluntary adoption by other international organisations and governments. As a general rule, standards are only as legitimate (and thus likely to be disseminated and effective) as the bodies that draft them. In turn, this puts a premium on widespread consultation and dialogue rather than a 'top-down' approach. Thus the FATF Forty Recommendations have been voluntarily endorsed and reinforced by other international organisations as diverse as the Black Sea Economic Co-operation Council, the Commonwealth Heads of Government, the Offshore Group of Banking Supervisors and the United Nations General Assembly (Galvao 2001), not because of coercion or inducements, but because they are seen as representing international best practice and endowed with the reputation and authority of their institutional author. For the OECD also 'influence ... depends critically on the OECD's identity as an unbiased source of knowledge and advice' (Porter and Webb 2004, 20). Even coercive strategies like blacklisting and sanctions indirectly rely on third parties judging that such penalties and threats are fair and legitimate in order to be effective. Once again, the extent that the particular sanction is accepted in the international community is closely linked with the reputation of the institution imposing such measures (Hurd 2002).

In light of the above, one of the most productive ways of generating public leverage over international organisations is to compare publicly articulated principles embedded in the regime with actual behaviour. Since the end of the cold war, international organisations have generally been founded to embody and propagate the importance of market competition, non-discrimination, consensual dispute settlement, good governance and so on, and bodies such as the FATF and FSF are no exception. These sort of public and frequently re-affirmed commitments provide an opening for outsiders to hold such institutions accountable to their principles. Tax havens did this well, contrasting the top-down exclusive cast of the OECD campaign with quotes from the official heading the initiative, for example:

The important thing is that as many people as possible have a seat at the table in setting what the rules would be. I see that as a general trend in a lot of our work. We must be opening up; we must become more inclusive; we must try not just be inviting countries to come and listen to what we have to say, but we've got to be inviting them and saying, 'You are here as partners. We're interested in what your views are, and your views will shape things that come out of the OECD'. (ITIO 2002, 19)

Declarations in this vein from international civil servants could be reproduced *ad infinitum*, but given the selectivity and discriminatory character of at least some of the multilateral initiatives they chair, the question is: are such public commitments anything more than just window dressing?

Taking the most pessimistic and cynical reading of recent efforts to regulate global finance (which is not the position of this chapter), namely that they are exclusively motivated by mercantilist concerns to entrench the G7 countries' dominance of the global financial services industry, there is still good reason to think that pronouncements on the virtues of economic competition and political inclusiveness are consequential. Even if they were never intended to be taken at face value, these sorts of public commitments can be used to bind international organisations and hold them accountable to principles which they may have introduced to the debate solely on pragmatic or instrumental grounds. Recent scholarship on the eastwards expansion of the EU has emphasised how what was at the time 'cheap talk' by existing member governments and Brussels institutions concerning the desirability of an enlarged union, came back to haunt them during the negotiation process. Despite operating from a very weak bargaining position, with little to offer the existing fifteen members in economic or security terms, post-Communist applicants have been able to capitalise on earlier rhetoric by their interlocutors on the need for an inclusive EU incorporating all European democracies. Even those within the EU unconvinced of the merits of expansion have so far been reluctant to admit that they had never really meant what they had said about including post-Communist states (Schimmelfennig 2001). This sort of 'rhetorical self-entrapment' means that parties looking to dishonour earlier public commitments must weigh costs of losing credibility and legitimacy in the eyes of bargaining partners and the international community at large against the advantage of preaching one thing and practising another. Although international politics is replete with examples of persistent and blatant hypocrisy, there are good reasons to think that international organisations are more sensitive to the costs of violating such norms than states. In their mammoth study of global business regulation in thirteen separate areas based on over 500 interviews, Braithwaite and Drahos (2000) come to the conclusion that by and large dialogue is not only more congruent with international norms of behaviour, it is also more efficient than coercion.

Building on these observations about the ability of outsiders to hold international organisations accountable to earlier commitments, it is also important to note that although these multilateral bodies are in many ways in the ascendent they can be individually quite vulnerable. The very proliferation and convergence of such institutions means that there are more and more competitors for any given policy area, and that member states are more and more insistent about getting 'value for money'. Although the World Bank and the IMF are well entrenched, even an institution of the pedigree of the OECD cannot be complacent about its survival. Its efforts to expand from being basically a think tank to a venue for regulatory negotiations have not been particularly successful (Marcussen 2004). Former British Chancellor of the Exchequer, Norman Lamont, stated that there is nothing the OECD does that could not be done by the IMF, except the statistical functions which could easily be hived off to another body (*Spectator*, 1 July 2000: 26). In late 2004 moves were afoot in the US Congress to cut off all funding to the institution as a direct result of its involvement in the tax competition campaign (*Financial Times*, 19 November 2004). Even representing as they do the world's most powerful countries, the congeries of international organisations currently involved in setting global tax and financial regulations can be successfully contested by groups of small and developing countries and NGOs through everyday tactics such as mimetic challenge.

Non-regulatory constructivism and social movements in international relations and sociology

So far this chapter has argued that small states can be effective in defending their interests by copying the tactics employed by NGOs, in particular using a mimetic challenge to point out the gap between principles that constitute regimes and the behaviour of dominant states and international institutions. In studying the activities of such groups in the international arena, international relations scholars have tended to adopt a particular approach formulated in sociology to analyse social movements. The defining example is Finnemore and Sikkink's piece in the 1998 golden anniversary issue of *International Organization*, representing the state of the art in the field. This section argues that there are important flaws in this approach, now conceded even by the sociologists who were most important in developing it (McAdam *et al.* 2001), while the next section presents the beginnings of an alternative approach.

The predominant approach to studying social movements in sociology in the 1990s built on the foundations of the resource mobilisation literature from the 1970s which saw groups as strategic actors. This has been reflected in international relations with the rise of such terms as 'norm entrepreneurs' for social movement leaders. Four basic assumptions are common to this strategic conception of social movements: that collective action is costly, that contenders count costs, that such action is undertaken in pursuit of collective goods and that contenders weigh up expected costs against expected benefits (Tilly 1978: 99).

In the 1990s there was an effort to combine the insights of resource mobilisation explanations with more directly political and cultural elements. This development occurred in part because of dissatisfaction with the confining economistic assumptions of resource mobilisation. A strict conception of self-interest and selective incentives was expanded to include notions of 'soft' or solidaristic incentives (McAdam *et al.* 1988). The main innovation, however, was the inclusion of 'framing processes': 'the collective processes of interpretation, attribution, and social construction that mediate between opportunity and action' (McAdam *et al.* 1996: 2). Frames or framing processes were incorporated into the study of social movements thanks in large part to the work of David Snow. He posed such questions as 'How do individuals decide to participate in a particular crowd or movement activity? What is the nature of decision-making process? What determines the kinds of meanings that are attributed to particular activities and events? How do these meanings get constructed?'(Snow and Oliver 1995: 582). The return of interest in such questions was somewhat hyperbolically referred to as 'bringing culture back in' (McAdam *et al.* 1996: 6).

In the most well-developed account of 'collective action frames' they are defined as an 'emergent action-oriented set of beliefs and meanings that inspire and legitimate social movement activities and campaigns' (Snow and Oliver 1995: 587). The 1996 edited volume, *Comparative Perspectives on Social Movements*, in many ways the culmination of writing in this vein, disaggregates the concept of frames in a manner that should now be familiar to constructivist international relations scholars: '(1) the cultural tool kits available to would-be insurgents; (2) the strategic framing effort of movement groups; (3) the frame contests between the movement and other collective actors – principally the state …; (4) the structure and role of the media in mediating such contests; and (5) the cultural impact of movement in modifying the available tool kit' (McAdam *et al.* 1996: 19). Despite references to social construction, scholars studying social movements in sociology then, and international relations now, stress the strategic 'tool kit' nature of frames, strictly in keeping with the general conception of social movements as strategic actors. The sociologist Sidney Tarrow explicitly argues against the view of 'movements as text', in favour of the view that 'meanings are constructed out of social and political interaction by movement entrepreneurs' (Tarrow 1994: 119). Tarrow cannot conceive of explanations of social movements based on cultural relations and the force of ideas: 'if meanings are "fixed" by … rhetorical renderings, who does the rendering and won't future movements require agency to be mobilised?' (Tarrow 1994: 121). Explanations based on frames are replete with voluntaristic accounts of how frames are chosen, manipulated and created by agents, how conflicting social movements and the state select and employ various elements of the cultural tool kit and so forth. Often the way in which such terms as 'framing contest' are used gives the impression that 'public relations campaign' would serve as an appropriate synonym. Once again, these features of the sociological literature have now been imported to international relations.

What are the weaknesses of this actor-centred view of social movements and frames in particular in sociology and sociological international relations? First and foremost is the convoluted treatment that reduces culture and a society's stock of shared meanings to a 'tool kit', to be raided and pressed into service when most convenient and efficacious. The idea that social movements may in fact be bound by or even a product of such shared meanings does not seem to be allowed. It is hard to imagine a concept less suited to this voluntaristic pick-and-choose treatment than culture; indeed, this has been one of the main reasons it has fallen into disfavour among wide sections of the discipline. Individuals and groups are enmeshed and socialised within such webs of meaning, even allowing a role for agency, movements could only employ frames in the manner Tarrow *et al.* suggest they do if actors were completely isolated from society and the dominant ideas of the time.

Thus despite the inclusion of what might initially be regarded as identity-based factors, strategy-based conceptions of social movements and international NGOs have tended to remain just that: focused on the actor, with a highly voluntaristic cast, and premised on rational maximising behaviour. Culture is only presented in the context of another menu of tactical options from which movement leaders can choose. This essential unity of the field is best captured by Munck, who points out that despite the new elements the 'conceptual framework is still actor-centred, and [the] . . . argument hinges on the strategic problem of getting "from here to there". Social movement theory is essentially about a variety of resources which organisers or leaders draw upon to constitute a movement' (Munck 1995: 670). For international relations scholars, constructivist accounts tend to lose their distinctiveness relative to the dominant rationalist theories. Symbols, argument and rhetoric become one more instrument to be pressed into service in maximising actors' utilities, akin to economic sanctions or military force. At a time when this view is still in the ascendent in international relations, Sidney Tarrow, Doug McAdam and Charles Tilly, the three most important sociologists behind this perspective, have now repudiated it (McAdam *et al.* 2001).

Rhetorical action as an alternative

Thus a potential problem with the idea of norms as 'framing', in which 'norm entrepreneurs' use appeals and audiences accept them in a highly calculating instrumental manner, is that it tends to over-correct for structural bias in earlier renditions of norms. If norms are just another resource to be pressed into service by rationally calculating agents in pursuit of their goals, why would anyone be moved or bound by them? (Elster 1989). 'Challengers cannot simply readily and instrumentally manipulate discourses for their own cynical ends, for this undermines the foundations of mutual understandings that explain the justice of their claims and actions to themselves and others' (Steinberg 1999: 753).

What is the alternative for international relations scholars? James Scott (1990) and Marc Steinberg see more powerful actors setting the dominant cultural and discursive features of the landscape, but also argue that the ambiguity and non-exclusive nature of rhetoric and culture mean that weaker actors have the opportunity to appropriate and subvert the language and values of the strong to even up the balance between them. Ideas and rhetoric cannot be controlled by the strong in the same way as money or weapons: 'if collective action discourse is contextual, public and emergent in the processes of mobilisation and action, as most accounts suggest, then exercising control and distribution of it as a resource is highly problematic' (Steinberg 1999: 742; see also Steinberg 1998). This difficulty in exercising control stems from the very nature of discourse which Steinberg, drawing directly from the Russian formalist literary theorist Mikhail Bakhtin, describes as a social process that is 'essentially dialectic, dynamic, and riven with contradictions' (Steinberg 1998: 852). Although elites may dominate the economy and maintain their monopoly of the means of violence, their control of linguistically mediated culture, ideas and norms is always contested and uncertain. The practical upshot of this is that those challenging the dominant elite generally do so using a vocabulary and values developed by the elite themselves, whether the challengers be nineteenth-century British textile workers, Malaysian peasants, international NGOs or tax haven states (Scott 1987, 1990). These features of language attest to 'the potential for persuasive communication to take a wolfish turn on the activists who rely on it' (Steinberg 1998: 861). The very principles put into play by the strong can be used to trip them up.

Bakhtin provides an attractive source of inspiration as a way of getting to grips with the tension between the structural nature of norms and agents' instrumental use of rhetoric, agents who are partly bound by collective understandings and community norms but also partly free to pursue their own selfish interests (Bakhtin 1985; Holquist 1990). Responding to the structuralist view of language as an unchanging system of rules existing outside the self and totally constraining the production of meaning, Bakhtin argued that there is scope for individual agency and innovation in producing meaning. He was also keen to establish, however, that each unit of discourse (utterance) could not be reduced to the intention of the speaker plain and simple because language is social and collective. Purely idiosyncratic speech is unintelligible to anyone else. Thus there is an analogy in international relations scholarship of dissatisfaction with determinative taken-for-granted norms coupled with unease about reducing normative appeals and moral suasion to a purely instrumental public relations campaign. The middle way for Bakhtin is to see the world as a vast system of contested meanings in which humans try to impose language as an ordering and simplifying system to render intelligible and communicable novel and chaotic events. Individual meanings are produced in a dialogic fashion, comprising an utterance, the social and historical context, and the relation between the two. Because what may seem to be a simple unambiguous statement has to be mediated through social context to be interpreted by the addressee, and this social context is conflicted and dynamic, many potential meanings attached to that particular utterance are put into play. What is the relevance of this for norms, power and international relations?

Bakhtin believes that no matter how much dominant classes or other elites try to establish their preferred norms and discursive themes, the complicating effects of dialogue prevent control over meaning, leaving room for subordinate populations to subvert the themes put into play by the rulers and appropriate them for their own ends. Bakhtin's work is thus described as fundamentally pluralist and anti-totalitarian (despite living and working in the Soviet Union all through the Stalin era), in that he finds discourse to be irreducibly 'multi-vocal' or 'polyphonic', creating 'heteroglossia'. This view thus contradicts international relations scholarship in the 'critical' constructivist vein, which sees norms as one more weapon in the arsenal of dominant states in extending their hegemony to the ideational sphere.

There are some parallels between the way tax havens made subversive use of principles of the powerful, and the way ideas developed by Europeans relating to human equality were used to delegitimise European colonial empires. For Crawford the same arguments that were important in shaping the practice of colonialism were ultimately used to bring about its undoing (Crawford 2002: 7). Robert Jackson has taken an even more direct line, noting that the ideational basis of the decolonisation movement 'flows from the heart of the Western political tradition', especially in relation to democracy and equality (Jackson 1993: 134). Drawing on the heritage of this movement, tax haven states in the Caribbean and Pacific often reprised anti-colonial themes in resisting core states' financial regulatory initiatives. The key difference in these two instances of self-assertion in the periphery, however, is that tax havens were drawing on the principles of the strong to uphold the status quo (a lack of global tax regulation), rather than to undermine it.

Returning to international organisations, writing on the United Nations (UN) Security Council, Hurd echoes these insights, observing that 'resistance works best when presented in terms borrowed from the language of the authority and where the point is . . . to argue that the existing authority is not being true to its own professed values' (Hurd 2002: 47). By this measure the 'Washington consensus', advanced by the IMF and World Bank among others, stressing robust competition, financial deregulation, the liberalisation of capital flows and the legitimacy of market outcomes occurring in the context of a level playing field, definitely constitutes a dominant discourse among economic policy-makers. Accentuating this identification is the way these values are epitomised in the OECD's convention and practices, and the specific principles put into play by the 1998 report and officials' subsequent statements relating to the tax competition initiative. These include the need to maintain fiscal sovereignty and appropriateness of dialogue and cooperation in setting up cross-border regulatory frameworks. Tax havens and their supporters took these themes and used them to undermine the OECD campaign, to show how core countries were not being true to their own professed values in working to overturn market results through coercively imposing biased regulatory standards on a global scale.

Conclusions

This chapter has briefly presented an explanation of how small states, NGOs and other marginalised actors in world politics can affect important policy outcomes even against the opposition of powerful core states. With reference to Stephen Krasner's quote in the Introduction, Luxembourg, Samoa, Grenada and others don't have to be hegemonic to use others' ideas for their own ends. Following on from the work of Bakhtin as mediated by Scott and Steinberg, the ambiguity of dominant ideas and principles that constitute regimes gives scope for weak actors to appropriate, subvert and reverse the interpretations of powerful actors for subaltern goals. As applied to international organisations by Schimmelfennig, this approach provides ample room for contestation and agency, unlike overly structural understandings of norms, but does not reduce features of the cultural and discursive landscape to tools to be selected by calculating asocial norm entrepreneurs trading off resource inputs and political outputs at the margin.

Although this chapter has aimed to advance the theoretical treatment of regime change in international political economy, there are also important policy implications. Probably the most apparent is the difficulty of using coercion to establish or modify a regime, especially those regimes that rely on international institutions for their functioning. Even in the limiting and atypical case of conditional lending, the IMF and World Bank have had great difficulty achieving their policy goals in the face of suspicion, hostility and covert opposition from poor, weak recipient countries. Those in international organisations and national policy-makers in the core involved in delegating an increasing range of functions to such organisations enhance their chances of success by promoting inclusive rule-making that at the very least does not leave weak states worse off. This is because securing the unwilling compliance of even small weak states is expensive and difficult. Conversely, those in small and weak states in the periphery may benefit from regimes founded on the ideas of the dominant states, even against the latter's wishes, by employing mimetic challenges to exploit the ambiguity and flexibility inherent in all such general propositions. By using mimetic challenges, critics in tax havens have been able to hold dominant states and international organisations accountable for their consistent support of markets and competition to delegitimise the OECD's campaign to restrict tax competition. To be sure, this room for manoeuvre does not erase power differences, but it does mean that contestation over regimes between core and periphery is not a foregone conclusion. One important current policy issue that may be susceptible to such treatment is the continuing protection of agriculture in the European Union, the US and Japan, in spite of these countries' purported commitment to free trade and market economics.

The final aspect of the issue is a normative one, in line with this volume's overarching concern with emancipatory politics. It is often too easy to make the transition from identifying small and weak actors, to identifying *with* such actors, attributing to them morally praiseworthy characteristics and finding them deserving of support merely by virtue of their marginality and vulnerability, especially in conflicts with other more powerful actors or ideas. Yet in the particular case of tax havens such a simplistic conclusion is premature, for even if talk of money laundering and 'harmful' tax competition has been exaggerated, this does not mean that some of the charges levelled against tax havens by the United States, the EU and the OECD are unjustified (UNDCCP 1998). In their more candid moments, officials in tax havens admit that much if not most of their business is derived from wealthy individuals and companies escaping tax liabilities in their home countries. Relating to considerations of justice more generally, governments in peripheral states have often perpetrated, ignored or excused human rights abuses at home and abroad, from Mauritanian slavery, to torture in Burma, state-sanctioned persecution of homosexuality in Africa and the Caribbean and severely discriminatory treatment of women in South Asia and the Middle East, even when these issues have been taken up by the United States and Europe. Weakness is not synonymous with moral virtue any more than strength entails villainy.

Note

1. Andorra, Anguilla, Antigua and Barbuda, Aruba, the Bahamas, Bahrain, Barbados, Belize, Bermuda, British Virgin Islands, Cayman Islands, Cook Islands, Cyprus, Dominica, Gibraltar, Grenada, Guernsey, Isle of Man, Jersey, Maldives, Montserrat, Netherlands Antilles, Niue, Liberia, Liechtenstein, Malta, Marshall Islands, Mauritius, Monaco, Nauru, Panama, Samoa, San Marino, Seychelles, St. Kitts and Nevis, St. Lucia, St. Vincent and the Grenadines, Tonga, Turks and Caicos Islands, US Virgin Islands, Vanuatu.

4 Southern sites of female agency: informal regimes and female migrant labour resistance in East and Southeast Asia

Michele Ford and Nicola Piper

Female migrant workers, especially the foreign domestic workers (FDWs) who comprise the majority of women migrants in Asia, are generally portrayed as having little or no agency in the world economy. Scholars of Asian migration have traditionally conceived of female migrant workers as either passive victims of global power structures (emphasising macroeconomic 'demand and supply' dynamics) or isolated actors exerting micro agency through acts of 'everyday resistance', while regulatory international political economy (RIPE) scholarship has largely failed to consider them at all. But while substantial evidence exists that reveals the extent to which the human and labour rights of FDWs are violated in East and Southeast Asia (Piper and Iredale 2003), it is wrong to portray these workers as either passive bearers of the weight of global structures or simply the objects of transnational advocacy campaigns (Keck and Sikkink 1998). Although FDWs are clearly subjected to structural oppression and are often objectified by well-meaning non-governmental organisations (NGOs), a significant number of FDWs attempt to mediate their experiences of work not only personally, but in conjunction with other migrant workers. When combined with the campaigns of middle-class activists associated with NGOs acting both within national boundaries and across them, these attempts at defiance constitute an informal regime that interacts with – and has the potential to influence – the formal industrial relations and immigration regimes that seek to control and regulate foreign domestic labour at the national and international levels.

This chapter focuses on FDWs' collective activism and middle-class campaigns in sending and receiving countries in East and Southeast Asia around foreign domestic worker issues. The chapter begins with a brief overview of female labour migration in East and Southeast Asia followed by a discussion of the formal regimes that seek to regulate it. It then proceeds to discuss the informal regimes that have emerged both within

63

and across national borders since the 1980s, using examples from several countries in the region. The final section focuses on the implications of interactions between the formal and informal regimes associated with foreign domestic labour. The chapter concludes that although serious obstacles continue to hinder migrant worker groups' and migrant labour NGOs' campaigns, these groups are engaged in an increasingly important form of transnational collective action that enables defiance and provides a mechanism through which to attempt to influence the formal regimes that regulate the personal and working lives of FDWs.

Female labour migration in East and Southeast Asia

Since the 1980s, large-scale labour migration has played a key role in the rapid development of East and Southeast Asian countries and their economies (e.g., Stahl and Appleyard 1992). By the early 1990s, labour migration had grown to the point that nearly all countries in the region were involved in either the sending or receiving of migrant labour, or in both (United Nations 2003: 2). For the governments of peripheral countries such as the Philippines, Indonesia and Thailand, rising demand for contract labour first in the Middle East from the mid-1970s and later in East and Southeast Asia provided a timely boost to sluggish economies and low foreign exchange reserves. Meanwhile, the importation of large numbers of migrant workers from poorer neighbouring countries provided a solution, in the short-run at least, to the shortage of labour experienced by industries and households in the core economies of Singapore, Malaysia, Hong Kong and Taiwan. Yet although sending and receiving countries in the region have become increasingly structurally dependent on this extremely flexible type of labour (Stahl 2000), migrant workers are largely left out of the equation when labour relations and industrial restructuring in the Asia Pacific region are discussed in the literature. Likewise, examinations of labour market flexibility largely neglect the contribution of short-term contracted labour performed by non-citizens (e.g., Gills and Piper 2002). With the notable exception of Hewison and Young (2006), more general RIPE analyses of the political economy of East and Southeast Asia also rarely discuss the issue of migrant labour in a region that collectively constitutes the largest labour exporter in the world, producing massive flows of documented and undocumented foreign workers every year (e.g., Rodan et al. 1997).

Migrant labour's position within regional economies cannot, of course, be divorced from regional patterns of capitalism and the labour regimes embedded in them, nor from their gendered nature. Domestically, patriarchal gender ideology and a strong sense of hierarchy in the countries of the region produce employment opportunities and entitlements segregated by sex. Migrant labour is affected in the same manner. Male migrants have been mobilised mainly in productive jobs in construction and manufacturing industries, while female migrants are largely concentrated in reproductive jobs in the household and the commercial service sectors (Yamanaka and Piper 2004). By 2000, more than two million women were estimated to be working abroad, accounting for one-third of approximately six million migrant workers employed in Asia. Recently, skilled and professional women have begun to migrate in response to expanding employment opportunities in business, health, education and services (see e.g., Raghuram 2000); however, these middle-class professionals constitute a tiny minority of female labour migrants, the majority of whom are overwhelmingly working class. Although a small but substantial proportion of working-class, migrant women are employed as assembly line workers and agricultural and fish farm hands (see e.g., Battistella and Asis 2002), the largest proportion of women migrating for work-related reasons, both documented and undocumented, are employed in a narrow range of reproductive, labour-related occupations such as live-in maids, caregivers, entertainers, sex workers and other service employees (e.g., Piper and Yamanaka 2003).

The transfer of foreign women within Asia to work as housekeepers and nannies has important implications for the construction and practice of household labour in both sending and receiving countries. East and Southeast Asian receiving countries are very different from Europe, where the trend towards an increasing presence of FDWs has to be understood in relation to analyses of the contraction of the welfare state (Kofman 2004). The expansion of the middle classes in Asian receiving countries by the 1990s brought with it increasingly strident household demands for domestic workers, not least because of the lack of European-style public welfare services. The ready availability of FDWs freed local, middle-class women from their household tasks, enabling them to participate in the labour market without questioning persistent assumptions about housework being women's work – a solution to labour market pressures which validates existing gender relations and the division of labour in the private sphere (Chin 2003). In sending countries, female labour migration also perpetuates gendered understandings of household labour by creating a 'care chain' as departing women hire maids to take care of their households while they work abroad (Ehrenreich and Hochschild Russell 2002). This hired woman typically comes from a poorer, non-migrant family with children of her own, and her absence from her own home creates a demand for care for her children. Since she cannot afford to pay a domestic worker this demand is typically met by her own oldest daughter (or another female member of the family), who takes on the household care work while the mother is away. The daughter or female relative thus represents the bottom of the global care hierarchy, whose household care work is diminished in value by virtue of being local and unpaid, and therefore totally outside the scope of formal labour regimes.

The main reason FDWs accept jobs abroad as maids is economic: the relatively high wages offered overseas allow them to save money to pay for the education of children, health services of various family members, housing and household commodities. There is, however, increasing evidence that women also exercise agency by migrating to escape difficult family relations, violent marriages, or the stigma of divorce or single parenthood (e.g., Scalabrini Migration Center 2004). FDWs are usually employed on two-year (often renewable) contracts that tie them to one specific employer, but many women remain overseas for several years. The main problem FDWs experience is separation from their families, in particular their children, in households where they are satisfied with their employment conditions. However, more serious problems related to the nature of their work do occur quite frequently. Working and residing in private homes, live-in maids incur the risk of suffering violation of contract terms and abuses by employers and family members with few formal avenues available for recourse (Human Rights Watch 2004, 2005).

Regulatory regimes and FDWs

Both local and foreign domestic workers are effectively denied legal protection in many jurisdictions (Chin 2003; Huang and Yeoh 2003; Lan 2003) because their work is viewed as an extension of the unpaid services 'naturally' provided by women. And because the work done by FDWs lies outside of sectors 'normally' regulated by industrial relations regimes, FDWs themselves do not conform to the concepts of 'work' and 'workforce' associated with those regimes. These concepts, derived from nineteenth-century definitions based on the experience of male industrial workers in the factory towns of Great Britain, have little room for migrants or women employed in formal sector occupations, let alone for female migrant workers employed outside the formal sector. It is not surprising, then, that FDWs are regulated by not one, but rather a whole range of formal regimes, each of which attempts (or fails) to deal with a particular aspect of FDWs' work or status as temporary migrants.

Most important among the regimes that seek to regulate FDWs are those concerned with industrial relations and immigration internationally and in sending and receiving countries, along with bilateral structures that seek to control labour migration flows. There have been attempts to include migration into the trade agenda of the World Trade Organisation (WTO), although to date its General Agreement on Trade in Services (GATS) negotiations on the 'movement of natural persons' (Mode 4) in the 'service sector' has excluded unskilled workers, including FDWs. There is no global coordinating mechanism or commonly agreed upon framework to guide policy-making on migration, leaving the international regulatory framework that protects migrants patchy and poorly developed (Ramamurthy 2003). However, regional and national regulatory mechanisms are theoretically informed by the global norms established by the United Nations (UN).

International structures

Migrant workers are recognised by the UN as a group that requires special protection. One of the UN's major initiatives on migrant workers is the 1990 Convention on the Protection of the Rights of All Migrant Workers and Members of their Families (ICRM). The ICRM is unusual in its usage of the male and female forms of personal and possessive pronouns (he/she, his/hers), thus making all rights provided applicable to men and women, but it does not address gender-specific needs of migrant workers in any way (UN General Assembly 2004; Cholewinski 1997). As noted in Truong's (1996: 32) discussion of protective mechanisms for female migrant workers, the ICRM has recognised female migrant workers, but not in their role as 'reproductive workers' – a term with which Truong refers to jobs in 'sex-affective services' and the 'caretaking economy'.

Within the UN's standard setting structure, it is in fact the International Labour Organisation (ILO) and United Nations Development Fund for Women (UNIFEM) which have most explicitly expressed a commitment to gender equality dimensions of migration and women's rights. The two relevant ILO conventions (Nos. 143 and 97) do not refer in any detail to female migrants' specific vulnerabilities, but the ILO's Gender Program has published numerous reports on women migrants in various countries; its Migration Section has also given much attention to migrants' rights with specific reference to gendered perspectives to such rights; and ILO reports have explicitly mentioned domestic work as a particular 'sector' prone to abusive and exploitative practices (ILO 2004; see also Esim and Smith 2004). Likewise, UNIFEM has paid special attention to domestic service, which is not surprising given that domestic labour is the most female-dominated form of work worldwide. UNIFEM runs a regional project entitled 'Empowering Migrant Workers in Asia' from its Bangkok office aimed at adapting the Convention on the Elimination of All Forms of Discrimination Against Women (CEDAW) to migration.

The effectiveness of these international instruments depends on how widely they are adopted, and how successfully they are implemented at the national and sub-national levels. For example, the ICRM only came into force in September 2003, having finally reached the required minimum number of ratifications. Furthermore, unlike CEDAW, the ICRM has only been ratified by a small number of countries, all of which are exporters of migrant labour (in the Asia Pacific). And although CEDAW has received much wider support, it is yet to be seen how successful UNIFEM's program will be in strengthening female migrant workers' rights through its application.

Immigration regimes

FDWs' immigration status is heavily regulated in both sending and receiving countries. Receiving countries in East and Southeast Asia practise a legal permit system on a long-term basis only for highly skilled or professional migrants. Unskilled migrant workers (who constitute the majority of foreign labour) are permitted to work under labour contract policies which stipulate clear limits on the duration of their employment and the industries in which they can be employed. In many receiving countries, the policies under which FDWs and other migrant workers are employed are periodically altered to meet changing labour market demands or on the basis of political or social considerations. Malaysia, for example, has a long history of attempting to regulate flows of Indonesian workers into both the Peninsula and Malaysia's eastern states in response to changing economic conditions and political pressures associated with race. Meanwhile, the Taiwanese government allowed women to be employed as domestic workers and carers after 1992, but officially suspended the use of foreign workers for domestic labour in 1996, although foreign workers continued to be brought in as carers for small children and the elderly. Receiving countries even regulate the extent to which FDWs are permitted to integrate into the host society. For example, in Singapore and Malaysia regulations include a prohibition on marrying local citizens.

Immigration regimes within receiving countries are only partially successful in regulating female migrant labour, not least because the effectiveness of border/entry controls varies dramatically. For example, Malaysia has an ongoing problem with undocumented workers from Indonesia and elsewhere, which it has attempted to address through punitive measures such as detention and mass deportation (Ford 2006) – a problem not faced to any significant extent by neighbouring Singapore. Similarly, despite policies mandating the return of unskilled migrants to their countries of origin upon expiry of their contracts, many migrant workers exercise agency by prolonging their employment and residence in the receiving country – either by overstaying (and thus slipping into a state of 'illegality') or by being given extensions on their work permits. Other migrants engage in a long-term cycle of contracts, either in a particular receiving country or in a range of countries: a practice which meets the letter, but not the stated aims, of the immigration regimes concerned. Regulations concerning the sectors and/or occupations in which migrant workers are employed after arriving in the country are also problematic. As Loveband (2003) demonstrates in the Taiwanese case, formal restrictions on the type of work undertaken by female migrant workers are extremely porous in practice, with many Indonesian women in particular continuing to undertake both domestic work and duties in their employers' small businesses in addition to (or instead of) working as carers. In Hong Kong, some FDWs circumvent regulations concerning the nature of their employment by working for several employers on an hourly basis instead of living-in with a single employer – an arrangement which gives them more freedom (Wee and Sim 2005). Ironically, this entails giving up their legal status by opting for unauthorised work.

Sending countries have also set up immigration procedures in an effort to control which workers go abroad, how they get there, and what they do once overseas. As early as 1974, the Philippine government recognised the importance of labour migration to the state economy and established the Philippine Overseas Employment Administration to promote contract labour emigration (Lindio-McGovern 2003). The Indonesian government followed suit, adopting a strongly interventionist approach towards overseas labour migration in the 1980s (see Ford 2006). The efficacy of these systems varies considerably. Most Filipino labour migrants leaving for destinations which have formal recruitment schemes do, in fact, depart through official channels, although there is evidence of migrants using unofficial channels to circumvent lengthy, expensive bureaucratic procedures. In contrast, the Indonesian government's migration regimes control a relatively small proportion of overseas labour migration: it is estimated that more labour migrants leave through unofficial channels than official channels, particularly those travelling to destinations within Southeast Asia (Hugo 2002). Sending countries' approach to the protection of their citizens working overseas varies dramatically. The government of the Philippines has become the most active protector of its migrant nationals by legislating the most comprehensive laws, at least on paper, enhancing migrant workers' rights. Its first major legislative achievement was the ratification of the ICRM in 1995. In order to appease the public outcry over the controversial case of Flor Contemplacion – a Filipina domestic worker executed in Singapore in the same year for allegedly killing another Filipina domestic worker and the child of the latter's employer (Hilsdon 2000) – President Fidel Ramos ratified the ICRM and legislated a domestic law, the Overseas Migration Act (RA 8042), to implement the ICRM. Indonesia signed the ICRM almost a decade later in September 2004.

Individual countries' attempts to control the flow of migrant workers are sometimes complemented by bilateral agreements (BLAs) between particular sending and receiving countries. For example, the Malaysian government has negotiated agreements concerning overseas labour migration with a range of countries including Indonesia, the Philippines, Thailand and Bangladesh. In the Philippines, BLAs have been widely promoted as a mechanism for ensuring more humane treatment of migrant workers, after the execution of Flor Contemplacion brought a heightened awareness of, and political sensitivity about, migrant worker abuse. However, relatively few BLAs have been signed given that the overseas employment program has been operating for over a quarter of a century. There are just fifteen such agreements between the Philippines and labour-importing nations, only two of which are with countries outside the Middle East, one of which is Malaysia. The BLAs in place are typically dominated by labour-importing countries' concerns, such as quotas and bureaucratic procedures, and hardly ever include protective clauses, let alone guarantees of migrant worker rights. More importantly, they generally make no reference to (or even specifically exclude) FDWs. For example the Memorandum of Understanding (MOU) which was signed by Indonesia and Malaysia in May 2004 did not deal with FDWs (Human Rights Watch 2004), although another MOU dealing specifically with Indonesian FDWs working in Malaysia was signed in 2006. Standard diplomatic channels are also sometimes used to address domestic workers' concerns. The Philippine government has stationed labour attachés in crucial labour-receiving destinations. In Singapore, the Philippine embassy is known as being 'interventionist', unlike its Indonesian counterpart (Abdul Rahman 2005); Filipino bureaucrats also raised objections to the Hong Kong government in 2003 when domestic workers were faced with a wage cut. However, severe budgetary constraints mean that sending country embassies find it extremely difficult to assist the large number of their migrant nationals in trouble, leaving most advocacy on behalf of FDWs to middle-class, feminist NGOs based in receiving countries.

Industrial relations regimes

NGOs' prominence in campaigns for FDW rights in receiving countries is at least partially explained by the fact that FDWs are excluded from those countries' industrial relations systems. As national employment acts or labour standards laws almost never recognise domestic work despite the high visibility of FDWs (e.g., Ford 2003), FDWs have few formal channels for seeking recourse in case of disputes over wages, working hours and conditions. Even in contexts such as Malaysia, Taiwan and Singapore where formal contracts for migrant workers exist, there is often a clause which explicitly excludes FDWs from national labour standards. In Taiwan foreign workers in industries such as construction and manufacturing are covered by the Labour Standards Law, but women working as carers are not (Loveband 2003). In Singapore FDWs do not fall under the Employment Act – not because they are non-citizens, but because of the nature of the work they perform (Yeoh *et al.* 2004). Although FDWs can in theory launch a civil court case if the problem is a matter pertaining to a contract (such as non-payment), in practice they have very limited access to the legal system because of the costs associated with engaging a lawyer and the fact that it is impossible for FDWs to testify if they have already been sent home. An exception to the exclusionary industrial relations policies that characterise most receiving countries in East and Southeast Asia is Hong Kong. Like Singapore, Malaysia and Taiwan, Hong Kong admits migrant workers on a strict contract system, but unlike FDWs in these countries, FDWs in Hong Kong are covered by the Employment Ordinance, which specifies their wage and leave entitlements (Wee and Sim 2005).

Although the ILO (2004) recognises female migrant workers as among the most vulnerable groups of foreign workers, FDWs have little access to trade unions in receiving countries in the region other than Hong Kong. The fact that non-state actors concerned with migrant labour in both sending and receiving countries in the region are typically NGOs (along with formal and informal groups comprised of FDWs themselves), rather than trade unions, reflects the history of unionism in the region (Ford 2004). Trade union structures in East and Southeast Asia are modelled on those of Europe and North America (Ariffin 1989), and women and migrant workers have traditionally occupied a marginalised position within unions. When women did become a focus for union organising in the latter part of the twentieth century, organising efforts concentrated on women employed in the formal sector, not women employed in informal sector occupations. Where trade unions have become more inclusive of migrant workers (traditionally seen as a threat to union members' interests) in contexts such as the United

Kingdom (Avci and McDonald 2000), the United States (Watts 2003) and Australia (Nicolaou 1991), they have focused on immigrant workers employed on long-term contracts in the formal sector.

FDWs are excluded, too, from the industrial relations systems of sending countries, partly because of the type of work they undertake, but mostly because industrial relations is defined as an activity which takes place on a national scale (see Andrew Herod in this volume), and thus excludes citizens who are employed overseas. In both the Philippines and Indonesia, FDWs fall under the umbrella of the same government department as industrial relations (in Indonesia's case, the Department of Manpower and Transmigration), but are handled by a separate section of the department from that which deals with industrial relations. Trade unions in sending countries have also paid little attention to overseas migrant workers. For example, the single official Indonesian union categorically excluded overseas migrant workers before the fall of President Suharto in 1998. Although migrant labour divisions have been formally established by some trade unions since restrictions on trade unionism were lifted in mid-1998, most migrant labour activism remains the province of NGOs.

Informal FDW regimes

Given these ambiguities surrounding formal representation, FDWs are largely left to seek to mediate the structures that dominate them by informal means. Research from both sending and receiving countries suggests that fluid and dynamic processes are emerging among FDWs as they develop increasingly individual autonomy and engage in both everyday resistance and collective action (Piper and Yamanaka 2003). However, existing studies of FDWs' collective activism and of NGOs' activities on their behalf often confine their attention to one destination country, which explains why migrant labour activism has been largely interpreted as a 'local' phenomenon with little influence on macro and meso politics (e.g., Abdul Rahman 2005). A different picture emerges when FDWs' agency and the agency of NGOs engaged in advocacy concerning FDW-related issues is recognised, and the nature of their activism is mapped not only within but across borders. It becomes clear that it collectively constitutes an informal regime which has the potential to interact with (and influence) the formal regimes regulating FDWs in the region.

Collective identity

One of the reasons why so much emphasis has been placed on FDWs' individual acts of 'everyday resistance' rather than their collective activism is because FDWs often have limited opportunities to meet with their peers. However, another is the fact that analyses of FDW agency have been strongly influenced by critiques of the expectation raised by some feminist scholars that feminisation of the transnational industrial workforce would result in growing female working-class solidarity. These critiques point to the plurality of subject positions occupied by women workers in peripheral contexts, drawing on ethnographic case studies that suggest factory women rarely construct identities or organise themselves in terms of collective or global interests, but rather engage in individual and even covert acts against various forms of control (Ong 1991). In contexts where industrial workers are employed within national boundaries, solidarity is linked to kinship and gender rather than class. For migrant workers, the issue of solidarity is further complicated by national and ethnic identity. As observed by Pinches (2001), for example, Filipino overseas workers (FOWs) are not simply workers – they are workers whose identities are founded in the Philippines. Pinches claims that the particular class experience of Filipino migrant workers tends to find expression in assertions of ethnic or national solidarity. The heightened politicisation of the hardships associated with overseas employment appears to have welded the identity of FOWs to that of all Filipinos. With the extensive state-led labour export policies and rising numbers of FOWs, certain types of jobs have become synonymous with Filipinos (such as domestic and 'entertainment' work) – arguably leading to the stigmatisation of Filipino ethnic identity in its entirety. This is especially evident for migrants who experience contradictory class processes as part of their cross-border mobility (such as a teacher taking on a job as a maid). Pinches argues that the international tendency to identify all Filipinos with FOWs led some middle-class nationalists to agitate for better state protection of FOWs to elevate the image of Filipinos as a whole. According to this reasoning, pro-migrant activism appears to be rooted in a strong sense of nationalism, rather than explicitly in class. It must be noted, though, that many middle-class activists have incentives for becoming politically active on behalf of migrants that have nothing to do with nationalism (see e.g., Courville and Piper 2004).

Class is an important factor in determining the geography of collective activism around FDW issues in the region. In particular, it manifests itself in the often contradictory processes of alliance formation between local women's organisations and FDW groups. This tension is clear in sending countries such as Indonesia, where middle-class women engaged in activism on behalf of FDWs do not generally raise issues faced by domestic workers employed locally by women like themselves with the same vigour as they promote the interests of Indonesian nationals employed as domestic workers overseas. Class intersects with national identity in receiving countries such as Hong Kong, Malaysia and Singapore, where middle-class women almost always employ foreign maids. In contrast to Japan and Korea, where advocacy is conducted by concerned citizens – and thus on behalf of migrants, rather than by the migrants themselves, because most labour migrants are undocumented (and foreign women work as entertainers rather than FDWs) – the majority of citizens and women's NGOs in these countries have remained aloof from, and indifferent to, issues of the welfare and rights of migrant workers. For example, in Hong Kong, middle-class women have largely failed to support FDWs' successful campaigns (Wee 2003), possibly because opposition to the government's proposal to lower the minimum wage is seen as an economic threat to working families who seek to minimise the costs of hiring a live-in maid.

Yet despite these contradictions the middle-class women active in these organisations have played an important role in both sending and receiving countries. A 2001 study of migrant education programs in six countries (Hong Kong, India, Indonesia, Japan, Philippines and South Korea) identified 248 groups which are directly involved in supporting migrants' issues (AMC 2001). Many of these migrant labour NGOs spend much of their time and efforts on service provision and immediate problem-solving rather than political advocacy or organising (Piper 2003), but their efforts to advocate for migrant women's rights have been influential at local, national and transnational levels in East and Southeast Asia.

Activism abroad

As cross-border labour migration flows accelerated and feminised from the 1980s onwards, many NGOs and other voluntary associations emerged that sought to address the needs and problems of migrant workers in receiving countries. As suggested above, activism on behalf of FDWs and other labour migrants takes multiple forms. Activism is primarily the domain of concerned citizens who campaign on behalf of migrants in contexts where political activism by foreigners themselves is impossible for a variety of reasons (for example migrants' legal status or the availability of political space), while in other contexts, migrant workers organise themselves. A third model is that citizens of FDWs' country of origin organise migrant workers in the receiving country, often in conjunction with NGOs in the sending country.

Hong Kong is one of the best researched examples with regard to NGO foreign worker activism, not least because FDWs and activists from FDWs' countries of origin have established a significant number of highly-visible NGOs and migrant worker organisations. Filipinas have played a particularly important role in the Hong Kong context. By 1984, United Filipinos Against Forced Remittance had been established (Constable 1997). Later this organisation became instrumental in the formation of the NGO coalition, United Filipinos in Hong Kong (UNIFIL), which is comprised of about twenty-five NGOs that monitor the working and living conditions of Filipina domestic workers in Hong Kong (Law 2002). Under its organisational umbrella, UNIFIL has successfully helped Indonesians, Sri Lankans and Indians to organise independent domestic worker unions. It has also spearheaded vigorous campaigns addressing Hong Kong immigration policies, fees imposed by the Philippine government, and changes to Hong Kong's minimum wage for domestic workers (Law 2002: 212). In contrast, in Singapore, NGO support for migrants has been comparatively muted, especially in the case of church-based organisations which have preferred to avoid human rights issues since 1987 when sixteen activists were arrested under the Internal Security Act (Yeoh and Huang 1999). In early 2003, however, The Working Committee Two was formed (later known as Transient Workers Count Too), which has engaged in both public and closed-door meetings campaigning about domestic workers' issues, primarily about 'Sunday Off' and 'Dignity Over Due', a campaign addressing various types of abuse (see Lyons 2005). Their less confrontational style has been quite successful, resulting in compulsory orientation for first-time employers implemented by the Ministry of Manpower and the setting up of a special unit offering conciliatory services (Abdul Rahman et al. 2005).

Activism at home

As noted by one Filipino activist, 'The key to successful campaigning abroad is a strong movement "at home"' (interview by Piper, Manila, November 2003). As this statement suggests, Filipino domestic worker activism in Hong Kong and elsewhere is influenced by many factors in their country of origin. Filipino citizens have long fought for human rights, specifically the rights of the poor and indigenous people, and for protection of the environment (Silliman and Noble 1998), and the Philippines has a long history of feminist activism. Migrant worker activism in the Philippines grew out of this grassroots democracy movement. From the onset of the government's efforts to promote labour exports in 1974, Filipino NGOs (along with the Catholic Church) have been heavily involved in public policy debates and campaigns. Filipino NGOs have been able to work in a comparatively open political system and even to have access to elite allies within the government. Although close connections with the government have created many frictions and conflicts in government-NGO relations, they indicate the centrality of labour migration issues in Philippine politics and the ability of NGOs to influence governmental policy-making (Villalba 1997).

Although Indonesia has a less-developed system of migrant labour advocacy than the Philippines, it is nevertheless home to many tens of migrant labour NGOs (interview by Ford, Jakarta, June 2003). Many of these are organised under the most prominent migrant labour umbrella organisation, the Consortium for the Defence of Indonesian Migrant Workers (*Konsorsium Pembela Buruh Migran Indonesia*, KOPBUMI). KOPBUMI has been extremely active in promoting migrant labour issues through the local media, and in advocating for changes in Indonesia's labour law, for example for a bill on the Protection of Indonesian Migrant Workers and their Families, which was introduced to parliament in 2002. In the same year, migrant labour NGOs filed a citizen's lawsuit against nine government officials, including President Megawati Soekarnoputri, in relation to the humanitarian disaster at Nunukan (Ford 2006). It has also sponsored the formation of the Jakarta-based Federation of Indonesian Migrant Worker Organisations (now the Indonesian Migrant Workers Union), whose local affiliates attempt to provide counselling and other assistance to prospective and former migrant workers at the local and provincial level (Ford 2004).

Activism across borders

The proliferation of NGO networks in Asia in the past two decades reflects the growing role that NGOs now play nationally and regionally in response to issues concerning migrant labour (Piper 2003; Ball and Piper 2005). Since the 1990s, two regional networks have emerged: the Migrant Forum in Asia (MFA) and the Coordination of Action Research on AIDS and Mobility (CARAM Asia). The MFA is a network of migrant support and advocacy groups based in South, Southeast and East Asia which focus on supporting migrant workers and their families. CARAM Asia, on the other hand, works with South and Southeast Asian NGOs mainly in the areas of migration and HIV/AIDS, but recently also on broader migration issues such as their 'domestic worker campaign'.

These transnational advocacy networks (TANs) have provided vital support for migrant labour NGOs in a range of countries. For example, in 2003 an Indonesian consortium of migrant worker organisations filed a court petition in order to pressure the Indonesian government to implement a Migrant Worker Bill modelled after the Philippines' Republican Act 8042 (interview by Piper, Jakarta, April 2003). In another example, staff from the Centre for Indonesian Migrant Workers have been seconded to the Asian Migrant Centre in Hong Kong. In addition to providing support for migrant labour NGOs, transnational networks have been used for other forms of migrant worker activism. In the Philippines, the 2003 enactment of the Absentee Voting Rights' Bill (RA 9189) could not have been achieved without the rallying of overseas Filipinos' support and financial donations, through the extensive transnational networks that connect worldwide efforts on behalf of more than five million Filipino overseas workers. This non-exhaustive list of examples shows that TANs constitute important informal channels through which FDWs express their everyday political agency that reflects the cross-border nature of their position within regional labour markets – channels that, along with activism in sending and receiving countries, constitute an informal regime that is capable of influencing the formal regimes which regulate foreign domestic labour.

Implications for formal regimes

The role of formal immigration and industrial relations regimes is to regulate and exploit migrant labour – which means, from the receiving countries' point of view, keeping foreign workers temporary and disposable; and from the sending countries' point of view, exporting as many workers as possible and reaping the largest possible benefit from their remittances. RIPE analyses of these formal regimes' impact on flows of foreign domestic labour may recognise their porousness. However, they seldom acknowledge the means through which FDWs and NGOs advocating FDWs' rights actively defy, and work to promote changes in, those regimes.

The informal regimes built up through FDW activism and migrant labour NGO activities on behalf of FDWs described above have the potential to influence the formal regimes upon which RIPE analyses focus. In sending countries such as Indonesia and the Philippines campaigns by migrant labour NGOs and ex-migrant workers have forced governments to put in place measures to improve the conditions of FDWs before they leave for overseas contracts and on their return, and to revisit labour migration policies (e.g., Ford 2006; Iredale et al. 2005). In Hong Kong, the receiving country in which informal regimes of migrant labour activism have been strongest, migrant worker organisations and migrant labour NGOs have succeeded in having FDWs incorporated in the formal industrial relations system, overcoming the barriers to unionisation imposed by nationality, temporary status and the nature of domestic work itself (interviews by Ford, Hong Kong, November 2005). A coalition of Hong Kong-based NGOs, through its member unions the

Indonesian Migrant Workers Union (IMWU) and Asian Domestic Workers Union (ADWU), drew on international resources to achieve this, filing a formal complaint with the ILO accusing the Hong Kong government of violating ILO Convention 97, of which Hong Kong is a State-party (Piper 2005).

It must be noted, however, that the extent to which the potential of these informal regimes is realised in particular places at particular times is often piecemeal and context-specific. In other words, patterns of FDW and NGO activism are themselves strongly influenced by another type of formal regime: the legal and policy regime regulating civil society activities in particular receiving countries. A strong contrast is evident, for example, between Singapore and Malaysia on the one hand and Hong Kong on the other. Political organising by, or on behalf of, FDWs is not always possible where governments do not make space for activism within civil society more generally, as in Singapore and Malaysia. In Malaysia, NGO activists' advocacy of foreign workers' rights has been a controversial and dangerous activity, subject to prosecution under Malaysia's infamous Internal Security Act and other punitive legislation. An example of this is the Printing Presses and Publications Act under which activist Irene Fernandez was charged in 1996 for publishing a document describing the experiences of migrant workers held in Malaysian detention camps in the previous year (Anon. 1996). In neighbouring Singapore, state controls on civil society mean that FDWs have little opportunity to organise at any more than the most informal of levels. In contrast, in Hong Kong, the government has been much more tolerant of civil activism aimed at helping migrant workers and even of contentious advocacy for their labour rights (Constable 1997; Ogaya 2003; Law 2003). State regimes of control over civil society also influence the level of activism around FDW issues in sending countries. The vibrancy of Filipino domestic worker activism in Hong Kong and elsewhere reflects political conditions in the Philippines, whereas although Indonesia's New Order regime (1967–98) was surprisingly tolerant of NGO advocacy on FDW issues, the New Order's long history of suppressing civil society activism clearly affected FDWs' willingness and ability to act collectively.

The collective agency of FDWs and FDW advocates in the face of such country-specific constraints plays itself out in a number of different ways. In Malaysia, engagement with transnational activism sustains localised NGO activism 'from the outside in' (Weiss 2004). In Singapore, NGOs avoid the framing of their activism as related to human rights, but try to appeal to employers' moral behaviour (Lyons 2005). Another way through which 'local' obstacles to organising can be at least partially circumvented is through TANs which target international regulatory regimes. In this regard, migrant labour NGOs have made significant progress. For example, in June 2004 representatives were invited for the first time to take part in an ILO annual congress, where they were able to make statements on issues of concern to FDWs and other migrant workers. Their input was built into the final Plan of Action, which highlighted the need for a rights-based approach to migration. Examples such as this demonstrate TANs' ability to affect the international system of norms against which national systems are measured. When combined with the support TANs provide for local migrant labour NGOs and migrant worker organisations through solidarity actions, and even financially, TANs' presence on the global stage makes them a very important component of the informal regime centred around FDW-related activism – a regime that, as demonstrated in this chapter, has significant potential to influence formal immigration and industrial relations regimes.

Conclusion

The intra-Asian movement of migrant workers constitutes an extremely significant phenomenon not just numerically, but in terms of regional geopolitics and human rights. As such, it is not surprising that issues surrounding FDW-related concerns have become a focus for widespread NGO activism in East and Southeast Asia, or even that migrant labour NGO networks have succeeded in affecting changes internationally and in particular sending and receiving country contexts. What is more difficult to explain is how RIPE analyses can ignore the effects of informal regimes, such as that comprised of local and transnational migrant labour NGO initiatives, on the formal regimes that regulate FDWs.

In this chapter, we have simultaneously emphasised the informal, 'everyday' nature of national and transnational activism by, and on behalf of, FDWs and identified the highly significant role that activism plays in bringing FDW concerns onto the agendas of national, regional and global policy-makers. In doing so, our discussion moves beyond conventional approaches favoured in RIPE to highlight everyday actions that provide a means to defiance for seemingly small actors. Using the examples from East and Southeast Asia, we have demonstrated that defiance can be seen in activism that collectively constitutes an informal regime which, although partial and fragmented, has the potential to influence the formal immigration and industrial relations regimes that seek, or fail, to regulate the movement and employment conditions of FDWs. These examples suggest that it is necessary to consider the impact of this informal regime in order to draw accurate conclusions about the nature and regulation of labour migration.

Part II

Global economic change from below

5   The everyday social sources of imperial and hegemonic financial orders

Leonard Seabrooke

Imagine that you are a member of the working or lower-middle classes. You scrimp and save to put together some savings with the hope of acquiring a home loan. Banks, however, refuse you credit on the grounds of your socioeconomic position and nobody will lend you money at anything but outrageously high interest rates. Such usury is apparently justified because your socioeconomic position suggests that you are an unsafe bet. And while you are going without, the talk on the street is that your government has been implicitly subsidising high-income earners' ever-increasing private international investments with public money. In particular, you hear complaints that publicly funded warships are being sent to far-off lands to ensure payment on private investments at a time when the domestic economy is stagnating. Worse still, some politicians want to raise tariffs on foodstuffs to pay for the construction of more warships on the grounds of protecting national security. You and your friends don't believe their claims to the legitimacy of such policy changes. If such a policy is pursued then not only will you not have access to a home loan but price increases on basic commodities will hurt your family and community. Unsurprisingly, your everyday frustration about lack of access to credit and property, as well as the prospect of increased relative tax burdens, builds. You wonder whether if the government intervened in the economy on behalf of the broader population, and against the narrow interests of rentiers (those who live off passive investments, like rents from property and arm's-length investments), foreign economic policy would change and the domestic economy could be reinvigorated. But the bottom line for now is that the government is not intervening in the economy in the way you think it *should*. You question the legitimacy of government policies and call others with similar frustrations to do the same with the hope of changing how the economy works both at home and abroad. Together you complain, in private and/or in public, with the hope of changing the system to be more in line with how you think the economy should work. Even if your capacity to act collectively is constrained due to political or economic considerations (such as getting arrested or losing your job), you can incrementally change your everyday behaviour to be more in tune with how you think the economy should work. You can also encourage others to change their everyday actions. If the government does not respond to such impulses its social legitimacy will weaken and there is a good chance that finance will become dangerously concentrated among rentiers. Such a concentration of financial wealth will leave the state more vulnerable to international financial shocks, with the fallout being further economic burdens for you and your kin.

This imagined scenario of everyday political action and institutional change in both domestic and foreign economic policy is not so far from reality, as this chapter illustrates. The imagined scenario reminds us that the legitimacy of governments' policies is not automatically generated and that while a state may *claim* the legitimacy of its policies, such claims can only be legitimated when they receive the *consent* of those on the receiving end of the policy change. The consent of seemingly small or ordinary actors is important for any political and economic system to have stability; a point often overlooked in the regulatory IPE literature (RIPE). In contrast, an important element of the everyday international political economy (EIPE) approach offered in this book is that legitimacy is not seen as a resource held by elite actors and that everyday agents provide impulses for government in accordance with their views about how the economy should work. Following an EIPE approach, actors' perception of the legitimacy of changes at the macro-level (such as a concentration of financial wealth among rentiers that changes the international financial order) can lead to contestation over micro-level phenomena (such as tax rates, credit access and property ownership) that then goes on to transform macro-level phenomena (like the state changing its engagement with the international political economy as a result of domestic contestation). There can be, therefore, a causal chain from the macro to the micro and then back to the macro (Schelling 1997). This reminds us that while the structures of the world economy do indeed constrain choices, everyday actors also have agency in transforming the world economy through the contestation of policies and institutions.

The threshold for contestation does not require blood to be spilled on the streets from open protest between the state and social groups. Everyday politics need not be only overtly 'political' but can also be a product of axiorational behaviour. Axiorational behaviour is neither purely instrumental nor purely value oriented. It is action that is grounded in *reason* that is likely to be seen as legitimate by a broader population (Seabrooke 2006a: Ch. 2; Boudon 2001: Ch. 4; also see the editors' introduction to this volume). Axiorational behaviour is 'every-day', and understanding it calls upon us to establish how actors attribute meaning to their actions and find empowerment through them in their everyday lives (Kerkvliet 2005). Contests to elites' and rulers' legitimacy claims are expressed by everyday agents who 'vote with their feet' through their belief-driven actions, by deciding to participate or withdraw from institutions in economic life (see also Seabrooke 2007c). Recognising this capacity among everyday agents reminds us that while social norms are important in informing behaviour 'all the way through' (Blyth 2002: 270), these norms must be recognised as violable and pliable through changing economic conventions – a point often missed by 'systemic' constructivist scholars (see the editors' introduction to this volume). In sum, everyday agents' *axiorational* behaviour has an evolutionary and cumulative impact upon institutional change, often providing the back-ground to what would otherwise appear to be 'revolutionary' change (Campbell and Pedersen 1996; Thelen 2004). It is the relationship between state and society on everyday matters that has the real capacity to transform environments (Weber 1978: 253; Bendix 1977: 19). Understanding such dynamics permits us to develop a deeper under-standing of the social sources of a state's financial power and its influence on the character of an international financial order in different periods of time.

The RIPE literature on the sources of financial power has seldom tackled such dynamics (with the notable exception of Germain 1997; and, within EIPE, Paul Langley in this volume). Rather, RIPE literature has concerned itself primarily with the external constraints that financial globalisation places upon economies (Strange 1996; Cerny *et al.* 2005), or the generation of financial power from the 'big end of town' – the brokerage houses, the exchanges, the large banks, etc. (see Mosley 2003a). While these institutions are undoubtedly important, states often draw their capital from a broader base than is commonly investi-gated by scholars working within the constraints of the RIPE framework. For the EIPE approach the everyday domestic legitimacy of economic relationships between social groups within states heavily informs its engagement with the international political economy. This is particularly the case with regard to policies that have a strong impact on everyday life, such as property access, credit access and tax burdens – what I term the 'financial reform nexus' (Seabrooke 2006a). In fact, how states treat people on below-median income *but well above the poverty line,* the 'ordi-nary folk' in lower-income groupings (hereafter LIGs), with regard to the legitimation of a financial reform nexus, tells us about the domestic foundations for influence in the international financial order.

Following this logic, this chapter discusses the everyday social sources of English imperialist influence in the international financial order of the late-nineteenth/early twentieth century and US hegemonic influence in the international financial order of the late twentieth century. In doing so, it investigates the imagined scenario of frustration outlined above to map links between how the English (not British – the vast majority of financial wealth was English and conformed to English norms) and US states treated LIGs (once again, those from the working to the middle classes, not who we typically consider 'the poor') and the character of their influence on the international financial order during periods of financial globalisation in which they were dominant. The above imagined scenario also suggests a hypothesis: that if a state can legitimate its financial reform nexus to help people on below-median income gain access to credit and acquire property, as well as lower their tax burdens, it can broaden and deepen the domestic pool of capital. Such a situation not only provides a positive benefit to LIGs, but enhances a state's financial power in the international political economy, specifically its capacity to draw capital from and export capital to the international financial order, as well as influencing this order's regulatory and normative structure (Seabrooke 2006a). Alternatively, states can choose to neglect LIGs and dismiss positive intervention into the economy to instead favour negative intervention that supports rentiers that benefit from the concentration of financial wealth, creating what I term a 'rentier shift'. This hypothesis helps us distinguish imperial from hegemonic financial orders.

This chapter provides two cases. The English case demonstrates that everyday actors were engaged in the financial system in its rise to dominance in the international financial order (1840–90). However, after 1890 negative state intervention enabled a rentier shift that damaged the legitimation of the financial reform nexus for LIGs and weakened English capacity to sustain its dominance in the international financial order despite increased volumetric influence in imperialist forms of investment. Everyday forms of defiance and axiorational behaviour from English LIGs highlight how the character of the domestic political economy informs the character of the international financial order.

The US case demonstrates a rentier shift during a period considered to be indicative of declining US hegemony, the early 1980s. But this rentier shift was challenged by everyday political action that led to positive state intervention that then bolstered US hegemonic influence in the international financial order (1985–2000). Here LIGs used everyday politics, including advocacy groups for 'community reinvestment' and 'fair housing', to challenge a rentier shift and enable positive state intervention to support LIGs' creditworthiness. Moreover, axiorational behaviour among LIGs led to the development of strong social norms that spread new financial practices including mortgage securitisation and financial innovation. As a consequence of everyday changes in the US, the state placed greater emphasis on forms of arm's-length credit-worthiness assessment that typify hegemonic rather than imperialist dominance in the international financial order. I conclude by reflecting on how differentiating domestic social sources of financial power permits us to identify changes in the Bush administration that portend of a shift from hegemonic to imperial influence in the international political economy.

The English financial reform nexus and the international rentier economy

Everyday sources of financial power in the mid-nineteenth-century order

Between 1840 and 1890, the bulk of capital within England was located in the provinces, not in the City of London. A key source of England's relatively deep and broad capital market came from its unique mixing of 'state capitalism' with private capitalism through positive state intervention that brought the middle classes into the national banking system (Weber 1956: 26). In the early nineteenth century the Bank of England (BoE) declared its interest in extensive branch banking to obtain even greater deposits from 'every quarter of the Kingdom' (Neal 1998: 72). More importantly, an important source of financial power for England during this period was the humble joint-stock bank. Following the 1825 bank crisis new financial regulations allowed joint-stock banks to gain capital 'from all classes without exception' (Weber 1902: 36–7). As such, placing capital with joint-stock banks became usual activity for everyday actors in the middle classes. Stanley Chapman, for example, describes the typical joint-stock bank in the 1840–90 period as comprising of deposits from nearly 70 per cent middle-class occupations (in order of representation: cotton spinners, retailers, corn merchants and linen merchants) with only 18 per cent represented by 'Gentlemen' and 10 per cent by professionals (mainly lawyers and doctors, see Chapman 1997: 59). As a consequence, during the 1840s and 1850s joint-stock banks held the largest share of capital within the English financial system, some of which was then placed through London's banks for international investment (Cameron 1967: 49–51).

A further example of positive state intervention in this period is provided by W. E. Gladstone's efforts in the 1860s to create a post office savings bank system to attract deposits from the working classes. This innovation was a response to the growing political power of LIGs (following the 1867 reform act that gave the vote to adult male householders) and recognised that private financial institutions' policies on the provision of mortgages to LIGs were becoming 'anti-social and immoral' (Offer 1981: 141). Gladstone's call was also responding to changes within the financial system and the need to alter the portfolio choices of the 'privately controlled institutions to finance [LIGs'] needs or other desired social objectives, e.g. housing' (Sheppard 1971: 4). Indeed, mortgages as a percentage of total financial assets declined from 15.4 per cent in 1880 to 7.6 per cent in 1915 as a rentier shift emerged in England that preferred foreign portfolio investment to domestic investment (Sheppard 1971: 184–5; Seabrooke 2006a: 80–1).

In addition to the post office savings bank system, trustee savings banks had grown rapidly, with their deposits doubling in the final three decades of the nineteenth century. However, these institutions stagnated during the Edwardian period due to a lack of state intervention. While the English state had positively intervened in fiscal affairs by raising income tax and reducing tariffs on foodstuffs, its efforts in altering depository financial institutions waned in the 1890s and it made no real inroads in bolstering property access for LIGs. As a consequence, a rentier shift was evident across the English financial reform nexus and informed international imperialist investment. This shift was a stark affront to English LIGs' expectations about how the economy should work and led to the weakening legitimacy of the financial reform nexus.

English credit politics

The biggest change in the credit system in the 1890s was the concentration of assets in the City of London that led to the relative impoverishment of the provinces. While the ratio of provincial assets to London joint-stock bank assets was 3.2:1 in 1844, it was 1:1.06 by 1880 and worsened thereafter (Collins 1983: 376). Edgar Jaffé's 1905 study of this process is worth citing at length:

Is it not amazing that only in the 90s was the survival of provincial banks threatened when capital city banks turned the tables and sought to get hold of an advantage through the extension into the Provinces … leading to today's principle, that only big banks that are established both in London and the Provinces are competitive enough to fight their way through with a view of success. (Jaffé 1905: 104, this author's translation from the German)

Along with the concentration of private financial institutions, the BoE also dramatically changed the functions of its provincial branches. Ernest Edye, the Principal of Branch Banking for the BoE in the early 1900s, wrote that the 'raison d'être of a Bank is to meet the legitimate requirements of its Customers' and that this legitimate purpose was being violated by the BoE's 'locks up' policy that drained capital from the provinces to the central office without reciprocal credit extension (see Seabrooke 2006a: 60–4). The combined effect of these private and public changes was to tighten credit access for LIGs in the provinces, while in London itself LIGs' access to credit continued to be blocked. Thus while the output of the financial services sector between 1890 and 1915 more than doubled compared with only a slight increase in the non-financial sector, credit provision to LIGs actually diminished (Cottrell 1991: 43; Jaffé 1905: 105). Bank concentration led to depersonalised and centralised credit allocation where LIGs were concerned, providing them with less credit. This was not, however, a process of economic rationalisation. Within the City of London creditworthiness *became* 'heavily dependent upon personal relations between the lender and the borrower' through gentlemanly networks (Capie and Collins 1996: 35). As such, while the pool of English capital became more concentrated, the breadth of the sources from which it was drawn shrank. The power of everyday actors to influence the financial system was being undermined while rentiers were being empowered. As a consequence LIGs withdrew in increasing numbers from the post office savings bank system, in part due to its association with supplementing government revenue (Davis and Gallman 2001: 134), and openly protested on the streets in 1914 when savings banks collapsed and were not adequately bailed out by the government (Seabrooke 2006a: 79–80). In short, credit politics for LIGs was a great source of frustration.

English tax politics

English tax politics was better for LIGs than credit politics. By the early 1900s direct taxes had increased to 38 per cent of government income from 19 per cent in the 1870s and 33 per cent in 1900 (Hobson 1997: 125). However, wealthy individuals were unwilling to permit further increases in direct taxes and pushed for a reversion to indirect taxes (through tariffs) through the Conservative Party. Joseph Chamberlain attempted to dress tariff protectionism as a condition for social reform and argued that income taxes would inhibit domestic economic consumption and lead to a stagnation of the economy. Such a policy shift was supported by financial elites despite the City's supposed belief in a free-trading world order (Cassis 1990: 13). At the same time 'social liberals' – most notably John A. Hobson – pointed to the potential for positive state intervention, through the implementation of increased income taxation on the wealthy, to boost broad domestic consumption and curb rentiers' 'unearned' and 'excessive' incomes, and thereby alter their support for imperialist foreign economic policies (Hobson 1906: 25; Seabrooke 2005b). Popular support from LIGs encouraged the Liberal Party to make social reform from *direct* taxation a cornerstone for institutional change. We must, however, separate the rhetoric from the reality to improve our understanding of state intervention in 'Liberal England'.

The most well-known consequence of the Liberal Party's socially progressive tax policies was the 'radical' 'People's Budget' of 1909–10 (Murray 1980). This budget *threatened* to transform the English financial reform nexus in favour of LIGs. But in reality the People's Budget was generally conservative and the Liberal Party was generally reluctant to redistribute income from the wealthy to LIGs. The budget itself only marginally enhanced national income while government expenditure actually dropped (Balderston 1989: 236). Furthermore, the vast majority of LIGs earned too little for any tax breaks and the only significant relief was for those far above median income. In short, the tax reforms were insufficient to assist the development of a broader social source of English financial power (through savings or consumption) and assisted the 'years of frustration' LIGs felt about the financial reform nexus immediately prior to the First World War (Bernstein 1986: Ch. 7). Such frustrations were expressed through everyday forms of actions that reflected the waning legitimacy of the English financial reform nexus. For example, despite increased real wages and declining property prices, LIGs did not save more but rather consumed more. Given a lack of access to credit and insufficient tax redistribution to support reform programs, short-term spending horizons were legitimate (Seabrooke 2006a: 77).

English property politics

If English credit politics was frustrating, and tax politics disappointing, for LIGs, property politics was infuriating. Despite persistent demand for property ownership the Liberal government did not positively intervene on behalf of LIGs but, instead, provided tax concessions to agrarian landholders and urban landlords (Offer 1980: 243). Nor did the government intervene to change creditworthiness assessments for LIGs. The dominant attitude among rentiers and the wealthy classes at the time was that investment in mortgages for LIGs was dangerous and that foreign portfolio investment in industries supported by imperial power, such as mining and shipping, was much preferred. Much of the reluctance towards mortgage credit came from the perception that the banker would accept 'urban land as collateral only with the gravest misgivings and placed it among the lowest grades of security' (Offer 1981: 114). This is not to say, however, that credit was not available for the right groups. There was real growth of 100 per cent, between 1900 and 1914, of 'small fry' landlords who owned more than seven or eight properties (Offer 1981: 119). In general, however, LIGs were disabled from property access at anything but usurious rates of interest to compensate for the apparent risk (Offer 1980: 244; such usury is referred to as 'sub-prime lending' in today's parlance, see below). As a consequence, LIGs' frustration with their lack of access became an especially touchy political nerve point.

The Liberal Party did not sufficiently respond to this impulse by altering creditworthiness assessments for LIGs. Rather, to quote George Dangerfield, the Liberal Party was stuck behind 'a barrier of Capital which they dared not attack' (1935: 8). The English state was unable to alter the 'positional premium' that rentiers and the landed classes attached to property as an explicit expression of 'wealth . . . traded above its economic value' (Nicholas 1999: 41–3; Offer 1981). As a consequence a rentier shift transformed the English financial system to focus on 'hands-off' international investments in imperialist ventures. Faced with no serious challenge from the state, English international financial capacity became increasingly dependent on fickle-minded rentiers. Accordingly, the dominant English legitimating framework of the international *rentier* economy rested on the increasingly shaky domestic legitimation of the financial reform nexus.

The international rentier economy

England's treatment of the Gold Standard, its treatment of international financial regulation and the types of investment predominant throughout the period reflected aspects of the domestic legitimation of the financial reform nexus.

First, the key characteristic of the English management of the Gold Standard was its 'hands-off' approach. Sir John Clapham, for example, argues that before 1918 the 'Bank was amazingly detached from international affairs; heard from no one; saw no one; only watched the gold and took the necessary steps automatically' (Clapham 1944: 400–1). While England was able to extract a 'fiscal transnationalism' as states conformed to the basic structure of the Gold Standard and used sterling, the extent of England's responsibility did not justify its domestic 'locksup' policy on provincial credit, as complained by Edye and others (Mann 1993: 291).

Second, domestic views towards the assessment of creditworthiness informed rentier-like behaviour in the international financial order. This could be seen in rentiers' dependence upon the imperial naval defence system to overcome problems in assessing the creditworthiness of states they invested in, as well as England's dismissal of any international financial regulation that would increase scrutiny on the creditworthiness of English investors themselves (Seabrooke 2006a: 184–5). In the early twentieth century, what would now be called 'emerging market economies' (hereafter EMEs) received 63 per cent of global foreign direct investment, whereas in the late twentieth century they received only 28 per cent (Baldwin and Martin 1999: 20). While this superficially seems progressive, 85 per cent of English overseas portfolio investment was in moderate-to-high risk debt securities, which financed governments that could be punished, or industries such as railways, mining and metallurgy that were under English control (Bordo *et al.* 1998: 17). Groups such as the Corporation for Foreign Bondholders provoked the English state into threatening EMEs to enforce the payment of private loans, or face international 'blacklisting' (Lipson 1985; see, for a modern case, J. C. Sharman in this volume). International creditworthiness reflected English rentier interests: that in the absence of face-to-face establishment of creditworthiness the only alternatives were denial of credit (in the domestic context for English LIGs) or the use of force (in the international context).

Third, the types of imperialist investment favoured by English investors, the rejection of international financial regulation and the attitude towards the use of force to secure returns on investment, typified English norms in the international rentier economy. As English primacy in the international financial order rested on rentier norms, its foundations were increasingly shaky, particularly as LIGs railed against rentier behaviour and English middle-class 'superloyal schizoids' came to question their strange combination of state liberalism and imperialism (Mann 1993: 292, 583). Given that England did not have a highly legitimate financial reform nexus, its means to cope with the financial shock of the First World War were much reduced. As a consequence it was unable to sustain its imperialist international rentier economy after the First World War. The link between militarism and rentier interests proved unsustainable as the rentier shift undermined the real social source of English financial power, everyday actors.

The US financial reform nexus and the international creditor economy

The Reagan rentier shift

Scholarship within political economy and international relations literatures during the 1980s emphasised the US's declining hegemony (Gilpin 1987; Keohane 1984). Other scholars have argued, with foresight and hindsight, that the US did not lose hegemony but lessened the influence of the state and permitted more 'market-based' influence to attain 'structural power' (Strange 1987; Helleiner 1994). Either way, the mid-1980s are viewed as a period of internal decline under the constraints of, or to the benefit of, international finance (Cerny 1994). In contrast, I argue that everyday resistance and politics provided impulses for positive state intervention that provided LIGs with increased representation across the financial reform nexus.

Let us be clear and not don rose-coloured glasses about the natural capacity of the US state to cater to LIGs. The first Reagan administration *did* enable a rentier shift that sought to disempower LIGs from credit access, property access and to increase their tax burdens – with even worse, and sustained, effects on the American poor. In the English case we found that there was a shift in power towards the conservative city and against the provinces from the 1890s that intensified after 1900. In the US case there was a massive increase in the amount of private capital in the international political economy after 1970 (Germain 1997), and by 1980 a conservative bloc under the Republican Party was elected on arguments for monetary responsibility and tax cuts (Blyth 2002: 167–70).

The Reagan administration in its first term pushed forward an agenda that directly supported rentiers across the financial reform nexus, on tax, on credit and on property. The Tax Reform Act of 1981 provided not only a 23 per cent income tax cut but, importantly, supported the deduction of payments on non-owner-occupied residential and commercial mortgage interest payments from income tax assessment (Epstein 1985: 633). Such changes encouraged the kind of 'small fry' landlordism that was so deeply unpopular in the English case, with similar results. On top of these reforms the Garn-St. Germain Act of 1982 permitted individual ownership of savings and loans banks (S&Ls), effectively encouraging what were community financial institutions to be taken up by individuals for speculative purposes. This reform encouraged S&Ls and commercial banks to speculate on real estate and junk bonds and generated the banking crises of the mid-to-late 1980s. Combined, these reforms represented a significant attempt at a rentier shift with state support.

In addition to these pro-rentier reforms, reckless international syndi-cated lending (which had persisted since the mid-1970s) led to the international debt crisis with its epicentre in Latin America (Seabrooke 2001: 119–23). Here US commercial banks complained that successive US governments had encouraged them to borrow as 'a matter of public interest' and sought potential access to taxpayer monies as a consequence (Cohen 1986: 40). A number of advocacy groups argued that under no circumstances should taxpayer monies be used to bail out 'bad bets' to sovereign debtors. Indeed, the 1983 International Lending Supervisory Act (ILSA) responded to such calls and legislated to punish banks that held large amounts of non-performing loans from sovereign debtors. In general there was a political shift within the US to encourage banks to securitise assets and deal in 'safe' domestic assets in preference to reckless international investments. The 1984 Secondary Mortgage Market Enhancement Act followed up on this by encouraging a more liquid secondary market for the supposedly safest of income streams – people paying off their home loans (Seabrooke 2006a: 125–6). In doing so, it signalled a reversal of the rentier shift that could be seen in the following years across tax burdens and property and credit access. During the second Reagan administration that rentier shift slipped into reverse gear and the legitimation of the financial reform nexus for LIGs became strongest under the Clinton administration.

US tax politics

While the Reagan administration is not commonly seen as progressive on tax reform, changes in 1986 were 'not consistent with the intent of the neoliberal program' (Campbell 2004: 161). Indeed, the 1986 tax reforms reversed many, but not all, of the rentier excesses of the 1981 reforms. The reforms shifted the emphasis away from the capacity to deduct interest repayments on commercial property, *non-owner-occupier* residen-tial property and consumer credit from one's income tax, and towards owner-occupier mortgage interest payment deductibility scaled to benefit LIGs (Lowy 1991: 132–3). These changes provided significant tax relief to LIGs, with their effective tax burdens decreasing and rentiers' burdens increasing during the late 1980s, especially following the closing of some (not all!) investment loopholes (Seabrooke 2006a: 121). When compared to the benefits of the much lauded People's Budget in England, the 1986 tax reforms represented significant positive state intervention that did address the early-1980s rentier shift for LIGs but did not compensate for the increasing impoverishment of the American poor (see also, on US tax progressivity, Prasad 2006).

On top of the 1986 reforms, the tax reforms of the Clinton adminis-tration were also particularly progressive for LIGs. The Tax Reform Act of 1993, for example, increased the top personal tax rate from 31 per cent to 39.6 per cent and created a new 36 per cent tax bracket for upper-level incomes. In addition, the 1997 Taxpayer Relief Act lowered the income tax rate for low incomes and put in place a fourfold increase in tax subsidies to very-low income groups (Steuerle 2001: 6–7). Clinton's boosting of the Earned Income Tax Credit scheme also provided relief to the lower-income end of US LIGs and the working poor. On the tax front, LIGs were consistently providing impulses to the government for relief, everyday actions that, contrary to our common neoliberal under-standing of the US, led to positively redistributive institutional change. While we can certainly note that tax reforms did not redress rising income inequality in the US, LIGs were given lower tax burdens than in many other advanced industrial states and, accordingly, had greater potential to save monies for property access.

US property politics

The rentier shift of the first Reagan administration provided a source of frustration for LIGs, who took up with other everyday actors to attempt to transform their political and economic environment. As we saw in the English case above, alienation from property is a key source of frustration for LIGs. To reverse the rentier shift of the early 1980s, from the mid-1980s advocacy groups campaigned for 'fair housing' and 'community reinvestment' (see also the following section) that were directly tied to a discourse on civil rights. In response, the US government sought to create an 'efficient and equitable financial structure . . . to legitimize itself in the eyes of the public' (Meyerson 1989: 164–5).

During the mid-1980s advocacy groups for LIGs, such as the Association of Community Organizations for Reform Now (ACORN), forcibly occupied housing that had failed from S&L collapses (sparked off by the Reagan rentier shift), and tied red ribbons around commercial banks accused of unfair housing practices, including racial discrimina-tion (Borgos 1986: 428–9, 445; Sidney 2003: 84, 116). Such commun-ity activism from everyday actors filtered through to Congressional committees, where Democratic control of both the House and the Senate from 1987 to 1994 assisted the coupling of pro-community fair housing with financial re-regulation. The Financial Institutions Reform, Recovery, and Enforcement Act of 1989, for example, included an Affordable Housing Program of impressive scope. At the same time the 1989 emboldening of the Home Mortgage Disclosure Act (HMDA) of 1975 required banks to provide data on the ethnicity, age, gender and other details of applicants for mortgages.

Also under scrutiny from community groups of everyday actors were what I call the 'Federal Mortgage Agencies' (FMAs) that provide mortgage securitisation services to financial institutions (Seabrooke 2006a). In 1981 only 4 per cent of mortgages were securitised, but mid-1980s legislation soon boosted this figure to 69 per cent in 1989 (Hendershott 1994: 70). FMAs were targeted by community groups for supporting 'infamous slumlords' and the 1991 Federal Housing Enterprises Financial Safety and Soundness Act (FHEFSSA) responded by obligating the largest two (who are also publicly traded companies), Freddie Mac and Fannie Mae, to cater to institutions lending specifically to LIGs (Seabrooke 2006a: 118–19). As a consequence from 1993 to 1997 mortgages for low-income borrowers increased by 31 per cent, with a 53 per cent increase for low-income minority groups compared with 18 per cent for all borrowers on 120 per cent of median income. By 1999 low-income borrowers received 30.7 per cent of all mortgage loans, compared with 18.5 per cent in 1990 (Avery et al. 1999: 88). This growth can be attributed to the role of FMAs, as owner-occupied mortgage indebtedness increased to historical highs while there was a reduction in landlordism. In addition, between 1985 and 2000 US commercial banks increased residential mortgages as a percentage of their assets from 21 per cent to 34 per cent (Bertraut and Starr-McCluer 1999: 26, 28). As a consequence of marrying FMAs to a broad and socially legitimate purpose and increasing LIGs' homeownership, the FMAs grew more than sixfold between 1985 and 2000 to become the world's biggest issuers of fixed income securities after the US Treasury (Seabrooke 2006a: 208). Put simply, the recycling of capital provided by FMAs through mortgage securitisation led to the 'transformation of the local mortgage loan market into the global securities giant it is today' (Santomero and Eckles 2000: 11). Importantly, this process led to changes in axiorational behaviour as everyday economic conventions transformed to embrace increased levels of homeownership alongside securitisation as a 'way of life' that permitted capital to be recycled from the local to the global. In doing so, US financial power in the late twentieth century increasingly rested on a safe and robust domestic foundation. This was further cemented by institutional reforms and everyday changes in behaviour that permitted LIGs greater access to credit.

US credit politics

On top of the emboldened role of FMAs, LIGs had greater access to credit due to the coupling of socially progressive reforms with financial re-regulation. Once more, this was due to a combination of LIGs' advocacy groups and everyday incremental behaviour that led to changing expectations about what economic social norms should guide institutional change. During the Clinton administration the revision of long-standing laws to restrict interstate banking led to the 1994 coupling of the Riegle-Neal Interstate Banking Efficiency Act with the Riegle Community Development and Regulatory Improvement Act. This second act provided for Community Development Financial Institutions, as well as the Home Owner Equity Protection Act (HOEPA), which required regulators to impose premiums on any financial intermediaries offering grossly sub-prime mortgage rates (recall the use of usury in the English case as a source of frustration). The important change here is the marrying of new practices of creditworthiness assessment with fair housing and civil rights norms that seek to counter discrimination.

Also important for LIGs during the 1990s was the augmenting of the 1977 Community Reinvestment Act (CRA), that monitors and penalises banks that either 'redline' (ban lending to) low income communities or target them for sub-prime lending (which is still a serious concern for the poor). The CRA appeals to 'the notion of corrective justice, the normative idea that compensation should be made for past inequities' (Lacker 1995: 24). A number of LIGs' advocacy groups ensured that CRA conditions were met. Groups such as the National Community Reinvestment Coalition (NCRC, which grew out of ACORN, no pun intended), the National People's Action and the National Fair Housing Alliance provided a watchdog function. The first two, in particular, provided an auditing function examining financial institutions' data for compliance with HMDA and HOEPA legislation. These advocacy groups also commented on the behaviour of the FMAs. Importantly, their propagation of conventions and norms on 'community reinvestment' and 'fair housing' informed LIGs' expectations, so that by the end of the century most Americans, across income groups, knew of fair housing legislation and their right to request that authorities enforce it if violated (Turner et al. 2002; Abravanel and Cunningham 2002).

It has been estimated that lending under CRA oversight from 1992 to 2000 amounted to just under $1 trillion, highlighting the importance of the regulation not only for legitimacy but the generation of credit for LIGs within the US financial system (Seabrooke 2006a: 133). Generally, the US emphasis on creditworthiness for LIGs provides a stark contrast with England during its period of dominance under financial globalisation. While banks became more concentrated in England during the 1890–1915 period and lent less domestically as they expanded their role internationally, US banks lent at home while also expanding their prominence internationally. Credit, after all, is not a zero-sum game but a 'cumulative process' (Wicksell 1997: 96–110). By the mid-1990s US banks were lending more than in 1985 and more to LIGs than ever before. This was a consequence of both everyday resistance through advocacy groups and everyday politics in changing expectations and conventions. Such everyday axiorational actions were incremental and when accumulated also led to a change in US hegemonic influence in the international financial order to create an international creditor economy.

The international creditor economy

US influence to create an international creditor economy was entirely in accordance with US domestic entrepreneurial norms but without the redistributive norm on property ownership. During the 1985–2000 period the US fostered assessments of creditworthiness by encouraging international institutions that were recognised as legitimate actors in the international financial order and officially separate from direct US control, an approach of 'strategic restraint' to bolster hegemonic influence (Ikenberry 2001). For example, the Bank for International Settlement's (BIS) Basle Accord of 1988 to regulate internationally active banks was cobbled together by the US Federal Reserve and the Bank of England following the ILSA legislation discussed above. The accord required banks to keep 8 per cent of their capital in safe reserves. It directly encouraged banks to make up part of their capital reserves in OECD government securities, of which US Treasury bills were commonly perceived as the safest and most liquid (Seabrooke 2001: 137–8). The accord therefore provided a fiscal windfall to the US (Oatley and Nabors 1998: 37–41). It also encouraged the purchase of FMA securities, which effectively permitted the FMAs to attract international investors and then use the capital to provide cheaper mortgages, through their institutional clients, to LIGs (Seabrooke 2006a: 157, 198–9). The Basle Accord therefore encouraged international assessments of creditworthiness that favoured the US trend towards securitisation, while not regulating international securities traders themselves. Such regulation provides a clear means to differentiate the direct control of imperialist investment in the international rentier economy, which ignored domestic LIGs' call for property, and the more diffuse means of control employed by US hegemonic power in the international creditor economy, which helped supply more capital to LIGs for homeownership, only to then recycle the capital back to the international financial order via mortgage securitisation.

The US's stress on creditworthiness also led to greater financial surveillance in the international financial order rather than direct military threats, as in the 1890 to 1915 period. From the late 1980s the Group of 7 industrialised countries (G7) met with the International Monetary Fund (IMF) to coordinate financial information and augment the IMF's surveillance capacities to become the 'very core of the institution' (Pauly 1997: 41, 129). But such surveillance did not provide the IMF with autonomy from US hegemony because of the US's veto power over IMF 'special decisions' required for large loans to states in crisis (as occurred during the Mexican and Asian financial crises of the 1990s, see Seabrooke 2001: 165–7, 180–7). This veto power also strongly correlates with LIGs' attitudes that disapprove of the use of *perceived* national tax monies for international 'bail-outs' (Broz 2005).

The US hegemonic emphasis on creditworthiness also led to a mixture of public, quasi-public and private agencies charged with the task of sharing financial information and assessing creditworthiness. From the mid-1990s the BIS and the IMF put in place data dissemination standards for their members and in 1999 the G10 created a Financial Stability Forum in coordination with the BIS, IMF and the World Bank. Greater financial inclusion also followed the sharing of information, with more developing states being consulted in discussions concerned with the 'global financial architecture' (Germain 2001: 422). In addition, much of the punishment for defaulters in the international creditor economy was in the hands of private credit rating agencies, who provided 'developed country "government-at-a-distance" over developing countries' (Sinclair 2005: 147). Ratings firms such as Moody's and Standard & Poor's rated the creditworthiness of all players within the international creditor economy, including EMEs who increased their own issuance of debt securities from $13.9 billion in 1991 to $127.9 billion in 1997, with such financing becoming their primary means of borrowing (rather than international bank lending) by the end of the century (Mosley 2003b: 108). So while EMEs were receiving less foreign direct investment than during the international rentier economy, they had a much greater capacity to attract investors to their debt. Such a capacity provided EMEs with greater agency within the US hegemonic system, giving them 'room to groove' as long as they signalled that they had the presence of the 'right' financial and regulatory institutions and disclosed financial data to credit rating agencies (Seabrooke 2006b). The US emphasis on creditworthiness underpinned its hegemony in the international creditor economy and was a reflection of everyday political changes in the domestic financial reform nexus.

Conclusions

Cast your mind back to where we began: the imagined scenario of your frustration with not having access to a home loan that soon translated into everyday political action and resistance. Now, given the above cases, where would you rather be? Let us briefly review the cases and return to the hypothesis outlined at the beginning: that the legitimation of a financial reform nexus for LIGs will help a state broaden and deepen its domestic pool of capital, to increase its capacity to export and attract capital and to have a regulatory and normative influence on its international financial order.

In the English case the state did not reverse a post-1890 rentier shift that undermined the social source of financial power prominent in the 1840–1890 period. The Liberal Party provided the rhetoric but not the action for LIGs to provide their consent to a high legitimation of the financial reform nexus, as while there was a progressive movement on taxation, property access was still disabled for LIGs and credit access stagnated. In short, the legitimation of the English financial reform nexus among LIGs weakened. Certainly the types of investment in the international rentier economy reflected the preferences of rentiers, with the bulk of investment being channelled into EMEs that had imperialist 'gunboat' diplomacy lurking in the background. As the First World War drew closer English dominance in its imperialist international rentier economy reflected the increasingly unsteady foundations on which it had been built.

In the US case the financial reform nexus was transformed during the 1985–2000 period in a progressive manner, as tax burdens for LIGs were lessened, while credit and property access was enabled. I find that in this period US social norms did not lead to rallying against income inequality but informed a discourse about entrepreneurship that assisted calls for access to credit and property, as well as lower tax burdens, for LIGs (but no extra welfare for an increasingly disenfranchised poor) (Gijsberts 2002: 280). Important here was the role of both advocacy groups, who provided everyday resistance to ensure that LIGs were heard, and also changing everyday conventions as LIGs evermore adopted financial innovations and, through their financial institutions, participated in mortgage securitisation. Furthermore, the widespread knowledge of fair housing legislation and support for discourses on community reinvestment and civil rights provided a form of everyday politics that provided checks upon US financial institutions and their regulators. As a consequence, US hegemonic power in the international creditor economy placed strong emphasis on creditworthiness assessment through external institutions and private agencies, as well as supplying the US itself with the means to generate, attract and recycle capital with significant international consequences.

We can see from our two cases that US hegemonic influence was bolstered by the high legitimation of its domestic financial reform nexus, while England's imperialist influence weakened because of legitimation problems with its domestic financial reform nexus. What, then, is your choice for the better state and society to alleviate your imagined (or perhaps real) frustrations? But before we all wish to join American society, we must note that the domestic social sources of financial power can change easily. Indeed, post-2000 the George W. Bush administration has actively encouraged a rentier shift that seeks to increase LIGs' tax burdens. This can be seen in all areas of the financial reform nexus (tax, credit and property).

On tax politics, the Bush administration has provided extraordinarily generous tax cuts to the US super-rich, including serious cuts to estate taxes and capital gains taxes, as well as other tax breaks. As a consequence, during the Bush administration tax revenue as a percentage of GDP was pushed back to 1950s levels (Seabrooke 2006a: 209–10). More important than these cuts, however, is the Bush administration's propagation of the idea that the ideal tax system for the US is to remove income tax and instead have a broad consumption tax. While this tax policy change has not occurred and faces, fortunately, serious impediments, the support it has received from the administration reflects the extent to which they are willing to impose costs upon LIGs, since a high broad consumption tax would seriously harm LIGs at the lower end of the income distribution and be disastrous for the poor (Seabrooke 2006a: 210–11).

On credit politics, the Bush administration has permitted regulatory changes to be made to the classification of US financial institutions that relax the scrutiny placed on them by enforcers and watchdogs of CRA legislation. It has also permitted regulatory changes that give banks more movement for speculative investment, recalling policy changes that ignited the S&L crisis in the 1980s (Seabrooke 2006a: 206–7).

On property politics, the Bush administration has viewed FMAs as having an unfair advantage within the US market (which it does, and puts, ideally, to progressive use). As such it has called for Fannie Mae, in particular, to not pool mortgages acquired from banks, but only to provide a 'pass through' service. Given that FMAs during the Bush administration have been increasingly associated with financial institutions that lend less to minority LIGs, the Bush administration's criticisms of them place even more pressure on them to move away from their socially progressive purpose and to act more like a purely private financial institution (Seabrooke 2006a: 208–9).

In sum, across the financial reform nexus the Bush administration is making domestic changes that portend of a rentier shift. And it is little coincidence that the changes made to tax, property and credit have been made during a time when the US has been accused of reigniting 'imperialism'. Indeed, the changes to the financial reform nexus have supported increased rentier-type investments in the international financial order. US influence in the international financial order post-2000 reflects a shift from hegemonic to imperialist/rentier norms, with increased emphasis on foreign direct investment backed by military force (Iraq), the increased use of tax havens for tax evasion and a shift from attracting investment into FMA securities into ever-expanding US Treasury debt (Seabrooke 2004). Such changes indicate how the character of US influence in the international financial order has shifted from hegemonic to imperialist. This change is a consequence of the domestic rentier shift.

In understanding links between the legitimation of a domestic political economy and changes in international financial orders it is crucial that we consider everyday actors (see also Paul Langley's chapter in this volume). Everyday conceptions of how the economy should work provide impulses to states to choose either positive or negative forms of intervention into the economy. States ignore such impulses at their own peril. After all, widespread frustration is a powerful force behind contests over the legitimacy of a financial reform nexus. By tracing everyday actions we may understand how agents are able to transform their own political, social and economic environments with strong consequences for hegemonic or imperialist influence in the international political economy.

6 Everyday investor subjects and global financial change: the rise of Anglo-American mass investment

Paul Langley

What's 'new' about contemporary global finance? Scholars in the field of international political economy (IPE) would almost certainly respond to this question by emphasising an unprecedented shift in the balance between state and market in favour of the latter (e.g., Cohen 1996; Germain 1997; Helleiner 1994; Strange 1998). This seemingly reflects what the editors suggest is a 'regulatory straitjacket' that dominates IPE inquiry into global finance. By contrast, my focus in this chapter is the exceptional growth of Anglo-American mass investment. Others have begun to reveal the importance to contemporary global finance of the millions of American and British investors who are habitually neglected by regulatory IPE (RIPE) inquiry (Harmes 2001a, 2001b). Yet even within this prescient work, individual investors remain portrayed as 'weak' and as passive dupes of the power and agency of globalising finance capital. Genuinely re-valuing mass investment in our understanding of global finance requires that everyday investment practices and investor subjects are viewed as constitutive in today's qualitatively distinct global financial order (Langley 2002a). All subjects' perceived self-interests as investors – and not just those of the financial elite – are discursively framed and manifest in their reflective practices. Accordingly, this chapter concentrates on developments in what the editors describe as 'axiorational' behaviour (see Chapter 1) in Anglo-American mass investment culture and how it contributes to our understanding not only of global financial change, but also of the making of everyday investor subjects.

Re-valuing everyday financial practices and subjects in our understanding of global finance clearly challenges many of the settled conceptual assumptions that are present in RIPE. Specifically, and as this chapter will show, the regulatory preference to define the core questions of the field of IPE through an ontology of states and markets is found to be seriously wanting. Only policy and financial elites are deemed consequential for change by regulatory IPE perspectives, while the vast majority remain largely submissive victims of external global financial developments that are 'out there' somewhere. Here I illustrate how exploring state and societal change, as opposed to simply state and market change, can highlight much of what is 'new' about global finance in the present era. In this way, my purpose is quite distinct from Len Seabrooke's chapter in this volume that focuses on the relationship between the development of axiorational behaviour surrounding credit-worthiness issues for lower-income groupings and its link to US influence in the contemporary international financial order (see Chapter 5). What follows below is divided into three parts. To begin, I briefly inves-tigate the cultural changes that have led to investment practices becoming the predominant form taken by everyday saving in the US and UK. The second part of the chapter argues that the everyday investor typically understands his or her calculative risk-taking practices in financial mar-kets, and the returns that are expected to follow, as integral to a successful life as a 'free' subject. Put differently, investment increasingly operates as a technology of the self in neoliberal Anglo-American society, that is, as a set of axiorational practices for embracing risk/return that are regarded as essential to material well-being and security and are engaged in willingly. The third part of the chapter explores the making of investor subjects in more detail with reference to current developments in Anglo-American pensions. I show how the individualisation of responsibility and risk produced by current pension restructuring – an example of what the editors of this volume call 'intra-systems change' – rests on the sidelining of collective insurance as a means of constructing, managing and pooling risks in favour of the promotion of individual investment to calculate, embrace and bear risk. My concluding remarks return to the implications of the chapter for IPE inquiry into global finance.

Mass investment culture

As sociologist Nigel Dodd (1994: 11) makes clear in his discussion of Adam Smith's *The Wealth of Nations*, saving tends to be regarded by liberal economists as 'rational from both the individual and collective point of view'. For Smith, individuals who do not save are guilty of 'prodigality and misconduct', while saving collectively provides the basis for economic growth as 'capitals are increased by parsimony' (in Dodd 1994: 10). The 'invisible hand' ensures that what is saved by individuals is automatically transformed into productive investment for the collective good. However, the rationality of saving that is assumed by liberal economics serves to obscure the multiple, multifarious and context-specific forms taken by saving practices. Saving can clearly take many forms – from commercial bank deposits to the purchase of property, from the hoarding of precious metals and objects of desire to the stuffing of mattresses with cash.

Our concern here lies with a particular form of saving, that is, contemporary investment in securities markets as an ordinary and habitual practice in Anglo-American society. At the time of the Wall Street Crash in 1929, only 3 per cent of US households had a stake in the stock market. By 2001, often indirectly as a consequence of occupational pension funds and mutual funds, 51.9 per cent of US households owned stock, up from 25 per cent in 1987 (Bygrave 1998; Reuters 2003). Indications are that financial market investment has become the predominant form taken by everyday saving practices in the US and UK, thereby making possible the New York and London-centred disintermediated capital and equity markets of global finance. For example, according to the Federal Reserve Board's Survey of Consumer Finances, by 1998 stocks, mutual funds and tax-deferred retirement accounts accounted for 71.3 per cent of the value of all US families' financial assets, up from 48.4 per cent in 1989. During the same nine-year period, the share of the value of all US families' financial assets accounted for by transaction accounts and certificates of deposit fell from 29.3 per cent to 15.7 per cent (Kennickell et al. 2000: 8). Given the many diverse forms taken by saving practices and contrary to liberal economics, however, 'simply assuming a natural propensity to invest on the part of the individual will not do; neither will it suffice for us to assume that financial investments are the actors' optimal choice for saving money' (Preda 2001: 206). Rather, we need to question how financial market investment has become the predominant form taken by everyday saving in Anglo-American society; we need to trace the development of axiorational behaviour.

The unprecedented scale of Anglo-American societies' everyday investment in securities is beginning to register among social scientists (Aitken 2003; Aldridge 1998; Clark et al. 2004; Harmes 2001a, 2001b; Ron Martin 1999; Randy Martin 2002; Preda 2001). When viewed collectively, this body of research provides us with some discerning and prescient insights into Anglo-American mass investment. First, it is made clear that the relatively settled post-war practices of intermediated saving (i.e., deposits in commercial bank accounts) have been ruptured. For Randy Martin (2002: 5–6), for example, intermediated saving practices have become 'nearly extinct', largely replaced by a 'new psychology' whereby 'money is not to be left untouched, but constantly fondled'. What is at stake in this change is a further partial loosening of the practices of Anglo-American saving from their moral grounding in the Puritan canon. Here saving practices take a rather conservative and prudent form, as the virtues of thrift and frugality are celebrated. Deposits in a commercial bank account are, after all, made on the understanding that savings cannot be 'lost' (apart from to inflation) and that returns (interest payments) are guaranteed. Lendol Calder (1999: 23–6) stresses that, since the late nineteenth century, periods of moral panic over the erosion of puritan attitudes to finance tend to coincide with innovations and increases in consumer credit. Yet mass investment also signals the erosion of risk-averse and thrifty savings practices such as placing deposits in commercial bank accounts.

Illustrative in this regard is the discourse of 'shareholder society' and 'popular capitalism' that framed Anglo-American privatisation programs during the 1980s in particular. As Financial Secretary to the Treasury between 1983 and 1986, John Moore was an important architect of UK privatisations such as that of British Telecom. His account of privatisation notes that 'Many politicians and financiers doubted whether ordinary people would ever be able to understand equity share ownership or *whether . . . it is "right" to let them take risks with their money*' (Moore 1992: 116, my emphasis). For Moore, however, it is the very promotion of the risks and potential returns of share ownership to the 'ordinary people' that provides the cultural basis for 'successful' privatisation programs. In his terms, privatisation becomes 'an educational process whereby the people of a country can grasp the fundamental beliefs and values of free enterprise' (Moore 1992: 115–16). It is clearly no coincidence, then, that the share allocation procedures for successive UK privatisations explicitly privileged applications from individuals who, in many cases, were making their first foray into securities investment. Between 1979 and 1991, the number of direct shareholders in the UK increased from three million (7 per cent of the adult population) to eleven million (25 per cent of the adult population), subsequently falling to nine million by 1995 as investors took the 'windfall' returns from the rising share prices of recently privatised companies (Ron Martin 1999: 268, 270).

Second and related, research into the emergence of contemporary mass investment is united in drawing attention to the significance of cultural change. Alex Preda's (2001) work provides perhaps the clearest example. He begins by asserting that 'A disposable income is of course a precondition of financial investing, as is a common institutional and juridical frame' (2001: 208). In terms of the former, investment practices are largely the preserve of the white middle and upper echelons of Anglo-American society. In terms of the latter, specific state legislation and regulatory change is necessary to permit mass investment practices. For example, the licensing of savings instruments such as personal equity plans (PEPs) and tax-exempt savings schemes (TESSAs) in the UK during the 1980s was essential in the forging of mutual fund practices that privileged stock market investment over commercial bank accounts through tax breaks (Knights 1997; such policies ran parallel to practices that also encouraged the use of tax havens, see, more generally, Jason Sharman's chapter in this volume). However, as Preda (2001: 208) continues, disposable income and institutional, legal and regulatory arrangements 'in themselves are not sufficient conditions' for mass investment. Also required is

a certain shared attitude with respect to financial markets, specific knowledge about financial products . . . a common way of talking about financial markets and products, and a shared framework in which such individuals can make sense of financial operations with respect to their lives. (Preda 2001: 208)

Similarly, in Rob Aitken's terms, the analysis of mass investment should treat 'culture not as secondary or derivative of larger, more material processes, but as constitutive of, and central to, the production and regulation of new economic practices, spaces and identities' (2003: 294). Gordon Clark et al. (2004) effectively concur. They argue that liberal economists' belief in so-called 'market fundamentals' as driving investment decision-making does not hold as 'the financial market' is itself increasingly constituted through cultural processes in which the media (e.g., 'how to . . .' investor guides, investor clubs and newsletters, advertising campaigns, magazines, websites, dedicated television stations and regular special sections in newspapers) and the public have come to occupy a central position.

Everyday investor subjects

While there is broad agreement among critical social scientists as to the significance of cultural processes for our understanding of mass investment, existing research offers a variety of approaches for understanding how investor identity is refracted through individual subjectivities. For example, Adam Harmes' (2001a) Gramscian-inspired reading represents individual investors as largely passive dupes of the financial fraction of capital. Here it is the strategic calculation of a structurally literate financial class that shapes global finance, their motivations deliberately obscured from the majority by the smoke and mirrors of 'false consciousness' that is created through mutual fund advertising and financial literacy campaigns. Not dissimilarly, Alan Aldridge's (1998) attempt to draw on Bourdieu to understand the emerging *habitus* of personal finance portrays individuals as unable to reflect upon their own investment practices and guilty of objective complicity. According to this view, individuals' 'cultural capital' – which, for Bourdieu, is the information necessary to make distinctions and value judgements – is undermined by the marketing of highly commodified financial products (e.g., index-tracker mutual funds). Such readings may help us to understand the creation of particular subject positions that are typically neglected by IPE inquiry into global finance, but cannot account for acting subjects.

By contrast, then, Aitken (2002, 2003) and Randy Martin (2002) suggest that all subjects' perceived self-interests as investors – and not just those of the financial elite – are discursively framed and manifest in their reflective practices. Here investor subjects are also the architects and not simply artefacts of global finance. For Aitken in particular, this view follows directly from his conceptual deployment of Michel Foucault's notion of 'governmentality'. As Foucault (1979: 20) described it, governmentality is 'the ensemble formed by the institutions, procedures, analyses and reflections, the calculations and tactics, that allow the exercise of this very specific albeit complex form of power, which has as its target population'. The act of government is not rule simply undertaken by the institutions, individuals and groups that hold authority over society (e.g., financial capital), but also the rationalities that connect 'government, politics and administration to the space of bodies, lives, selves and persons' (Dean 1999a: 12). Foucault's concept of governmentality is of particular utility in furthering our understanding of (neo)liberal programs of government that hinge on the government of the self by the self (Miller and Rose 1990). (Neo)Liberal government simultaneously respects the formal freedom and autonomy of subjects on the one hand, and governs within and through those autonomous actions on the other by promoting the very disciplinary technologies deemed necessary for a successful autonomous life. For actors governing rationalities become axiomatic, but they are chosen rather than adopted in an unreflective manner (see also the editors' introduction, Chapter 1, and Len Seabrooke's Chapter 5 in this volume).

From the perspective provided by Foucault's notion of governmentality, three key sets of related insights into contemporary Anglo-American investor subjects can be singled out and developed. All follow from Aitken's (2002, 2003) call for sensitivity to historical continuities and discontinuities as we seek to understand the making of contemporary investor subjects. For him, 'the connection of an autonomous self with practices of mass investment' (2003: 310) is not exclusive to contemporary neoliberal programs of government. Rather, important discontinuities mark out the making of contemporary investor subjects. First, the investor subject invoked by the liberal programs of government which prevailed in North America in the first half of the twentieth century was 'not organized around a monolithic or disconnected identity' (2003: 303), but was often enmeshed with images of nation-building and citizenship. Contemporary investment is often sheared of its associations with the collective good of the nation as investors are encouraged to take a global perspective and diversify their portfolio in order to maximise their individual returns. For example, of the eighty-four million direct and indirect US shareholders identified by the New York Stock Exchange, 45 per cent were found to hold shares in non-US companies (NYSE 2000).

Second, the discourses of investment found in contemporary media advertising attempt to overcome 'prudential masculinity' (Aitken 2002). This is one particular form of 'ethical' and masculinised financial subjectivity that, throughout the nineteenth and much of the twentieth century, encouraged saving as an obligation to the household. For example, investors in railway stocks during the later half of the nineteenth century were represented almost exclusively as 'family fathers' who could look to their wives to 'provide them with moral support' (Preda 2001: 216). By contrast, contemporary investor subjects are represented in media advertising campaigns as both men and women. While the presence of women in these campaigns is an important discontinuity with the past, this does not mean that contemporary everyday investment is less gendered than previously. Particularly revealing in this regard are the self-help financial guides and websites produced specifically for women that, at once, both transform and re-inscribe gendered financial identities (e.g., Blake Goodman 2000). 'Prudential masculinity' is no longer a defining feature in representations of the investor, but the portrayal of male and female investors remains highly differentiated. By comparison with their male counterparts, women are typically characterised in financial guides as lacking investment experience and large sums of capital, and as emotionally disposed not to undertake 'risky' investment strategies.

Third, while Aitken's observation that the relationship between investment practices and the autonomous self is not exclusive to neoliberal programs of government is insightful, it should not obscure contemporary change in how that relationship is represented and perceived. I would contend that the practices of investment occupy a more elemental position in contemporary governmentality than was the case previously. In the words of Joseph Nocera, a former senior editor at *Fortune* magazine, 'For the first time in history, average Americans view the stock market as both necessary and safe . . . People are in the market these days because they're afraid not to be' (in Bygrave 1998: 25). Everyday investment can be conceived of as a neoliberal 'technology of the self' – that is, a contemporary practice engaged in willingly as part of producing ourselves as 'free' subjects (Peters 2001: 78). Contemporary neoliberalism is characterised by the re-definition of the relationship between state and economy, and the application of the classical liberal model of the rational economic subject (*homo oeconomicus*) to all areas of social life. Contrary to previous liberal programs of government, the market is not supervised by the state, but instead provides the organisational principles for state, society and the individual. The result is 'a political rationality that tries to render the social domain economic and to link a reduction in (welfare) state services and security systems to the increasing call for "personal responsibility" and "self-care" ' (Lemke 2001: 203). As Michael Peters has it, 'the responsibilization of the self' associated with neoliberal government calls up 'new forms of prudentialism (a *privatized* actuarialism) where risk management is forced back onto individuals and satisfied through the market' (2001: 91, emphasis in original). It is no coincidence, then, that the notion of 'risk' is replacing 'need' as a core guiding principle of social policy-making and welfare delivery (Kemshall 2002). Entrepreneurial technologies of the self that enable individuals to successfully engage with risk become necessary to the production of the self as a 'free' subject (O'Malley 2000). It is here that the 'present invitation to live by finance' – where finance 'presents itself ... as a means for the acquisition of the self ... a proposal for how to get ahead' (Randy Martin 2002: 3) – becomes significant. Financial self-discipline (rationality, planning and foresight, prudence, etc.) broadly is integral for the autonomous neoliberal subject (Knights 1997: 224), and investment is increasingly essential to the course of self-realisation. Individual welfare, security and thus 'freedom' appear to require not only a set of entrepreneurial work-related skills that will be rewarded by employers (Amoore 2004), but also a portfolio of financial market assets that, carefully selected through the calculated engagement with risk, holds out the prospect of returns.

Perhaps the most stark example of investment as a neoliberal technology of the self at work in Anglo-American society is found in the practices of the so-called 'day trader'. Day traders are represented as 'ordinary' Americans who give up their day jobs to become full-time investors in the financial markets through the channels supplied by internet trading platforms and discount brokers (Randy Martin 2002: 46–9). According to NYSE (2000) figures, the average number of daily trades made through US online brokerage accounts increased from 96,200 in March 1997 to 1,371,000 in March 2000. The proliferation of day trading has been simply attributed by some observers to the 1990s bull market and the associated promises of massive returns on investment present in the 'new economy' discourse (e.g., Gross 2000). Yet the proliferation of day traders should not be understood merely as a passing moment in everyday financial subjectivity called up by a fleeting, speculative discourse. Rather, as Tom Baker and Jonathan Simon put it, 'the popular interest in day trading seems . . . to reflect less the promise of easy wealth than the cultural attraction of embracing risk. It represents the possibility of attaining autonomy, leaving behind the frustrations of working for someone else, by risking your own capital' (2002: 6). Simply attributing the emergence of day trading to the new economy bubble obscures its moral, political and technological context. The neoliberal morality of providing for one's material independence as the central component of one's 'freedom' increasingly draws on the rationality of financial investment as a technique that rewards those showing enterprise and good economic judgement.

Despite the apparent 'ordinariness' of the day trader, a very small number of individuals have, of course, given up their day job to compete with the professional financial traders. Anglo-American mass investment in financial markets is characterised not so much by the rise of the day trader, but by individual portfolios built up through contributions to mutual funds and pension plans. Indeed, the development of mass investment has actually coincided with a decline in the share of the US and UK stock markets that are owned directly by relatively wealthy individuals (Ron Martin 1999; NYSE 2000). While not as stark as in the instance of day trading, investment in mutual funds also nevertheless appears as central to the production of the 'free' self. The growth of mutual fund investment could, of course, also be ascribed to the 1990s 'new economy' bull market. Indeed, no less an authority on financial affairs than Charles P. Kindleberger described the boom in US stock markets throughout the 1990s as 'a mutual funds mania' (quoted in Clayton 2000: 16). The pouring of savings into mutual funds, rising stock markets and (in the US) cuts in capital gains taxes were clearly co-constitutive (Stiglitz 2003), a relationship in which the growth of the financial media also undoubtedly played a very important role (Clark et al. 2004). If this were the whole story, however, it would be fair to expect that mutual fund investment would have collapsed as the new economy bubble burst in early 2000. In January 2004, Americans poured $40.8 billion into mutual funds. This was the third highest monthly growth since 1992 (Fuerbringer 2004). Such growth is perhaps even more revealing given the ongoing investigations, led by New York Attorney General Eliot Spitzer, into improper trading at the height of the bubble by asset managers (Atlas 2004). As the perceived relationship between material wealth, individual freedom and finance has tightened, mutual fund investment for many Americans is not just a passing adventure in speculation. It is not, in Daniel Gross's terms, 'a do-it-yourself hobby for the vast middle and upper-middle class' (2000: 5). Rather, achieving returns from mutual funds is perceived as leading to future happiness, improved social standing and, ultimately, greater freedom.

Retirement, responsibility and risk

During the post-1945 period, retirement in North American and European societies in particular came to be funded for the most part through the state's taxation of current workers (so-called 'pay-as-you-go' or PAYGO pensions). At the same time, the further development of retirement saving practices through Anglo-American occupational pension schemes created a network of investment relationships between workers (largely skilled, unionised and male), their employers and financial markets (Cutler and Waine 2001). Changes in these investment relationships since the mid-1970s and early 1980s, and their significance to the constitution of disintermediated and globalising financial markets, are the focus for a growing body of cross-disciplinary research (e.g., Blackburn 2002; Clark 2000; Clowes 2000; Engelen 2003; Minns 2001; Seabrooke 2001). Robin Blackburn (2002: 6) reckons that in 1999, prior to the stock market downturn, the global assets of pension funds were valued at $13,000 billion. Around 60 per cent of these assets, or $7,800 billion, belonged to US savers, with those of UK savers worth $1,400 billion. He places these figures in perspective by noting that, according to OECD calculations, the worldwide value of stock markets at the time stood at $23,000 billion. In our terms, what has received very little attention in this literature is the extent to which investment as a neoliberal technology of the self has come to loom large in Anglo-American pensions. Two key developments mark the recent restructuring of pensions that, taken together, are furthering an individualisation of responsibility and risk.

First, the last couple of decades have seen moves to further minimise the share of total retirement income that is provided through state-based pension arrangements. Such attempts to discipline individual responsibility for pensions provision are, of course, not limited to the US and UK, but are part of a wider assault on PAYGO pensions led by the World Bank (1994) and the OECD (1998). While the share of total retirement income provided for by occupational and personal pensions in the US and UK is high by comparison with Germany, France and Spain, for example, the Anglo-American attack on state-based pensions is nevertheless being pursued with considerable zeal. By way of illustration, the headline objective of the Labour government is to transform the structure of UK retirement income by reversing the current 60:40 ratio of state to occupational and personal pensions (Department of Social Security 1998). To this end, they have maintained the indexation of basic state pension (BSP) benefits to prices as opposed to earnings that was put in place in 1980 by Margaret Thatcher's first government. At the same time, the centrepiece of government policy is the 'stakeholder pension', introduced in April 2001. Stakeholder pensions are a form of tax-favoured occupational pension scheme where asset management costs are capped at 1 per cent of assets per year. Employers that do not have an existing occupational fund are legally bound to offer (but not provide) a stakeholder pension to their employees. The stakeholder thereby targets three to five million low- to middle-income workers who would have otherwise relied solely upon the state in their retirement (Ring 2002). In the US, meanwhile, George W. Bush's 'President's Commission to Strengthen Social Security' of December 2001 offered a range of options to cut state pension benefits and partially marketise and individualise social security (*Economist* 2002: 14–15). With Bush's victory in the 2004 Presidential election, the discourse proclaiming the need for reform (e.g., SSA 2004) appears likely to finally generate firm legislative proposals (Halbfinger 2004).

Second, restructuring is also well underway in occupational pensions. Since the mid-1980s in the US, and more recently in the UK, an accelerating shift from defined benefit (DB) to defined contribution (DC) occupational pension provision has taken hold (Mitchell and Schieber 1998). Anglo-American pension funds take two principal forms: DB or 'final salary', and DC or 'money purchase'. Both have legal standing as trusts and translate tax-favoured contributions by employees and sponsoring employers into collective holdings of equities, bonds and other financial instruments. While the scale and ratio of employer and employee contributions varies across both DB and DC, it is the difference in terms of benefits paid that primarily distinguishes final salary from money purchase schemes. As UK Government Actuary Chris Daykin (2002: 10–11) summarises, DB arrangements 'offer benefits which are either specified in absolute terms or are calculated according to a prescribed formula, usually based on [final] salary or period of service or both'. DC schemes 'offer no particular commitment regarding the benefit to be paid, which is dependent on what is paid in by way of contributions. Contributions are invested and the benefit reflects the results of that investment.' The shift from DB to DC has reached a crescendo in the UK since the turn of the century during the so-called 'final salary pension crisis' (Langley 2004). In 1975, for example, 87 per cent of American workers that were members of an occupational pension scheme were part of a DB plan. By 2001, 58 per cent of those covered by a scheme were members of a DC scheme, a further 23 per cent enjoyed membership of both DC and DB, and 19 per cent were members of a DB plan only (Aizcorbe et al. 2003).

DC plans, which are commonly known as 401(k) plans in the US as around three-quarters of DC plans use the 401(k) tax code, permit employees to reduce their current tax liabilities by taking income in the form of pension contributions (Munnel and Sundén 2004). What is most significant for us is the individualisation of responsibility and investment risk that the shift from DB to DC necessarily implies. Contributions to DB schemes are invested on the behalf of workers by scheme trustees and the asset management industry, and the employer bears the risk that returns on investment may not be sufficient to meet guaranteed benefits. As Harmes (2001a: 106) observes, workers contributing to DB schemes are 'more akin to passive savers than active investors', their benefits appearing as 'more of an entitlement than a return on investment'. In contrast, as the Director of the Office of Policy and Research at the US Department of Labor (DoL) Richard Hinz summarises, under DC schemes 'workers are often responsible for deciding whether to join a plan by contributing, determining the percentage of pay to contribute, deciding between different investment options, and deciding what to do with vested account balances when changing jobs' (2000: 33).

As the neoliberal state undertakes programs to minimise the share of total retirement income that is provided through welfare, and as employers' commitments to DB occupational pension schemes wane, individuals are cut loose from previous arrangements to become increasingly responsible for their own retirement income. A mixture of disciplinary disincentives (e.g., cutting benefits from PAYGO, closing DB schemes to new entrants), incentives (e.g., tax breaks on DC pension contributions) and new regulatory regimes (e.g., UK stakeholder legislation, 401(k) tax code) are necessary in producing the individualisation of responsibility and risk in pensions. Financial market investment appears as the only means of securing material well-being and therefore freedom in retirement. In the words of Assistant Secretary of Labor Ann L. Combs (2004), for example, the Bush administration sought throughout its first period in office to work to ensure that 'the 401(k) plans of America's workers and their families continue to provide the flexibility, freedom, and security inherent in a vibrant "ownership society"' (see also Seabrooke 2006a: 206–13). This work has included increasing the limits on tax-preferred contributions to

401(k)s and individual retirement accounts (IRAs), and enabling 401(k) plan administrators to provide workplace investment advice (Andrews 2003; Leonhardt 2003).

Given that state-based pensions rest on a collective 'social contract' of solidarity across generations and between rich and poor, the revision of that contract tends to be associated with a discourse that views contributions to PAYGO (e.g., National Insurance in the UK) in negative terms as a tax on both the economy and the individual. This is especially the case when contributions to occupational and personal pension plans are simultaneously portrayed as individual investment that realises returns, manages risks and contributes to overall economic growth (e.g., Clowes 2000). For Martin Feldstein, President of the US National Bureau of Economic Research and key adviser to Bush in the 2000 Presidential election campaign, for example,

The Social Security program today is a very risky 'asset' for anyone who expects to depend on Social Security benefits as the primary source of retirement income. . . . Participants in a pay-as-you-go system are always at the mercy of the political process. The political support that previously came from the program's popularity is declining rapidly as voters recognize that the return on their Social Security taxes has fallen close to zero . . . There is no way to avoid the political risk to benefits inherent in a pay-as-you-go system. By contrast, the risks of market fluctuations of a funded system can be avoided by a relatively small increase in the savings rate during working years, effectively building up a financial cushion to absorb fluctuations in stock and bond prices. (Feldstein 1997: 37)

It is not simply that the so-called 'unfunded liabilities' of PAYGO and the 'pre-funded assets' of occupational and personal pensions carry clear normative connotations (Minns 2001: 63). At the same time, to paraphrase Feldstein, little can be done about the 'political risks' of unfunded arrangements, but 'the risks of market fluctuations' present in pre-funded arrangements can be measured and responded to by the individual through the technology of investment.

It is important to stress that the individualisation of risk that Feldstein applauds is not, contrary to Joseph Stiglitz (2003) for example, simply a transfer of responsibility for the management of investment risks (e.g., falling stock prices). Such a reading would require us to understand 'risks' as objectively identifiable dangers. But, as Mitchell Dean puts it, 'There is no such thing as risk in reality. Risk is a . . . set of different ways . . . of ordering reality, of rendering it into a calculable form' (1999b: 131). Once we recognise the category of 'risk' as a means to the calculation of an uncertain future, then the individualisation of responsibility and risk in pensions comes to be viewed quite differently. In our terms, the individualisation of risk in pensions is only achieved through the cultural displacement of one technology of government (insurance) by another (investment).

At first blush, there are several important similarities between insurance and investment as technologies of government. The calculation of and engagement with risk is, of course, integral to both. Indeed, the prospect of individual security offered by both insurance and investment practices rests upon the construction of the uncertain future as a set of calculable, measurable and manageable risks. Both also 'rely in crucial respects upon "expertise": the social authority ascribed to particular agents [i.e., insurers, asset managers, etc.] and forms of judgement [i.e., probability, actuarialism, portfolio theory, etc.] on the basis of their claims to possess specialized truths and rare powers' (Miller and Rose 1990: 2). Furthermore, the operation of insurance and investment as technologies of the self would appear to be similar: both offer neoliberal subjects the prospect of the very welfare and financial security that appears, at the same time, as a primary means of acquiring material well-being and producing and maintaining freedom. For example, an individual in the UK who contributes to a private health insurance program in the face of state cutbacks may similarly contribute to a stake-holder pension plan against a backdrop of falls in the BSP.

Despite these similarities, investment practices differ from insurance practices in two important respects. First, insurance and investment represent 'risk' in very different ways. Insurance developed throughout the twentieth century to protect the individual against loss or hardship from a diverse range of risks (e.g., accidents, unemployment, poverty, old age, premature death). Here risks are constructed through expert probability calculations as an actuarial phenomenon that can be managed, pooled and spread across a population (Ewald 1991). Such a view of risk as a possible hindrance or loss to be shared and minimised contrasts with the representation of risk present in investment practices as an incentive or opportunity to be embraced (e.g., Ben-Ami 2001). The move from collective insurance to individual investment in pensions – that is, the shift from state-based and DB occupational pensions to DC and personal pensions – is perhaps the exemplar of a broader trend in neoliberal society that Baker and Simon (2002) call 'embracing risk'. This is the 'historic shift of investment risk from broad pools (the classic structure of risk spreading through insurance) to individual (middle class) consumers and employees in return for the possibility of greater return' (Baker and Simon 2002: 4).

Second, unlike insurance, responsibility for the calculation, measurement and management of investment risks ultimately lies with the individual. Consider the example of a typical DC pension plan. The nature of the DC plan available to an individual in the US and UK is likely to be determined by the trustees appointed by the plan sponsor (i.e., their employer) who selects the plan and the plan administrator. The plan administrator plays the role of record keeper, provider of investor education and information (including regular account statements) for participants, and intermediary for participants' investment decisions. All features of plan administration may be 'bundled' and provided by a single company, or 'unbundled' and contracted between a range of service providers to a greater or lesser degree. DC plans tend to offer individuals a menu of mutual funds covering a range of asset classes and sub-asset classes from which to create their own portfolio. In a so-called 'closed menu plan', all funds are from a single company which is also likely to be the plan administrator. Conversely, several separate fund providers may feature in the increasingly common 'open menu plan'. DC plans can also offer individuals a choice between a range of diversified portfolios (so-called 'life-style funds') which are each created to meet various risk/reward targets. Whatever its form, investors in a DC pension plan do defer day-to day financial management to expert asset managers, yet their investment decisions within a scheme (e.g., the choice of 'blue chip' or an 'emerging market' mutual fund) entail a calculative engagement with risk/reward. In sum, the individual that embraces the opportunity of investment can receive financial rewards and the freedom that is assumed will follow, but the risks that an investment turns sour and that freedom will be compromised are not pooled or spread. Individual retirement investors are, in short, both calculative risk-takers and risk-bearers.

Conclusions

I began this chapter by highlighting the ways in which IPE inquiry into global finance tends to marginalise and obscure the constitutive role of everyday spaces, practices and subjects in the changes that mark the contemporary era. I subsequently focused on the development of Anglo-American mass investment and the reflective practices of everyday investor subjects. The argument that investment operates as a neoliberal technology of the self – that is, as a set of practices for embracing risk/return regarded as essential to the production of the material well-being and security of a 'free' self – was explored both in general and in relation to recent restructuring in Anglo-American pensions. Rather than reiterate these points once again, I would like to conclude by briefly considering some of the implications of the chapter for IPE inquiry into global finance.

As I suggested at the outset of the chapter, what the editors of this volume call RIPE is found seriously wanting in conceptual terms once we attempt to re-value the place of everyday life in our understanding of global finance. As I hope my research here into Anglo-American mass investment has made plain, exploring state and societal change, and not just state–market change, may indeed be key to understanding the development of axiorational behaviours that inform much of what is 'new' about global finance. In general, IPE scholars of global finance could, then, learn much from those within their field who have sought to raise the profile of women (e.g., Marchand and Runyan 2000), the workplace (e.g., Amoore 2002) and cities (e.g., Drainville 2004) in order to socially situate their accounts of global restructuring. The common representation of global finance in IPE as 'out there' and above and beyond everyday life also follows from a conception of finance as cross-border capital flows. As sociologists and geographers are beginning to realise (Larner and Le Heron 2002), analytical frameworks that conceive of the global economy through the metaphor of 'flows' position material changes (e.g., disintermediation) in a consequential relationship to states, societies and individuals. The result is disembodied and somewhat structural accounts of change. For IPE scholars of global finance, an embodied and constitutive understanding of global finance would seem to require a move away from the metaphor of 'flows', a move that would be greatly assisted by an engagement with inter-disciplinary innovations in the social theory of money and finance (e.g., Dodd 1994; Leyshon and Thrift 1997; Ingham 2004). In addition, IPE inquiry into the legitimacy or otherwise of global finance has concentrated almost exclusively on the institutions of governance that attempt to manage stability. Legitimacy is thus seen to hinge upon the technical proficiency and democratic credentials of governing institutions (e.g., Germain 2001; Porter 2001). My intervention in this chapter suggests, however, that the legitimacy or otherwise of the new financial order may also turn on the capacity of globalising markets to be perceived as meeting the expectations of return held by Anglo-American everyday investors (see also Seabrooke 2006a). Further research is required in this regard, as there are contradictions present in all claims to manage the uncertain future through the techniques and calculations of risk/return (Crook 1999).

Re-valuing the constitutive role of everyday spaces, practices and identities in global finance also has implications for the politics of transformation. IPE writers on global finance have tended to concentrate their attention on the political prospects for emancipatory change that follow from either state re-regulation of financial markets, or the capacity of a nascent global civil society to renovate the institutions of the financial architecture. The former typically seeks to rebuild the national political economy in the name of social democracy, while the latter seeks to reorient multilateralism in the name of global inclusion (see Langley 2002b: 161–7 for an overview). The possibilities for transformation grounded in everyday axiorational practices are usually overlooked. Yet as disintermediation and Anglo-American mass investment have developed, for example, alternative practices emerge in a dialectical manner as the 'ownership' of the economy changes hands. In Robert Pollin's (1995: 29) terms, the relatively broadly based social ownership that results from mass investment could provide a starting point from which to replace an 'elite-voice' with a 'democratic-voice' in economic decision-making. The political prospects of so-called 'ethical investment' and 'shareholder activism', and their capacity to contest and confound investment strategies based solely on 'shareholder value' and the maximisation of returns are, then, long overdue for critical consideration in the field of IPE.

7 Peasants as subaltern agents in Latin America: neoliberalism, resistance and the power of the powerless

Adam David Morton

Eric Hobsbawm long heralded 'the death of the peasantry' as the most dramatic and far-reaching social change to mark the twentieth century, resulting from transformations in agricultural production. In his trilogy on the 'long nineteenth century' (from the 1780s to 1914), he argued that the peasantry as a social class were destined to fade away, a possibility that became more actual by the late twentieth century. Across Latin America the percentage of peasants halved, or almost halved, in twenty years in Colombia (1951–73), Mexico (1960–80) and Brazil (1960–80) while in the Dominican Republic (1960–81), Venezuela (1961–81) and Jamaica (1953–81) the decline was by almost two-thirds. By the 1970s there was *no* country in Latin America in which peasants were not a minority with the continents of sub-Saharan Africa, South and continental Southeast Asia and China standing as the only regions of the globe still essentially dominated by rural production (Hobsbawm 1987: 137, 1994: 289–91). For Hobsbawm the epochal significance of this transformation was clear.

The mere fact that the peasantry has ceased to constitute the actual majority of the population in many parts of the world, that it has for practical purposes disappeared in some . . . and that its disappearance as a class today is quite conceivable in many developed countries, separates the period since the eighteenth century from all previous history since the development of agriculture. (Hobsbawm 1999: 198)

Stemming from this he proposed that the specific variety of subalternity, poverty, exploitation and oppression encapsulated by the peasantry and their relation to land and production would lead to the gradual political disintegration of their class identity. Peasantries, in his view, would become more and more incapable of enforcing their class interests, or organising themselves as a class through representative organisations, while nevertheless stepping back from their complete dismissal as a source of agency for political acts of defiance (Hobsbawm 1999: 219–22). Elsewhere, one can find similar support for these claims about the gradual

120

erosion of the peasantry as a social class. One example is in the analysis of the impact of globalisation in Latin America and the ways in which a proletarianisation of the peasantry has ensued in light of the restructuring of traditional agricultural production towards non-traditional agricultural exports (NTAE) such as fruit, cut flowers, ornamental plants, winter vegetables and spices (Robinson 2003: 252–8; Cammack 2002: 126–7).

What these broad claims tend to neglect, though, is precisely the constitution and reproduction of peasantries through the dynamics of capital accumulation. While the trend at the heart of claims about the 'death of the peasantry' may be evident there is, at least, a twofold neglect. First, of the processes of class formation evident in the transformation of the peasantry through which a range of productive activities are combined and, second, of the purposeful agency articulated by the peasantry as a subaltern class linked to their (re)constitution within the changing dynamics of capital accumulation (Bernstein 2000). The action of groups like the Zapatista Army of National Liberation (EZLN) in Mexico and similar agrarian-based movements such as the Landless Rural Workers Movement (MST) in Brazil and the National Confederation of Indigenous Nationalities (CONAIE) in Ecuador calling for agrarian reform, or regional peasant movements such as *Via Campesina* with its ties to 'anti-globalisation' fora, would all seemingly challenge the thesis about the inevitable demise of the peasantry. Contemporary features of these rural movements in Latin America, while resonating with familiar motifs of peasant movements in earlier transitions to capitalism, thus raise new issues about the old 'agrarian question' (Brass 2002).

Most pivotal here is the importance of recognising what has been referred to as 'the power of the powerless': the everyday modest expressions of volition that often remain anonymous but whose political impact often transcend individual revolt to transform consciousness and structure purposeful agency (Havel 1985: 64–5). While power is expressed through the habitualisation and internalisation of social practices – organising and dividing subjectivities – it also provokes acts representative of what the editors refer to as everyday forms of defiance agency (see Chapter 1). Yet focus on the latter has predominantly and adroitly been evaded within regulatory international political economy (RIPE) debates. The claim has long been made that the focus on the supposed hegemony of transnational capital has been privileged at the expense of a consideration of conditions of transformation in world order. As André Drainville (1994: 125) noted, 'analysis must give way to more active sorties against transnational neoliberalism, and the analysis of concepts of control must beget original concepts of resistance'. Here the importance of focusing on peasant movements of resistance

and their claims to counter-hegemonic strategies of structural transformation becomes acute (Morton 2002). This is the aim of the present
chapter: to retrace and represent a novel form of defiance agency in
the form of the agrarian-based EZLN resistance that was itself cognisant
of the local and global dynamics of capital accumulation in Mexico.
This aim is in keeping with the recent and growing focus on the diverse
array of so-called 'anti-capitalist' resistance movements and the move to
recognise neoliberal globalisation as a highly contested set of social relations through which practices of *class struggle* are articulated (Bieler and
Morton 2003, 2004).

In order to realise this aim the chapter investigates the role of the
peasantry in Latin America, or the power of the powerless, through a
focus on the EZLN in Mexico. Three main sections bring the argument
into focus. First, the point of departure is the consideration of the peasantry as a *subaltern class* through the use of Antonio Gramsci's own
methodological criteria in understanding the history of subaltern classes
to analyse the interplay of ruler and ruled within resistance struggles.
What Gramsci (1996: 21) recognised as the 'anxious defence' of subaltern classes is linked to issues of defiance agency through a focus on the
case of the EZLN in Mexico. What emerges from this is a consideration of
the growth of radical peasant organisations in Chiapas, Mexico linked to
transformations in property relations within the context of the restructuring of capital and the rise of neoliberalism on a global scale. Hence in this
section the response of the EZLN is also situated within an era of structural change in the 1970s within which the logic of capitalist social
relations shifted towards neoliberal policy priorities (Morton 2003a).
The roots of the rebellion are therefore analysed by focusing on the
changing forms and relations of production in Chiapas during the
1970s, which led to a growth of radical peasant organisations that
would influence the formation of the EZLN. As a result of this analysis,
issues arise concerning the intersection of class-based and indigenous
forms of identity asserted by the EZLN, hence appreciating how the
movement is situated within the recomposition of class struggle in
Mexico (Veltmeyer 2000). In the second section, the immediate context
of the rebellion is then discussed in relation to the restructuring of capital
represented by the rise of neoliberal globalisation understood as the
expansion of the interests of capital accumulation on a global scale
through policies favouring market-imposed discipline, monetarism and
the logic of competitiveness, the latter most significantly epitomised
by the coexistent implementation of the North American Free Trade
Agreement (NAFTA) in Mexico. Third, the innovative methods of struggle developed by the EZLN will then be analysed within the context

and categories of counter-hegemonic forms of resistance developed by Gramsci. The forms of political representation developed by the EZLN in resisting neoliberal restructuring are thus analysed in terms of how they pressed claims and asserted autonomy within a critique of social power relations in Mexico. Hence the account encompasses both specific changes to production relations that affected the rise of the EZLN as well as the subjective implications of political consciousness. What emerges, in conclusion, is an appreciation of the peasantry as a subaltern class that in the case of the EZLN focuses on processes of defiance agency – or the power of the powerless – while contesting assumptions about the inevitable demise of the peasantry in the modern world.

Subaltern class agency and changes to the social relations of production in Chiapas

Through an emphasis on the socio-cultural interplay between ruler and ruled, Gramsci advocated a focus on struggles over hegemony within which both domination *and* resistance could be analysed. Here, Gramsci's own criteria on the history of subaltern classes are useful as a point of departure to analyse alternative historical and contemporary contexts (Gramsci 1971: 52–5; Morton 2003b). According to Gramsci, the specific history of subaltern classes is intertwined with that of state–civil society relations more generally. It is therefore important to try and unravel such contestations (for more detail see Morton 2007). One way of doing so is to identify the 'objective' formation of subaltern social classes by analysing developments and transformations within the sphere of production (Gramsci 1971: 52). This advances an understanding of the 'decisive nucleus of economic activity' but without succumbing to expressions of economism (Gramsci 1971: 161). For example, historical and contemporary research needs to incorporate, as much as possible, a consideration of the mentalities and ideologies of subaltern classes, their active as well as passive affiliation to dominant social forms of political association, and thus their involvement in formations that might conserve dissent or maintain control (Gramsci 1971: 52). Additionally, such a method entails focusing on the formations which subaltern classes themselves produce (e.g., trade unions, workers' co-operatives, or peasant associations) which press claims or assert autonomy within the existing conditions of hegemony. Questions of historical and political consciousness expressed by subaltern classes can then be raised with the ultimate aim of appreciating the common terrain dialectically occupied by both structure and agency (Bieler and Morton 2001). 'The history of subaltern social groups is necessarily fragmented and episodic', writes Gramsci, to the extent that 'subaltern groups are always subject to the activity of ruling groups, even when they rebel and rise up' (Gramsci 1971: 54–5).

This method of analysis can be useful in tracing the combination of developments that exacerbated the agrarian landscape in Chiapas to precipitate social mobilisation. From the 1970s onward there was a conjunction of factors in the region that involved migrant flows influenced by changes in production and land demands, the expansion of cattle-ranching forcing the relocation of peasants, ambitious state projects negatively impacting on peasant subsistence, an energy boom skewing peasant and commercial agriculture and the subsequent impact of neoliberal policies on state programs and policies of support. Therefore, rather than peasants being unaccustomed to change, communities underwent constant readjustment during the 1970s, which led to a crucial reorganisation of local social organisation. One of the major transformations at this time was the way energy development and the linked oil boom of the 1970s changed the material and social bases of community existence in Chiapas. Emblematic here was the impact of the Organization of the Petroleum Exporting Countries (OPEC) oil crisis on communities in Chiapas that skewed production away from the fragile agricultural sector towards large-scale development projects. According to George Collier, one of the roots of the Zapatista rebellion can therefore be linked to the pernicious impact the oil boom had in restructuring local social relations of production in Chiapas.

After the OPEC oil crisis in 1972, Mexico borrowed internationally to expand oil production for export and to finance ambitious projects of development. During the resulting development boom, Mexico's agriculture declined from 14% of GDP in 1965 to just 7% of GDP in 1982, as resources for production flowed into other sectors. Mexico, propelled by energy development, became more and more oriented towards foreign markets and away from food self-sufficiency. (Collier 1994a: 16)

Hence large-scale development projects (hydroelectric dams, populist agricultural policies, petroleum exploration and extraction) increased throughout the presidential administrations in Mexico of Luis Echeverría (1970–76) and Lopez Portillo (1976–82). These state-led projects of development had several consequences in the central highlands of Chiapas, principally drawing peasants into off-farm wages and entrepreneurial opportunities in transport and commerce, linked to the energy industry, or out of agriculture and into wage work as unskilled labourers in construction. These changes in the social relations of production resulted in distinctions being drawn between subsistence-producing peasants and those involved in wage labour.

In particular, productive relations became more class-based while gender and generational differences were also heightened by new meanings associated with work. This change in the social relations of production signified a move away from the politics of rank-based forms of organisation based on community hierarchies to the politics of class-based forms of organisation in Chiapas (Collier 1994b). It was a process of class formation, to draw from E. P. Thompson (1978), whereby particular communities experienced new structures of exploitation and identified new points of antagonistic interest centred around issues of class struggle; even though forms of class-consciousness – involving a conscious identity of common interests – may not have immediately emerged. In Chiapas, these issues of class struggle arose when peasant communities sought to resolve antagonisms less through the rank-based social ties and communal commitments of civil-religious hierarchies and more through cash derived from wage work or through factions associated with political parties (Collier 1994b: 9–16). Yet this transformation did not simply equate with the death of the peasantry as a social class and thus as a source of agency to express defiance. Instead the situation was a mix of agricultural petty commodity production alongside the exchange of wage labour and other economic activities (Kovic 2003: 61).

For instance, the attractiveness of wage work over peasant agriculture during the 1970s did draw communities in Chiapas into a capitalist social division of labour but this became an especially vulnerable and acute situation after the collapse of Mexico's oil-fuelled development in 1982. This meant that peasants had to then return to agricultural production alongside developing a mix of economic activities within the context of growing class-stratification and changing processes of capitalist accumulation. Such reaction to the dynamics of capitalism and fundamental changes to the way of life for certain communities in Chiapas also posed challenges that undermined the institutionalised control of social conflict organised through the ruling Institutional Revolutionary Party (PRI). This entailed peasant movements embracing new forms of political organisation outside the institutionalised presence of the PRI to assert a greater degree of autonomy.

Prior to the EZLN rebellion in 1994, initially involving the seizure of several towns in Chiapas through an assault against the army, the increasingly class-based conflict represented by the above changes to the social relations of production in Chiapas was also the context for radical consciousness-raising efforts. This was crucially related to the pastoral and community work of Bishop Samuel Ruiz García. Ruiz became the Bishop of San Cristóbal in 1959 and cultivated contacts with French and Italian intellectual priests, clerical sociologists and anthropologists of development throughout the 1960s. As a result, there were efforts in Chiapas to promote forms of social action and consciousness-raising within the diocese, to the extent that Ruiz's role can be understood as the agency of an organic intellectual in shifting people's ideas about the changing social situation. This refers to the action of somebody organically connected to social forces, here at the grassroots level, with the task of 'systematically and patiently ensuring that this force is formed, developed, and rendered ever more homogeneous, compact and self-aware' (Gramsci 1971: 185). The active construction of an awareness among the people of the exploitative nature underpinning social relations linked to changes in production was therefore brought about through education and the development of a critical consciousness in an attempt to overcome everyday taken-for-granted attitudes. From this activism, heightened cultural and historical awareness ensued among indigenous groups and a realisation of their role as protagonists in, rather than passive victims of, history. Equally crucial at the time was the invitation Ruiz extended to Maoist groups to carry out community organising in Chiapas in the 1970s that then eventually consolidated social and autonomous forms of radical peasant organisation outside the institutional control of the PRI. It was from within the waxing and waning of such peasant organisations throughout the 1970s and 1980s that the EZLN would eventually emerge (Harvey 1998). The formation of radical peasant organisations, within the context of changing forms of social relations of production in the 1970s, also began to experience the assault of neoliberal restructuring in the 1980s. This was a trend that was emblematic of a reconfiguration of state–civil society relations across Mexico marked by increased repression, massive arrests and the assassination of agrarian leaders.

The accumulation strategy of neoliberalism: NAFTA and agrarian reform

The recomposition of capital on a global scale under the rubric of neoliberal restructuring proceeded in Mexico along lines that involved attempts to consolidate a neoliberal accumulation strategy while rearticulating the fractured form of hegemony articulated by the PRI. This was conducted through the material and political discourse of *salinismo* during the administration of Carlos Salinas de Gortari (1988–94) that involved reorienting relations among dominant factions of capital as well as the balance of class forces across state–civil society relations in Mexico (Morton 2003a). The EZLN rebellion on 1 January 1994 was thus a response against both the global strategy of neoliberal capitalist accumulation as well as the specific discourse of *salinismo* in Mexico that peaked with the implementation of NAFTA. Hence NAFTA was denounced by the Zapatistas as 'the death certificate for the ethnic peoples of Mexico' and Subcomandante Marcos, as the figurehead of the movement, observed that the rebellion 'isn't just about Chiapas – it's about NAFTA and Salinas's whole neoliberal project' (as cited in Ross 1995: 21, 153). It was therefore no coincidence that the EZLN rebellion was orchestrated on the very same day that NAFTA came into effect.

One of the principal measures of neoliberal restructuring in Mexico was reforming the agrarian sector. During the 1970s increases in state revenues from petroleum exports helped to sustain agricultural subsidies, which became embodied within the state-run Mexican food system (SAM) in 1980. However, although annual subsidies stimulated national maize production among peasant producers, the international market for oil prices and the debt crisis eliminated the financial base of SAM and the attempt to implement redistributive food policies. During the administration of Miguel de la Madrid (1982–88), rather than public programs to stimulate maize production, marketing and consumption,

the Mexican government reaffirmed its commitment to meet its international financial obligations, thus committing a major proportion of the federal budget to debt servicing, and began a process of crisis management, oriented towards markedly reducing the level of subsidies and cutting back social services, selling off state-owned enterprises and postponing investment in the physical infrastructure of the country. (Hewitt de Alcántara 1994: 8)

Between 1987 and 1989 the price for maize plummeted, contributing to a deepening recession in the countryside, while those maize producers operating at a loss increased from 43 to 65 per cent between 1987 and 1988 (Hewitt de Alcántara 1994: 12). Within the context of neoliberal restructuring there was, then, an overhaul of the agricultural sector that involved the privatisation of state-owned enterprises and the withdrawal of price supports and subsidies linked to World Bank demands. Notably the state-owned Mexican Coffee Institute (INMECAFÉ), established in 1958, was also dismantled under the privatisation policies of *salinismo*, which meant a withdrawal from purchasing and marketing functions and the reduction of technical assistance. The collapse of world coffee prices by 50 per cent in 1989 compounded this withdrawal and exacerbated the plight of rural communities, with small-holders in parts of Chiapas abandoning production between 1989 and 1993. The reform of the agricultural sector also involved altering the status of collective *ejido* land-holdings (common land owned and used by independent producers with usufruct rights to individual parcels).

This entailed reforming Article 27 of the Mexican Constitution of 1917 that enshrined the *ejido* as central to collective land ownership. Yet the *ejido* also ensured a form of political and organisational state control because it became the principal vehicle for state regulation of peasant access to land and therefore helped to maintain political control over the peasantry. Under the *ejido* reform, though, lands could now be legally sold, bought, rented, or used as collateral for loans; private companies could purchase lands; new associations between capitalist developers and *ejidatarios* (*ejido* owners) were allowed; and provisions for peasants to petition for land redistribution were deleted, formally ending a process of land distribution, with primacy given to the security of private property (Harvey 1996: 194–5). Although the collective status of such landholdings was more apparent than real, as there was an ongoing capitalisation of rural production even before the reform of Article 27, the symbolic break with past agrarian reform based on the ideals of the Mexican Revolution was pivotal and destroyed any future hope of land redistribution among the peasantry (Harvey 1998: 188). This loss of hope would be compounded by the realisation that reform of the agrarian code would *accelerate* the capitalist transformation of agricultural productive relations. The gradual elimination of restrictions on maize imports initiated over a fifteen year period under NAFTA – with average yields of maize in Mexico at 1.7 tons/hectare compared with 6.9 tons/hectare in the US – would tend to support this view (DeWalt *et al.* 1994: 56).

One result of this neoliberal restructuring of the agrarian sector was that social and institutional bases of peasant representation linked to the *ejido* system were fundamentally altered. This meant that, as the privatisation of communal *ejido* landholdings proceeded, alternative institutional organisations had to be constructed in an attempt to re-establish and re-define the broader hegemonic process. Yet this proved increasingly difficult in light of the more autonomous forms of peasant mobilisation in Chiapas, discussed earlier, which developed outside the institutional organisation of the PRI. At the same time, during the neoliberal phase of agricultural restructuring, conflicts between and within peasant groups in the highland communities of Chiapas were also encouraged. The EZLN thus emerged within a looming crisis of authority in Mexico, meaning that the hegemonic basis of support for the basic structure of the political system was unravelling resulting in a breakdown of social consensus. As Luis Hernández Navarro (1998: 9) put it, the crisis in Mexico resulted from, 'contradictions between a set of political institutions based on top-down corporatist and clientelist relations on the one hand, and an increasingly mature civil society which seeks full participation on the other.' Following Gramsci (1971: 275–6), it is a situation when 'the ruling class has lost its consensus, i.e. is no longer "leading" but only dominant, exercising coercive force alone', it means, 'precisely that the great masses have become detached from their traditional ideologies, and no longer believe what they used to believe previously etc.'. It is within this crisis of authority that the defiance agency of peasant-based resistance in Chiapas embarked on a counter-hegemonic movement by publicly emerging on 1 January 1994 as the EZLN with a mass base of support and a well-organised army. The following section now highlights the counter-hegemonic aspects of the EZLN to further understand it in relation to Gramsci's strategic thinking and practice, which stresses the importance of subjective factors of subaltern agency within concrete processes of class struggle that assist the development of defiance agency.

Aspects of counter-hegemony as the power of the powerless

'The ethnic identity of an oppressed people – the Maya – is embraced proudly', observes Bill Weinberg (2000: 193), 'but not exalted to the exclusion of common class concerns'. At a time when utopias across Latin America were declared by Jorge Castañeda (1994) as unarmed, the EZLN initiated a military offensive on 1 January 1994 against the above processes of neoliberal restructuring, which raised new questions about the options and innovative techniques open to resistance movements.

Almost immediately there was a mobilisation of different weapons, fusing the materiality of armed struggle with the symbolic importance of particular images and discourses. Within counter-hegemonic forms of resistance a combination of strategies are available. Specifically, Gramsci differentiated between those based on a 'war of manoeuvre' and those involving a 'war of position', although these should not be regarded as different extremes or mutually exclusive options but, rather, possibilities located on a continuum. A 'war of manoeuvre' is analogous to a rapid assault targeted directly against the institutions of state power, the capture of which would only prove transitory. Alternatively, a 'war of position' is comparable to a form of trench warfare involving an ideological struggle on the cultural front of civil society: to overcome the 'powerful system of fortresses and earthworks' requiring a concentration of hegemonic activity 'before the rise to power' in an attempt to penetrate and subvert the mechanisms of ideological diffusion (Gramsci 1971: 59, 238). Thus the initial military assault by the EZLN begun in January 1994 was a transitory phase in a 'war of manoeuvre', reflected in the 'First Declaration of the Lacandon Jungle' that declared the intention to advance onto the capital of the country and defeat the Mexican Federal Army (Marcos 1995: 53). Since this phase, although the armed option has been present but limited, it is possible to highlight the strategy of a shifting 'war of position' conducted by the EZLN. This has involved asserting intellectual and moral resistance to confront both the ideological apparatus of the PRI but also wider material social class interests in Mexico that have subsequently been supportive of the accumulation strategy of neoliberalism. Within this war of position strategy various novel features have been adopted by the EZLN with five standing as particularly noteworthy: 1) the activation of national and international civil society; 2) the aim to address and establish indigenous rights; 3) the appeal to interests beyond the ascriptive identities of ethnicity; 4) the campaign for wider democratisation; and 5) the constant goal of innovation through new forms of governance within the communities of Chiapas.

First, in terms of the activation of civil society, the EZLN has promoted various forms of mobilisation and new forms of organisation to gain wider national appeal. This initially included calling for a National Democratic Convention (CND), in the 'Second Declaration of the Lacandon Jungle', which was part of the strategy of building up an overall counter-hegemonic project within civil society. As a result the CND was organised between 6–9 August 1994, in San Cristóbal and a place in the Lacandon jungle renamed Aguascalientes, which brought together more than 6,000 delegates to deliberate on the need for a transitional government and strategies to promote democracy and develop a coordinated national project. Despite ultimate failure in influencing the outcome of the national elections on 21 August, this was a clear effort to mobilise civil society as a site of popular antagonism to try and develop a solidarity of interests as the basis for a counter-hegemony.

Similarly, the aim of activating civil society has had both a national *and* international dimension, for example represented by the attempt to form an additional political force on 1 January 1996 called the Zapatista National Liberation Front (FZLN), which aimed to support the EZLN as an urban counterpart organisation through a wider, more organic structure based on common consent. A crucial feature of both fronts was the continued emphasis on links between the leaders and the led that drew on the earlier practices of social mobilisation within the indigenous communities. Globally, the impact of the EZLN has also been noted in terms of inspiring the broad round of recent anti-globalisation resistance movements. As Luca Casarini, the main spokesperson of autonomist resistance active within the European Social Forum, has indicated, the recent practical activities of anti-globalisation resistance in Europe and elsewhere unfolded in the wake of the EZLN (Hernández Navarro 2004: 3–4). Various international meetings convened by the EZLN both in Mexico (July–August 1996) and in Europe (Spain, July–August 1997), known as intercontinental meetings against neoliberalism, demonstrated the insertion of such resistance within the global conditions of neoliberalism. Albeit with modest outcomes, the EZLN became a backstop for the global justice movement and set precedents for the 'anti-globalisation' movement by subsequently targeting initiatives such as the Free Trade Area of the Americas (FTAA). There are now over eighty EZLN solidarity communities in Europe and approximately fifty such communities in the United States that have supported the autonomous municipalities in Mexico while simultaneously campaigning closer to home against neoliberalism. Many of the characteristics of anti-globalisation resistance are thus seen as debuting in the rebellion of the EZLN in Mexico with the latter consistently demonstrating an ability to mediate between the particular and the universal to forge a global consciousness of solidarity (Olesen 2004). The EZLN has thus witnessed many of its vocal claims echoed in the activities of the global social justice movement, albeit most recently sanitised within initiatives such as Make Poverty History, the launching of the Commission for Africa report, *Our Common Interest* (March 2005), and the proposed International Finance Facility (IFF), a scheme whereby aid can be provided in advance to assist states in reaching the 'Millennium Development' goals set out by the United Nations.

The second area of importance in the expression of resistance has been the EZLN's involvement in peace talks and assertion of indigenous rights at San Andrés Larráinzar, a small town in Chiapas, with two intermediaries in dialogue with the state, the Commission of Concord and Pacification (COCOPA) and the National Mediation Commission (CONAI). The peace process hoped to address a series of issues revolving around indigenous rights and culture, negotiations on democracy and justice, land reform and women's rights. It resulted in the San Andrés Accords on Indigenous Rights and Culture, signed on 16 February 1996, which laid the groundwork for significant changes in the areas of indigenous rights, political participation and cultural autonomy. Concretely, this inspired the founding of the National Indigenous Congress (CNI) in 1996 as representative of Mexico's indigenous peoples who make up between 10 and 14 per cent of the country's population. While, again, advances such as the CNI and the San Andrés Accords should be seen as limited in terms of securing substantive gains for the indigenous communities in Mexico, they should not be totally discounted. For instance, some have swayed towards the former stance by drawing a comparison between talks with the EZLN and the overall process of electoral reform in Mexico. 'Everyone agrees the dialogue must be pursued, there is a broad consensus regarding the worthiness of the cause,' averred Jorge Castañeda (1995: 258), 'but few are terribly excited either about the outcome itself or its urgency. As long as the process continues, there is little concern about its results, or absence thereof.' Thus it can be agreed that little progress has been made since the San Andrés Accords were signed on 16 February 1996. However, presaging a continuation of resistance after the national elections on 2 July 2000 – which witnessed the defeat of the PRI and the presidential victory of Vicente Fox backed by the centre-right National Action Party (PAN) – the EZLN has embarked on renewed forms of resistance to assert indigenous rights. On 21 March 1999 both the EZLN and FZLN organised a strategically important 'Consulta for the Recognition of the Rights of the Indian Peoples'. This was a mobilisation of 5,000 Zapatista delegates consisting of teams of two people – one male, one female – visiting every municipality across Mexico to promote participation in a referendum on the peace 'process' and the future of the EZLN. The consulta resulted in some 3 million votes with 95 per cent of the participants voting in favour of honouring the San Andrés Accords, recognising Indian rights and supporting military withdrawal from Chiapas. The Zapatistas also subsequently set the date of 25 February 2001 for the 'March of Indigenous Dignity' to leave San Cristóbal in Chiapas, to cross through various states, and arrive in Mexico City on 6 March, in order to promote support for their latest demands. This was designed to mount increasing pressure in support of the fulfilment of the San Andrés Accords and the bill on indigenous rights that followed the original COCOPA legislative proposal. Between 28 April and 2 May 2001, Congress approved a watered-down version of the original COCOPA bill on indigenous rights and culture. This failed to recognise communities as legal entities and their rights to natural resources or to hold communal property, which could have threatened the property rights of landowners. Hence the conservative view of *The Economist* (2001: 59) that there will be a return to *status quo ante bellum* in Chiapas. Although the outcomes might seem disappointing, the endeavour to constantly innovate with new forms of political mobilisation and expression in the name of indigenous rights is itself significant.

What these tactics have meant in practice is, thirdly, an endeavour to appeal to various forms of identity as the basis for a counter-hegemony linked through common points of convergence grounded in capitalist relations of exploitation. Primarily, the ambiguities of identity have been embraced by constructing and mobilising ethnic identity while also maintaining a degree of anonymity through the wearing of masks. This helps to project issues of ethnicity while creating new social spaces within which alternative forms of identity coexist. At one level this has involved making an equation between indigenous identity and poverty to recognise that socioeconomic exclusion has an ethnic dimension. At another level it has involved promoting indigenous identity within the context of Mexican nationalism and appeals to the workers' movement and trade union struggle in Mexico. Additionally, there have been attempts to reinvent group identities by emphasising the struggle against gender inequalities and by affirming sexuality rights. However, this does not mean that the new discourses and challenges to power relations have become part of everyday practice or that there is complete internal democratisation within the communities of Chiapas. Yet the struggle initiated by the Zapatistas has transcended its particular aspects to engender a movement of Zapatismo in and beyond Mexico in relation to the wider anti-globalisation movement. This has been expressed within the European Social Forum (ESF), for example, where the notion of 'another Europe' was directly linked to regional struggles in Latin America, including the EZLN rebellion (Bieler and Morton 2004). As Marcos (1997) himself has stated, explicitly critiquing neoliberal globalisation, the EZLN struggle is a search for 'a world in which there is room for many worlds. A world capable of containing all the worlds.'

The fourth focus area that the EZLN has promoted since the beginning of the rebellion has been the rallying cry for democracy in Mexico. Initial communiqués in 1994 signalled the demand for work, land, housing, health, education, independence, freedom, democracy and justice (Marcos 1995: 51–4). It has therefore been possible to witness the EZLN's contribution, along with other civil society organisations in Mexico, to the cleanliness of elections, the importance of electoral monitoring, the transparency of civil servant practices, the need for independent media reporting and the popularisation of civic participation (Gilbreth and Otero 2001). The historic defeat of the PRI and the victory of Vicente Fox may have drained some of the potency away from this demand, in terms of the consolidation of democratisation in Mexico. However, one can remain circumspect about the formalistic degree of such 'democratic transition' and the equation of democracy with the periodic circulation of elites (see Morton 2005). Most significantly, the fact that neoliberalism can be upbraided as thoroughly *un*democratic in both national and transnational contexts is significant, although perhaps the Zapatista's unwillingness to participate in conventional electoral politics has seemed costly. 'The *Partido Revolucionario Democratica* [PRD: Party of the Democratic Revolution] is a vote', the Mexican cultural critic Carlos Monsiváis has declared, but 'the Zapatistas are a cause' (personal interview, Mexico City, 20 March 1999). The pursuit of this tactic, however, may have resulted in a series of missed opportunities. Not only has the chance to forge common links with the centre-left PRD been missed during national elections but such tactics may also have cost the PRD electoral gains at the local level in Chiapas (Vilas 1996: 277–81).

In Chiapas itself, the election of a new state governor on 20 August 2000 led to the victory of Pablo Salazar, representing an eight-party 'Alliance for Chiapas', which again would seemingly detract from the EZLN cause of democratisation. The sanguine view is that these polls have been turning points in the Zapatista conflict because peace proposals – backed by a 'democratic' mandate – would be difficult to rebuff (*The Economist* 2000: 53–4). Likewise, Luis H. Alvarez, the coordinator of governmental peace efforts in Chiapas under the new Fox administration, announced the partial withdrawal of the army in Chiapas in December 2000, although the army still maintains a large presence throughout the state alongside paramilitaries. Breaking their silence with the new administration, the Zapatistas embarked on a whole series of new initiatives from 2002 onwards with new demands focusing on 'three signals'. These were: 1) fulfilment of the San Andrés Accords, following the COCOPA legislative proposal; 2) release of all Zapatista prisoners held at Cerro Hueco state prison in Chiapas and in the states of Tabasco and Querétaro; and 3) a large process of demilitarisation that would go beyond prevailing troop movements. While there has been partial compliance with these 'three signals' – Chiapas state Interior Minister, Emilio Zebadúa, even acknowledged that the autonomous municipalities in Chiapas created by the EZLN represent legitimate aspirations that could be regularised through constitutional means – there are still major stumbling blocks to such negotiations. Not least of these is the fact that there are 20,000 refugees in Chiapas internally displaced by armed conflict, a condition exacerbated by the decision of the International Committee of the Red Cross to close its office in 2004, leading to the cessation of food distribution to 8,000 refugees in the communities of Pohlo and Chenalhó.

Yet, picking up the common national and transnational denominator of neoliberalism, the Zapatistas have also roundly criticised recent development proposals promoted by the Fox government with Marcos (2000) stating that, 'although there is a radical difference in the way you came to power, your political, social and economic program is the same we have been suffering under during the last administrations'. Perhaps more ominously, Marcos (2001) went on to state in an interview with the national newspaper *La Jornada*, 'I don't know if our plans are terribly subversive, I don't believe so, but I do know that, if this isn't resolved, something terrible is going to explode, even without us.' Fifthly and finally, therefore, the EZLN has continued to innovate with new forms of governance to challenge the Mexican state alongside pursuing tactics of land occupation. This initially led Richard Stahler-Stock (1998: 14) to observe that, 'the real challenge to PRI hegemony lies in the Zapatista's development projects, including collective agriculture, building local infrastructure, piping water from streams, training health promoters and starting up small enterprises'. Since the Zapatista uprising in 1994, land seized by various peasant organisations and indigenous communities has been estimated to be between 60,000 and 500,000 hectares with government distribution in reaction to such seizures amounting to 180,000 hectares, although retaliation by landowners has reduced these figures (Barmeyer 2003: 133–4). More recently, it has been expressed through the creation since August 2003 of five *caracoles* (or 'spirals') in the communities of Chiapas (La Garrucha, Morelia, Oventic, La Realidad and Roberto Barrios) to replace the former autonomous municipalities that covered more than 30 townships. These *caracoles* are based on five Juntas of Good Government in an attempt to further redefine and assert autonomy as well as promote economic development. The *caracoles* cover the Guatemala border region, the southern and northern canyons, the northern zone and the highlands of Chiapas. They are responsible for carrying out legal, judicial and economic policies across the range of education, healthcare, justice and development. Further Zapatista communities have relocated from isolated communities, in the Montes Azules bioreserve, to move to lands with easier access to the regional Juntas of Good Government to establish easier access to education and health care. Some Zapatista communities within the Juntas have also implemented a strategy of raising income from coffee throughout the state of Chiapas by pushing up the price paid to peasant producers from 12.5 to 15 pesos per kilo (or US$0.54 to US$0.68 per pound). While the EZLN has difficulty in protecting, defending and expanding development initiatives and land redistribution in Chiapas it would again be precocious to simply dismiss such efforts.

The autonomous communities no longer recognise government-imposed authorities but democratically install their own community representatives. Within the newly created municipal structures, the Zapatista communities name their authorities and commissions for various spheres of duty such as land management, education, health, justice, and women's rights. (Barmeyer 2003: 135)

It is to these endeavours that the achievements of the EZLN should be recognised while remaining open as to what further lasting effect it will have on the terrain of social struggle in Mexico. Importantly, developments in such 'spheres of duty' produce important forms of defiance agency that are not captured in conventional thinking about peasant resistance. They speak more about how everyday politics, rather than resistance alone, informs defiance agency (cf. Kerkvliet 2005).

Conclusions: on the terrain of class struggle and the power of the powerless

The EZLN has clearly struggled to maintain momentum for the rebellion, most significantly in relation to the San Andrés Accords centred on indigenous rights and attempts to reorganise peasant autonomy through community development projects. However, it would be too pessimistic to accord with Jorge Castañeda (personal interview, Mexico City, 9 and 13 March 1999), one time Secretary of Foreign Relations within the Vicente Fox administration, that 'despite having enormous international support and the emblematic aspects of a just cause, the movement has gone absolutely nowhere. The Zapatistas have been nowhere, gone nowhere and they are nowhere.' To accord with such a view would be too dismissive of the modest acts of volition emblematic of the defiance agency of the 'power of the powerless'. After all, as Gramsci (1996: 60–1) forewarned:

A realistic politics must not concern itself solely with immediate success . . . it must also create and safeguard those conditions that are necessary for future activity – and one of these is the education of the people. This is the issue. The higher the cultural level and the greater the development of the critical spirit, the more 'impartial' – that is, the more historically 'objective' – one's position will be.

Instead, then, the conclusions to draw from this chapter centre on three dimensions related to the question of resistance within the global conditions of capitalist restructuring.

First, in terms of unpacking a sociology of power, due recognition has to be granted to the intertwined histories of hegemonic *and* resistance practices. This entails recognising the 'power of the powerless' or the modest expressions of human volition, the vast majority of which might remain anonymous but at the same time demand greater attention in order to understand forms of defiance agency within broader structures of governance that seek to constrain peasant action. The case of the EZLN under analysis here highlights different dimensions of peasant-based defiance agency and their demands for control over land in Mexico, therefore vitiating claims about the disappearance of the peasantry as a meaningful social class engaged in active forms of resistance. Regardless of whether such agency results in repeated cycles of mass protest/ negotiation/agreements/broken promises/mass protest (Petras and Veltmeyer 2002: 64–8), it is clear that the Zapatista rebellion has acted as a catalyst for wider resistance against the neoliberal project in and beyond Mexico.

Second, the EZLN demonstrates that the existence and reproduction of indigenous identity largely depends on access to land, meaning that there is a class basis to their actions due to the combination of their role as peasant producers and wage labourers. As Gerardo Otero (2004) has outlined, class grievances and ethnic identity issues are important in the constitution of the peasantry within the EZLN movement, which shapes both their material interests and cultural aspects of identity set against the context of changing social relations of production. Issues of class struggle therefore matter. While the EZLN itself is struggling to retain a presence in leading social movements in Mexico, the wider formation of class struggle through the intersection of labour and social movements in Mexico continues. Indicative here is the forming of the Labour, Peasant, Social and Popular Front (FSCSP) – founded in 2002 by independent labour unions such as the National Union of Workers (UNT), the Permanent Agrarian Congress (CAP) and the Mexican Union Front (FSM) – to stand in opposition against the effects of the neoliberal agenda in Mexico. Demonstrations and work stoppages have thus far been organised through the FSCSP against the reform and privatisation of the social security system, the proposed reform of the Federal Labour Law to increase flexibilisation and employers' rights, and the privatisation of the energy sector in Mexico. The EZLN has been important in drawing attention to the transformation of class identities and forging links between labour and social movements. It has conducted its own understanding of class struggle. How such resistance mutates will therefore increasingly become an especially acute matter in the face of second-generation neoliberal reforms.

The third and final conclusion to draw in terms of the 'power of the powerless' relates to the politics of scale of defiance. At the heart of the spatial terrain of both hegemony and resistance is a combination of logics driven by transnational, regional, national and local dynamics. One cannot afford to impute a singularly transnational logic to the domains of hegemony and resistance at the expense of local context and texture. 'Global solidarity activities', as Thomas Olesen (2004: 265) avers, 'in fact often originate at the local and national level and revolve around cultural and identity characteristics tied to these spaces.' Initiatives for defiance are themselves embedded in the local experiences of wider capitalist processes. This demands due recognition of the different spatial scales of hegemony and resistance that work through transnational, state and local power matrices without collapsing into a logic that privileges any single domain (see Morton 2007). Nevertheless it should be clear that how transnational hegemony becomes translated and/or contested through local social formations is an intrinsic part of the picture of domination and defiance. This point should be at the forefront of analysis in the consideration of the second generation of neoliberal reforms in Mexico and Latin America, when further changes to property relations will reveal new social bases of discontent, resistance and forms of class struggle, articulated in the form of the power of the powerless.

Part III

Bringing Eastern agents in

Eastern agents of globalisation:
Oriental globalisation in the rise
of Western capitalism

John M. Hobson

In this chapter I seek to critique the Eurocentrism of mainstream 'regulatory theory' by restoring the lost theme of Eastern agency to the study of
international political economy (IPE). This is undertaken in the context
of two main empirical areas – globalisation and international economic
systems change. While globalisation is now a major topic on the IPE
research agenda, the study of international economic systems change
has yet to be considered. In the Introduction we presented one rationale
that justifies the topic's inclusion in IPE – namely that it enables us to
problematise the present international economic order by revealing the
'small actors' that played a formative role in its creation. But a second
rationale for its inclusion lies in the point that studies of globalisation
often implicitly presuppose the prior importance of the European transition from feudalism to capitalism. That is, globalisation is thought to be
the expression of the 'triumph of the West'. Accordingly, the two processes are conventionally understood to be fundamentally entwined. But
the conventional way of thinking about these two entwined processes
reflects a Eurocentric predisposition to the study of the world economy
insofar as the agency of the progressive and pioneering West is thought to
provide the vital link. I argue that the two processes are indeed entwined
but that the link between them is provided by the role performed by
progressive, pioneering Eastern capitalist agents.

This chapter focuses on the *cumulative impact* of the myriad forms of
axiorational behaviour and agency that has been conducted by numerous
everyday Eastern agents which, in aggregate, led on to the rise of globalisation and the rise of capitalist modernity. Thus as Eastern agents went
about their everyday activities, many of which were not motivated by pure
economic instrumental rationality, they unwittingly enabled progressive
global-economic outcomes. In the critical period, c. 500–c. 1800, defiance agency was not important either because much of Asia was at that
time more advanced than the West or because the West was spared
colonial conquest by the more advanced Eastern societies such as Islam

and China. And while Western imperialism was undoubtedly important in the Americas in the latter part of the period, it is significant that in Asia, Western imperialism only began in earnest at the end of the eighteenth century. Hybridised mimicry was also important insofar as Eastern agents refracted other Eastern ideas through their own specific cultural lenses, as did the Europeans as they emulated and borrowed the many Eastern ideas, technologies and institutions that diffused across from the East through Oriental globalisation. Nevertheless in this particular chapter I shall focus on the everyday axiorational behaviour of Eastern agents to make my case.

Before proceeding to set out my own argument it is useful to briefly consider how Eurocentrism conflates the two processes of globalisation and the rise of capitalist modernity within a Western triumphalist narrative. Let us take each in turn beginning with globalisation. In the conventional Eurocentric historiography, the year 1492 traditionally represents the moment when the Europeans came of age and then launched the 'Voyages of Discovery'. And their significance derives from the assumption that they served to project outwards the Western capitalist system as the Europeans 'battered down the walls' of the so-called inward-looking, back-ward Eastern regions, thereby transforming them into outward-looking capitalist economies. From there, globalisation is allegedly propelled forwards in a linear way by successive Western pioneers down to the end of the nineteenth century before culminating with the post-1945 era when the global economy acquired its 'thick' and fullest form under the aegis of American hegemony or the *Pax Americana* (e.g., Held *et al.* 1999). Such an analysis elevates the Westerners to the status of global history's progressive subject – past, present and future. The Eastern peoples, by contrast, are dismissed as but globalisation's passive object, simply awaiting the arrival of the Westerners who could deliver them into the bright light of (Western) 'progressive global modernity', though always under conditions, if not terms, laid down by the more advanced West.

As with the conventional analyses of globalisation, the major theories of the rise of Western capitalism – including liberalism, Weberianism and Marxism – also suffer from a pervading Eurocentric bias (see Blaut 2000; Frank 1998: Ch. 1; Hobson 2004: Ch. 1). Eurocentrism effectively imposes a constructed or imaginary line of 'civilisational-apartheid' between the East and West, in which the former is separated off from the latter and is simultaneously denigrated as the West's inferior opposite Other (Said 1978; Amin 1989; Bernal 1991). Simultaneously the West was inscribed with uniquely progressive characteristics that distinguished it from an East that was defined only by regressive properties. This Eurocentric premise infects the major theories in that they view the rise of capitalism as occurring not merely in Europe, but that it was achieved single-handedly by the superior Europeans. And this in turn derives from the Eurocentric assumption that Europe is and always has been 'unique' or 'exceptional' in that it contained within itself the seeds of progress. Moreover, it is axiomatic that these seeds did not exist within the East or that if they did so they landed on fallow ground only to be choked during the germination process by repressive Eastern political, ideological and social institutions.

Accordingly, the path that such Eurocentric analysts take is to scan a very narrow patch of turf – Western Europe – in order to select the critical progressive variables that made Europe's rise inevitable. Certainly by the end of the twentieth century (if not well before) it became apparent that the European patch had been exhaustively ploughed by generations of Eurocentric scholars. Indeed this has occurred to the extent that it is now suffering from 'intellectual-ecological breakdown', given that Eurocentrism has largely failed to uncover any fresh variables that can provide a new account (Blaut 2000). And while debate between the different theories continues to rage, this turns out to be an internecine debate. For when viewed from a non-Eurocentric vantage-point, they appear as but minor variations on the exact same Eurocentric or Orientalist theme.

In this chapter I develop an alternative non-Eurocentric account to explain the rise of both the global economy and modern capitalism. As already noted, I too envisage the relationship between these two processes as entwined. But in contrast to the Eurocentric perspective, I argue that the emergence of the global economy long predated the rise of Western capitalism. And I see the link between these two entwined processes as lying not with the 'West' but with the 'progressive East'. A panoply of pioneering Eastern capitalist agents set up a global economy after the sixth century, along the sinews of which the more advanced Eastern 'resource portfolios' (ie., technologies, ideas and institutions) diffused through Oriental globalisation to be subsequently assimilated or copied by the Europeans, thereby fuelling the rise of Western capitalism.

As a result of this argument it becomes apparent that scanning only the European patch either for the causes of Europe's breakthrough or for the origins of globalisation, as Frank (1998) notes, is in effect to shine the spotlight in the wrong place. For when we illuminate the much greener field of the Afro-Asian region, we rediscover or bring to light the many Eastern factors that made the rise of globalisation and Western capitalism possible. In short, deconstructing Eurocentrism by erasing the imaginary line of 'civilisational-apartheid' reveals the manifold ways in which the West has been a promiscuous or hybrid entity that has been fundamentally embedded in the East – reflected in my preferred label of the Oriental West. Accordingly, I argue that the East should not be denigrated as a passive object, but should be appreciated as a progressive subject or pioneering agent of global and economic world history. I make my case in two parts. Part one examines the progressive actions undertaken by a panoply of Eastern agents as they set about building and maintaining a global economy, while part two reveals briefly how Eastern agency and Oriental globalisation enabled the rise of Western capitalism.

Oriental globalisation: Eastern subjects as pioneers of the global economy, 500–1800

The standard picture of the world *before* 1500 presented by Eurocentrism comprises two core features: first, a world mired in so-called stagnant 'tradition'; and second, a fragmented world divided between insulated and backward regional civilisations that were governed by 'irrational' growth-repressive despotic states (outside of Western Europe). Accordingly, it becomes inconceivable to imagine a globally-interdependent economy at any point before 1500. And it is this enduring belief that has preserved the integrity of Eurocentrism precisely because it justifies the equation of the emergence of the global economy with the rise and thrust of a superior Europe outwards into the world after 1492/98.

This familiar Eurocentric picture is a myth in the first instance because a global economy that broke down civilisational isolationism began as early as the sixth century during what I call the Afro-Asian Age of Discovery. Accordingly, Eurocentrism's celebrated post-1492/1498 European 'Voyages of Discovery' might be more appropriately labelled the *Voyages of Rediscovery* given that large parts of Asia and Africa had been interconnected for up to a millennium previously. The Eurocentric picture is also a myth because it obscures the considerable vibrancy of many Eastern economies (Hobson 2004: Ch. 2–4), some of which came to occupy the leading edge of global economic power. And it is noteworthy that none of the leading economies between 500 and 1800 were Western.

There are two generic types of global economic power: what may be called, borrowing from Michael Mann, 'extensive' and 'intensive' (Mann 1986: 6–10). Extensive global power refers to the ability of an economy or region to project its tentacles outwards in order to bind the world together through economic interdependence. Intensive global power refers to a high degree of 'productive' power within a particular region, which enables that economy to provide high levels of supply and demand for global trade and other capitalist transactions. We need to differentiate these precisely because different regions have enjoyed prominence in one or both of these forms of global power at different times. Between roughly 650 and 1100 Islamic West Asia/North Africa had the highest levels of extensive and intensive power, though by about 1100 the *leading edge* of intensive global power passed to China (where it remained well into the nineteenth century). Nevertheless, West Asia/North Africa and increasingly India maintained the leading edge of extensive power until about the fifteenth century when China once more took over in this respect, even though the former powers continued to enjoy significant levels of intensive and extensive power well into the eighteenth century. Nevertheless this picture was re-imagined by Eurocentric intellectuals in the nineteenth century, so that first Venice and later Portugal, Spain, The Netherlands and Britain were (re)presented as the leading global powers in the post-1000 period.

The claim that a global economy or globalisation existed prior to 1500 is usually rebutted on six main grounds (e.g., Held *et al.* 1999). Refuting these in turn enables me to provide an initial justification for my claim that globalisation predated 1500. First, the world before 1500 was not segmented into isolated components. Rather, after about 500 CE Persians, Arabs, Africans, Javanese, Jews, Indians and Chinese created and maintained a global economy until about 1800, in which the major civilisations of the world were *at all times interlinked* (hence the term *Oriental globalisation*). Second, the portrayal of the Eastern states as but growth-repressive oriental despotisms is incorrect given that Eastern rulers often provided a pacified environment and kept transit taxes low precisely so as to facilitate global trade. Third, in contrast to the assumption of an absence of sufficiently rational institutions to enable global capitalism, there was in fact a whole series of such institutions in place after 500 to support global trade. As Janet Abu-Lughod noted:

Distances as measured by time, were calculated in weeks and months at best, but it took years to traverse the entire [global] circuit. And yet goods were transferred, prices set, exchange rates agreed upon, contracts entered into, credit – on funds or on goods located elsewhere – extended, partnerships formed, and, obviously, records kept and agreements honored. (Abu-Lughod 1989: 8)

Fourth, *contra* the view of inadequate transportation to support global interactions, while transport technologies were obviously nowhere near as advanced as they are today, nevertheless they proved to be conducive for global trade. Moreover, the Eurocentric assumption that global trade affected only about 10 per cent of the world's population – and was therefore inconsequential – is based on the assumption that such trade was in luxury goods which were consumed only by the elites. But this obscures the point that the majority of global trade was actually conducted in mass-based consumer products, which affected considerably more than 10 per cent of the world's population (Chaudhuri 1978; Frank 1998).

Fifth, while the velocity of global transmissions was indeed very slow, nevertheless global flows had a major re-organisational or high (trans-formative) 'impact' on societies across the world. The ultimate significance of the global economy lay not in the type or quantity of trade that it supported, but that it provided a ready-made conveyor-belt along which the more advanced Eastern 'resource portfolios' diffused across to the West. Indeed, as section two of the chapter argues, the high impact propensity of Oriental globalisation is confirmed by my point that it promoted the transformation of Europe from an agrarian peripheral back-water to a modern capitalist economy.

Sixth and finally, it is often asserted that a global economy could not have existed prior to 1500 (or even the nineteenth century) because not all parts of the globe were tightly interconnected. But the assumption that the whole world should be tightly linked before we can declare that it is global is problematic even for the modern period. Again as Abu-Lughod (1989: 32) points out:

No world system is *global*, in the sense that all parts articulate evenly with one another, regardless of whether the role they play is central or peripheral. Even today, the world, more globally integrated than ever before in history, is broken up into important subspheres or subsystems, such as the northern Atlantic system . . . the Pacific rim . . . China, still a system unto itself, and [so on].

Indeed the vast bulk of 'global' trade today is confined within the trilateral bloc, while economies are still primarily national in scope given that about 90 per cent of production in the major economies is for the domestic market (Weiss 1999: 63). Moreover, domestic investment by domestic capital far exceeds direct investment overseas plus foreign investment at home, with the latter being financed mainly from domestic savings (Wade 1996: 66, 86; Weiss 1999: 63). We need not conclude from this that globalisation is non-existent today; merely that it is neither no less 'perfect' today than it was under its historical Oriental incarnation, nor does it have to be 'perfect' for us to accept its existence.

Overall, the Eurocentric narrative displays a strong sense of ahistoricism because those who argue that globalisation did not exist in any form prior to 1500 do so by analysing the world through the presentist lens of modern globalisation (e.g., high velocity or high intensity of transactions). Thus teleologically scanning the past for the features of globalisation's modern format not surprisingly enables them to 'confirm' its absence prior to 1500. But a slightly looser definition reveals the presence of early and modern globalisation. Thus we can say that globalisation existed prior to (and indeed after) 1500 insofar as *significant flows of goods, resources, currencies, capital, institutions, ideas, technologies, diseases and peoples flowed across regions to such an extent that they impacted upon, and led to the trans-formation of, societies across much of the globe.*

I take the post-500 era as the approximate starting date of Oriental globalisation. The revival of camel transport was important because it enabled the long overland routes across Central Asia to be relatively easily traversed (McNeill 1995: 314). But the key development here was the emergence of a series of interlinked 'empires' that enabled a significantly pacified environment within which overland and seaborne trade could flourish (Bentley 1993: Ch. 1 and 3; Wink 1990). These comprised T'ang China (618–907), the Islamic Ummayad/Abbasid Empire in West Asia (661–1258), the Fatimids in North Africa (909–1171) and the Ummayad polity in Spain (756–1031). Moreover, the kingdom of Śrīvijaya in Sumatra was also important because it constituted a vital entrepôt that connected China to the Indian Ocean between the seventh and thirteenth centuries. In short, the prosperity and commercialisation of the Arab and Chinese (as well as the South Asian and North African) world acted like a huge bellows that fanned the flames of an emergent global economy (McNeill 1995: 316).

Noteworthy here is that Henry Pirenne's famous thesis – that the Islamic invasions broke the unity of Western Europe from Eastern Europe (Byzantium), and that it was only by the turn of the millennium when trade resumed – needs to be inverted:

There was a close connection between the Frankish and Arab worlds, and . . . the Carolingian Renaissance, the successes of the Italian city-states, and the growth of the Hanseatic League were all enhanced rather than retarded by contacts with the Muslim East . . . . It seems quite certain that trade revived at many places in the late eighth and ninth centuries [in Europe] . . . . Contradicting Pirenne, therefore, historians now speak of the economic 'Islamization of early medieval Europe'. (Wink 1990: 35–6)

Indeed, in contrast to Pirenne (1939), without Muhammad, medieval European commercial development would have been virtually inconceivable. Thus by the eighth century, Europe had become integrated within the emergent Afro-Asian-led global economy. While there were many important groups who helped build the global economy, especially the Jews, North Africans, Indians, Chinese and Javanese, nevertheless the birth of Oriental globalisation owes most to the Muslims.

The Islamic global pioneer

The West Asian Muslims built upon the earlier achievements of the Sassanid Persians, which stem back possibly to the third and certainly to the fourth century. After 610, West Asia began its rise to global power with the 'revelation' of Muhammad. While previously West Asia was highly fragmented and subject to various colonising efforts by Persia, Syria and Byzantine Egypt, thereafter one of Muhammad's greatest contributions was to forge a unity through the power of Islam. And one of the most significant aspects of Islam was its penchant for trade and rational capitalist activity.

Ultimately Islam's comparative advantage lay in its considerable 'extensive' power. That is, Islam was able to conquer horizontal space, realised most fully in its ability to diffuse across large parts of the globe, as well as in its ability to spread capitalism. The centre of Islam, Mecca, was in turn one of the centres of the global trading network. Islam's power spread rapidly after the seventh century with the Mediterranean becoming in effect a Muslim lake, and 'Western Europe' a promontory within the Afro-Asian-led global economy. Islam also spread eastwards to India, Southeast Asia and China, as well as southwards into Africa through either religious or commercial influence (and often both). Its economic reach was extraordinary for the time, constituting the pivot of world trade. And certainly by the ninth century – as various contemporary documents confirm – there was one long, continuous line of transcontinental trade pioneered by Islamic merchants, reaching from China to the Mediterranean (Abu-Lughod 1989: 62; Wink 1990; Bentley 1993).

The Islamic Ummayads, Abbasids and North African Fatimids were important in that they united various arteries of long-distance trade known in antiquity between the Indian Ocean and the Mediterranean (to be discussed below). The Abbasid capital, Baghdad, was linked to the all-important Persian Gulf route. The contemporary, al-Ya'qūbi (c. 875), described Baghdad as the 'water-front to the world', while al-Mansūr proclaimed that 'there is no obstacle to us and China; everything on the sea can come to us on it' (cited in Hourani 1963: 64). Other Islamic ports were also important, especially Sīrāf on the Persian Gulf (on the coast of Iran south of Shīrāz), which was the major terminus for goods from China and Southeast Asia. The Red Sea route, guarded over by Egypt, was also of special importance, as was the overland route to China, along which caravans passed through the Iranian cities of Tabriz, Hamadan and Nishapur to Bukhara and Samarkand in Transoxiana, and then on to either China or India (see below). Ultimately, Islam constituted the *bridge of the world*, enabling the diffusion of global trade as well as all manner of Eastern resource portfolios into Europe between 650 and c.1800 (see the second section below).

It deserves emphasis that this immediately stands at odds with the Eurocentric assumption that Islam was a regressive religion that blocked the possibility of capitalist, let alone *rational* capitalist, activity. Moreover, this assumption is often deployed so as to deny the existence of a robust global economy prior to 1500 (if not 1850). But it appears to have been forgotten, wittingly or unwittingly, that Muhammad himself had been a *commenda* (or *qirād*) trader. In his twenties he married a rich *Qurayshi* woman (the *Quraysh* had grown rich from the caravan trade as well as banking). Interestingly, the

Meccans – the tribe of Quraysh – caused their capital to fructify through trade and loans at interest in a way that Weber would call rational . . . . The merchants of the Muslim Empire conformed perfectly to Weber's criteria for capitalist activity. They seized every and any opportunity for profit and calculated their outlays, their encashments and their profits in money terms. (Rodinson 1974: 14)

Indeed there are many points in the Qur'ān that suggest a clear link between rational capitalist behaviour and Islam (Rodinson 1974; Hodgson 1974; Hobson 2004: Ch. 2). And while we usually consider the *Sharīa* (the Islamic sacred law) as the root of despotism and economic backwardness, it was in fact created as a means to prevent the abuse of the rulers' or caliphs' power and, moreover, it set out clear provisions for contract law. Not surprisingly there was an entirely rational reason why the Islamic merchants were strong supporters of the *Sharīa*. Moreover, Islam was 'no "monotheism of the desert", born of the Bedouins' awed wonder at the vast openness of sky and land . . . Islam grew out of a long tradition of urban religion and it was as city-oriented as any variant of that tradition' (Hodgson 1993: 133).

The thrust of this claim is supported by the point that Islamic West Asia constituted the leading edge of global *intensive* power right down into the eleventh century. Eric Jones points out that the Abbasid Caliphate was the first region to achieve *per capita* economic growth – supposedly the *leitmotif* of modern capitalism (Jones 1988: Ch. 3). Moreover, manufacturing existed throughout West Asia/North Africa. For example, paper manufacturing began after 751; textile-manufacturing was important and widespread, as was sugar refinement; and Islamic iron and steel production outpaced in quantity and quality that produced by the Europeans right through the eighteenth and into the nineteenth centuries. Moreover, Islam held a comparative advantage over Europe with respect to scientific knowledge and rational thinking (see the second section below). Notable too is that the Muslims created a whole series of capitalist institutions (concerning partnerships, contract law, banking, credit and many others), upon which not only Islamic production, investment and commerce rested but also global trade. In sum

the density of commercial relations within the Muslim world constituted a sort of world market . . . of unprecedented dimensions. The development of exchange had made possible regional specialisation in industry and agriculture .... Not only did the Muslim world know a capitalistic sector, but this sector was apparently the most extensive and highly developed in history before the [modern period]. (Rodinson 1974: 56)

One final point here is noteworthy. For today we are used to thinking of a stand-off between Jews and Muslims, with the two being apparently irreconcilable. But under Oriental globalisation Jews and Muslims peacefully intermingled and worked symbiotically as vital agents in the global economy. Indeed Jewish traders, financiers and intellectuals were very important in Baghdad until about the tenth century and subsequently in Cairo in Fatimid Egypt after 969. And their roles are described in rich detail in the contemporary Geniza papers held in Cairo (Goitein 1964). Moreover, Jews, Muslims and Christians also coexisted in symbiotic relationships in Ummayad Spain for many centuries (Menocal 2002).

Oriental globalisation intensifies: Eastern hegemony over Europe continues, 1000–c. 1800

Following Abu-Lughod's discussion in her magisterial book, *Before European Hegemony* (1989), there were three principal trade routes that linked up with eight regional sub-systems, which I shall discuss in turn. And while these were important in the centuries before 1000, after that date they intensified further.

The Northern route and the economic gift of the Mongol Empire A significant boost to Oriental globalisation was provided by the emergence of the Mongol Empire in the thirteenth century. By the latter part of the thirteenth century the majority of the Eurasian landmass was held under Mongol control. The critical point is that this relatively unified territorial empire – the *Pax Mongolica* – provided a pacified region for capitalism to flourish. It promoted very long-distance, or global, overland trade covering the 5,000 miles between China and Europe. Institutional constraints and political costs along this route came down, not least because the Mongols proved to be receptive towards the many merchants who traversed the Empire. Indeed the famous contemporary of Marco Polo, Balducci Pegolotti, described the Silk Road as 'perfectly safe by day and night'.

The common Eurocentric dismissal of the Mongols as ravagers of economic progress is problematic. That they indeed engaged in brutal killing (especially in China) does not undermine the point that the Mongol Empire provided highly benign services for Europe by enabling the diffusion of trade and many advanced Eastern resource portfolios into

Europe (Fernández-Armesto 2001: 120–31). Nevertheless, this influential trade circuit was in decline by the mid-fourteenth century. But this did not mark the end of the Eastern-led global economy, since trade was increasingly channelled through the Middle and especially Southern routes.

The Middle route: the maintenance of Islamic global extensive power
According to Abu-Lughod (1989) this route began at the Mediterranean coast of Syria/Palestine, crossed the small desert and then the Mesopotamian plain to Baghdad, before finally breaking up into a land and sea route. The land route continued across Persia to Transoxiana and then either southeastward to northern India or due eastward to Samarkand and then across the desert to China. The sea route followed the Tigris River down to the Persian Gulf from Baghdad via Basra and then passed the trading kingdoms of Oman, Sīrāf, Hormuz or Qais (guardians of the link between the Gulf and the Indian Ocean beyond). While this route became important after the sixth century, it became extremely influential when Baghdad was the prime Muslim centre of trade after 750. But when Baghdad was plundered by the Mongols in 1258, the route underwent a temporary decline. However, with Iraq being subsequently ruled from Persia, the Gulf route revived. This Middle route was also important because it enabled a deeply symbiotic trading relationship between the Crusader kingdoms and the Muslim merchants who brought goods from as far away as the Orient.

The chief Crusader port in West Asia – Acre – was controlled up to 1291 by the Venetians, and there they excluded their Pisan and Genoese rivals. Nevertheless, although the Venetians dominated the *European* trading system, they always entered the global system on terms dictated by the West Asian Muslims and especially the North Africans. When Constantinople fell to the Byzantines in 1261, the Genoese were favoured over the Venetians, thereby pushing the latter to focus more on the Southern route. But with the Fall of Acre in 1291 the Venetians had no choice but to rely on the Southern route which was dominated by the Egyptians.

The Southern route: Europe's dependence on Egypt's trading hegemony, 1291–1517 This route linked the Alexandria-Cairo-Red Sea complex with the Arabian Sea and then the Indian Ocean and beyond. The fall of Baghdad in 1258 saw the capital of the Islamic world shift to Al-Qahirah – later Europeanised to Cairo – which then became the pivotal centre of global trade (though this latter process began during the Fatimid era in the tenth century). As Abu-Lughod claims, 'Whoever controlled the sea-route to Asia could set the terms of trade for a Europe now in retreat. From the thirteenth century and up to the sixteenth that power was Egypt' (Abu-Lughod 1989: 149). Indeed between 1291 and 1517 about 80 per cent of all trade that passed to the East by sea was controlled by the Egyptians.

Eurocentric scholars emphasise that European international trade with the East dried up after 1291 (with the Fall of Acre) as Egypt dominated the Red Sea trade to the East *at the expense* of the Christian Europeans. But despite the numerous prohibitions on trading with the 'infidel' issued by Pope Nicholas IV, the fact is that the Venetians managed to circumvent the ban and secured new treaties with the Sultan in 1355 and 1361. And right up until 1517, Venice survived because Egypt played such an important role within the global economy. Moreover, Venice and Genoa were not the 'pioneers' of global trade but *adaptors* or *intermediaries*, inserting themselves into the interstices of the Afro-Asian-led global economy and entering the global economy very much on the strict terms laid down by the West Asian Muslims and especially the Egyptians. Nevertheless, the Venetians and other Europeans accepted this dependent relationship because it was through this that they gained access to the many goods produced throughout the East.

As an aside here it is worth noting that it was at this time that the Portuguese had set off on their 'voyages of discovery' to the East. But to return to the point made earlier, it should be clear by now that they in fact 'discovered' nothing given that the East had been in contact with Europe for many centuries. For what the Portuguese learnt might well have been a revelation to the backward Europeans, but it was yesteryear's news to the many Eastern peoples. Moreover, the Portuguese were 'the last' to discover the Cape. In the mid-fifteenth century the famous Arab navigator, Shihāb al-Dīn Ahmad Ibn Mājid, sailed from West Asia to the Cape and then up the west coast of Africa and then on into the Mediterranean. Moreover, the Chinese (Islamic) admiral, Chêng Ho, sailed up the east coast of Africa in the early fifteenth century, though it is also possible that Chinese sailors had made it across in the eighth century. And the Javanese had made it to Madagascar and had settled in North Africa as early as the second century. In sum, it is clear that all the Portuguese were doing was *directly* joining the Afro-Asian-led global economy that had emerged after the sixth century.

Notable too is that even *after* 1517 the Islamic trading hegemony over Europe was maintained (despite Portuguese pronouncements to the contrary). For the baton of *Islamic* extensive power was passed from Egypt to the Ottoman Empire, which maintained its hold over the Portuguese in the Indian Ocean (see also Hodgson 1974). Moreover, other centres of Islamic economic power – Mughal India and Southeast Asia – remained strong enough to resist and dominate the European traders right up until about 1800 (Hobson 2004: Ch. 4 and 7). Nevertheless, while West Asia/North Africa remained the *bridge of the world* for much of the second millennium, the leading edge of global extensive power passed neither to Portugal after 1500 nor to Britain after 1600, but to China between c. 1450 and 1800.

China at or near the centre of the global economy, c. 1450–1800
Before discussing China's move towards the centre of the global trading system around 1450 it is important to preface this by returning to the point made earlier: that China had come to occupy the leading edge of global *intensive* power by about 1100. This was the result of the 'industrial miracle' that occurred largely under the Sung dynasty. A few key points are worth noting to illustrate my claim (but for a full discussion see Hobson 2004: Ch. 3). At the centre of this miracle was an iron and steel revolution. By 1078 the amounts of iron produced in China, as well as its cheapness, were only matched by the British as late as 1800. Significantly, Chinese iron was deployed in mass-based products, from knives to drill bits, ploughshares, chains for suspension bridges and a host of everyday items. Moreover, China's production of cast iron as well as wrought iron enabled the Chinese to produce cast iron cannon, which were far more effective than the European wrought iron cannon. In turn, all this was based on the use of blast furnaces which used piston bellows. Importantly, Chinese iron production goes back to the sixth century BCE during the Warring States period. And the double-acting piston bellows were deployed for iron production as early as the fourth century BCE. No less impressive was that as early as the second century BCE the Chinese were producing steel and by the fifth century CE steel was produced using a 'co-fusion' process whereby wrought and cast iron were melded together. Finally, the familiar claim that eighteenth-century Britain was the first country to substitute coke for charcoal in the production of iron under conditions of deforestation misses the point that this first occurred in eleventh-century China.

Also of note here is that Chinese textile production was considerably superior to Europe's, and stemmed back to the fourteenth century BCE. Striking too were the transportation and energy revolutions. The former saw the creation of an extensive canal system that rested on pound-locks, while the latter *inter alia* led to the use of water mills which were deployed for manufacturing purposes – most notably to fuel the water-powered bellows in the furnaces (which began as early 31 CE). Last, but by no means least, almost all of the ingredients that went into making the

European agricultural revolution of the eighteenth and nineteenth centuries had already been invented and were in place in China by the sixth century CE. Accordingly, the industrial (and agricultural) miracle placed China at the centre of global production, which in turn was vital in enabling China to move to or near the centre of the global trading system by about 1450.

One of the enduring myths of Eurocentric world history is that China withdrew from international trade in 1434 into its own regressive imperial tribute system, the significance of which was that it created a vacuum into which the more pioneering Europeans poured (e.g., Landes 1998: 96). But in fact after 1434 the Chinese economy came to occupy the leading edge of global extensive power. The conventional Eurocentric picture of a withdrawal errs initially because Western historians take too literal a view of both the official ban and the Chinese tribute system. The official documents are distorted by the Chinese government's attempt *at being seen* to maintain a Confucian (i.e., isolationist) ideal. Moreover, the withdrawal is wrongly confirmed by the existence of a regressive imperial tribute system, which was supposedly based on coercion and state-administered forms of tribute rather than commercial trade. But a number of points can be marshalled to refute this superficial reading.

First, the tribute system was in fact a disguised trading system that permitted considerable amounts of Chinese foreign trade (Hamashita 1994; Deng 1997). Second, 'vassals' were keen to become part of the system because for nominal amounts of tribute offered to the emperor they could gain access to China's highly lucrative economy. So keen were they that they often fought each other to become part of the system. And how else can we explain the point that the Portuguese, Spanish and Dutch repeatedly asked to join the system as vassals? Moreover, some – such as Japan in 1557 – even threatened an invasion of China if they were ejected from the system.

The ban was also a myth for various reasons. First, many Chinese merchants circumvented it in all manner of ways, for example by carrying a Portuguese Cartaz which enabled them to masquerade as Portuguese shipping, or alternatively by engaging in a thriving smuggling trade (Hobson 2004: Ch. 3; Deng 1997). Second, not all trade was banned since large amounts were officially sanctioned in three key ports: Macao, Chang-chou in Fukien Province and Su-chou in western Shensi Province (and through Amoy, Ningbo and Shanghai in Ch'ing times). But the clincher surely lies with the point that most of the world's silver was sucked into China, thereby confirming that the economy was both fully integrated within the global economy and was robust enough to enjoy a strong trade surplus. The key turning point here lay in the mid-fifteenth century when the Chinese economy was converted to a silver currency. Moreover, the high demand for Chinese exports ensured that much of the world's silver – especially that plundered in the Americas by the Europeans – was sucked into China. In turn, gold bullion spewed back outwards (having been exchanged for silver), where it was then sold in Europe only to be converted back into silver before re-entering China once more (Flynn and Giráldez 1994; Frank 1998; Pomeranz 2000). I call this continuous loop the 'global silver-recycling process', and its presence confirms the importance, if not the centrality, of China in the global economy. For it was ultimately China that sucked Europe and the Americas into a tight and interdependent global economic web through the strong demand that it provided for the American silver that was plundered by the Europeans.

All in all, as Jacques Gernet aptly notes, 'there was a big gap between the official regulations [i.e., the ban on foreign trade] and the reality of the commercial situation; the [official] restrictions imposed on trade might lead us to suppose that China was isolated at the very time when maritime trade was most intense' (Gernet 1999: 420). Thus while West Asia (the Ottoman and Persian empires), India and Southeast Asia all continued to play important roles in the global economy down to the nineteenth century, undoubtedly the most important role was performed by China between about 1450 and 1800. But to sum up this first section, it seems clear that globalisation is not unique to, or consequential only for, the twentieth century. Moreover, not only did (Oriental) globalisation begin during Europe's 'Dark Age', but its ultimate significance lay in the fact that it was the midwife, if not the mother, of the modern West.

Oriental globalisation and Eastern pioneers in the rise of Western capitalism, 500–1800

For many theorists, globalisation's ultimate importance lies in its ability to shape and transform societies across the world – what has been referred to as 'high impact' propensity (Held et al. 1999). It is therefore incumbent on me to reveal the high impact propensity of Oriental globalisation in order to secure acceptance of its robustness. The robustness of Oriental globalisation is confirmed by the claim of this section: that it promoted no less than the radical transformation of Europe from a backward agrarian society lying on the margins of the Afro-Asian-led global economy into a modern capitalist economy. My central claim is that every major turning point in the rise of Western capitalism was informed by the assimilation of the more advanced Eastern resource portfolios, which in turn had diffused across the Afro-Asian-led global economy into Europe through

Oriental globalisation. I shall draw on a few examples of these turning points to illustrate my claim (see Hobson 2004: Ch. 5–9 for a full account).

Most Eurocentric accounts begin with the commercial and financial revolutions that washed across Europe after about 1000. The standard view credits the Italians as the prime agents or movers in all of this. But while the Italians were undoubtedly the prime movers *within* Europe, they only were so because of their privileged trading connection with West Asia and North Africa – especially Egypt (Abu-Lughod 1989: 35–8; Braudel 1992). For a significant amount of trade from the East passed across the Islamic 'bridge of the world' into Italy and thence across Europe. That is, the Italians were not pioneers, but intermediaries, of the global trade that flowed across from the East. Moreover, Italy's financial success owed much to the Islamic financial institutions that also diffused across (Hobson 2004: Ch. 6). The Italian *collegantzia* partnership ('invented' in the eleventh century) was in fact an exact replica of the Islamic *commenda* agreement that had been invented at least four centuries earlier (Udovitch 1970). But this should hardly come as a revelation given that Muhammad himself was originally a *commenda* merchant. Moreover, all the major 'Italian' financial institutions – bills of exchange, cheques, credit institutions, banks and insurance – originated many centuries earlier in Islamic West Asia before they diffused across to Europe.

Before turning to the Renaissance which is conventionally thought to have originated in Italy, the next major turning point comprises the Voyages of (Re)discovery. These allegedly represented the sign of Europe's scientific, military and nautical/navigational superiority. But virtually all of the navigational and nautical technologies/techniques deployed by Da Gama and Columbus – the square hull and stern post rudder, the lateen sail and triple mast system, the astrolabe and compass, as well as lunar cycle charts, solar calendars, latitude/longitude tables and trigonometry – were borrowed either from China or Islamic West Asia. Put simply, had it not been for the diffusion of these Eastern portfolios there might never have been a European Age of Rediscovery. For without them, the Iberians would surely have remained confined to the Islamic Mediterranean. In turn the European excursions to the East are often linked to the European military revolution (1550–1660), which is viewed as the sign of Europe's military technological genius. But this obscures the point that all of the crucial military technologies were in fact borrowed from China where the world's first military revolution occurred between 850 and c. 1290. Indeed the Chinese invented gunpowder (850), the first metal-barrelled gun (1275) and the first cannon (1288). And in all cases, there is good circumstantial evidence for their diffusion across to Europe (Hobson 2004: Ch. 3 and 8).

As noted above, the Voyages of Rediscovery allegedly reflected the intellectual breakthroughs associated with the so-called European Renaissance (and which would later be complemented by the European scientific revolution). Moreover, these two intellectual movements are singled out by many Eurocentric historians as constituting the vital turning points that enabled Europe's breakthrough to modern capitalism. But while many Europeans trace their modern heritage back to the Renaissance, and hence to Ancient Greece, the fact is that many of its central ideas were derived from the world of Islam, all of which were pioneered after the eighth century CE (Hobson 2004: Ch. 8; Goody 2004). Islamic breakthroughs in mathematics including algebra and trigonometry were vital. The former term was taken from the title of one of al-Khwārizmī's mathematical texts. And by the beginning of the tenth century all six of the classical trigonometric functions had been defined and tabulated by Muslim mathematicians. Developments in public health, hygiene and medicine were also notable. Al-Rāzī's medical works were translated and reprinted in Europe some 40 times between 1498–1866. And Ibn Sīnā's *Canon of Medicine* became the founding text for European medical schools between the twelfth and fifteenth centuries. The Muslims developed numerous medicines and anaesthetics and pioneered the study of anatomy. They were also keen astrologers and astronomers, and their ideas were avidly borrowed by the Europeans. Ibn al-Shātir's mathematical models bore a remarkable resemblance to those used by Copernicus 150 years later. And as early as the ninth century, al-Khwārizmī calculated the circumference of the Earth to within 41 metres. Last but not least, the Baconian idea that science should be based on the experimental method had already been pioneered by the Muslims (not the Greeks).

Finally, for Eurocentrism the culminating point in the rise of the West is that of the British industrial and agricultural revolutions. But behind the headlines of pioneering British inventors lay the Chinese who had undergone their own industrial miracle during the Sung dynasty in the eleventh century (Hobson 2004: Ch. 3 and 9). Eurocentrism preaches that the British agricultural revolution was allegedly spurred on by a series of brilliant British inventions, including the curved iron mouldboard plough, Jethro Tull's seed drill and horse-drawn hoe, the horse-powered threshing machine and the rotary winnowing machine. Added to this were breakthroughs in crop rotations. But in each case, these had been invented in China by the sixth century. In the case of the plough and rotary winnowing machine, Chinese models were directly brought across (either by the Jesuits, European scientists or Dutch sailors). And the remaining inventions were most likely copied from Chinese manuals that flooded Europe after 1650 (some of which were transmitted by the Jesuits).

Much the same story applies to the British industrial revolution. Thus while Eurocentrism celebrates James Watt for his pioneering skills in inventing the steam engine, the fact is that he owed much to the Chinese. The essentials of the steam engine go back to Wang Chên's *Treatise on Agriculture* (1313), which in turn goes back to the Chinese invention of the water-powered bellows (31 CE). Moreover, Chinese breakthroughs in gun and cannon manufacturing were also important in enabling the later invention of the steam engine (given that the cannon or gun is in effect a one-cylinder combustion engine and all of our modern motors are descended from it). Interestingly, a further link here is that one of the major challenges confronting Watt was the need to bore an airtight cylinder: interesting because he turned to John Wilkinson for help, given that Wilkinson owned a boring mill that was designed for cannon production.

While Eurocentrism axiomatically assumes that it was the British who first used coal to produce iron ore, this in fact began in eleventh-century Sung China under similar conditions of deforestation. And the famous Martin-Siemens steel process of 1863 was pre-empted by the Chinese 'co-fusion' process that was developed in the fifth century CE. Given China's substantial lead in iron and steel production, it was not surprising that British producers (including the famous Benjamin Huntsman of Sheffield) undertook detailed studies of Chinese production methods in order to develop their own steel manufacturing techniques. It is true that the European invention of the Bessemer Converter (1852) was significantly derived from the breakthroughs made by the American, William Kelly, in 1845. But what is not usually pointed out is that Kelly himself had brought over four Chinese steel experts to Kentucky from whom he learned the principles of steel production.

The other great pillar of the British industrial revolution was the development of cotton manufacturing. But while British inventors such as John Lombe are usually singled out for praise, this misses the point that some of their inventions had been pioneered in China many centuries earlier. For example, Lombe's silk machines became the model for the Derby cotton machines. But while Lombe's 'invention' is recognised as a copy of the Italian machines, what is not usually admitted is that they in turn were a direct copy of the earlier Chinese inventions that had been assimilated in the thirteenth century (Pacey 1991). Notable too is that in textiles, the Chinese had long developed machines which differed in only one detail to that of James Hargreaves' famous 'spinning jenny' and John Kay's equally famous 'flying shuttle'. All in all, therefore, it is debatable as to whether there would ever have been a British industrial revolution had it not been for the much earlier pioneering Chinese breakthroughs, the knowledge of which (if not the actual technologies) were transmitted to Britain through a host of Oriental global channels.

Conclusion

I began with the premise that mainstream analyses of globalisation and the rise of modern capitalism are distorted by a Eurocentric prejudice that *selects* the West as the progressive subject of progressive global economic history and simultaneously *de-selects* the passive East. But when we do away with Eurocentrism we can reclaim what George James (1954) properly called the 'stolen legacy' of the East, and thereby restore the Eastern peoples to the status of creative and pioneering agents of global economic history. Indeed *contra* Eurocentrism it is clear that the Easterners have been many 'peoples *with* history' (to borrow the title of Eric Wolf's 1982 book). For this is illustrated by two key points: first that the many Eastern peoples have significantly contributed to the rise and development of the global economy. And second, the Eastern peoples have no less enabled the very breakthrough to modern capitalism that the West and its theoretical spokespersons have for too long unjustly claimed as their own unique creation. Accordingly, these two claims undermine the traditional Eurocentric assumption that the West has been the prime mover of capitalism and the global economy. And thus it seems fair to conclude that the need to challenge the Eurocentrism of mainstream IPE seems long overdue.

9   Diasporic agents and trans-Asian flows in the making of Asian modernity: the case of Thailand

Ara Wilson

This chapter explores Asian agency in the making of capitalist modernity in Thailand. The previous chapter, by showing how the West was shaped throughout its formative period (500–1800) by all manner of Eastern agents and influences, argues that East and West have never been discrete civilisations but are better understood as 'creolised formations'. This chapter brings the critique of Eurocentrism up to the present day. It challenges the Eurocentric view that Asian modernity has been con- structed by, or is derivative of, the West. Instead, I show that Asian modernity has been significantly produced by the agency of the Chinese diaspora and trans-Asian flows (for a full account see Wilson 2004).

This chapter analyses the making of modernity in Thailand through a social history of the consumer economy in Bangkok, which has materially and symbolically created a modern infrastructure in Bangkok. Drawing on historical, ethnographic and feminist approaches, I present an extended discussion of one major Sino-Thai family business in order to illustrate the grounded practices and processes – including kinship and gender relations – behind capitalist development in Thailand.

As the discussion of Bangkok's department stores makes clear, Thailand's capitalist modernity was produced by Asian actors and trans-Asian flows. The key entrepreneurs in Thailand's development came from the Chinese diaspora in Southeast Asia. The role of the over- seas Chinese in the region's economies is a well-rehearsed topic, first as 'aliens' subject to anxious scrutiny from nationalist states and Western powers and more recently as heralded models of 'Asian values' that promote capitalist ethics and stable investment climates. Although these views credit Asian economic agency, their Orientalist lens obscures the concrete social processes that fostered modernity within Thailand. A better understanding of these developments requires conceptualising culture, identity and modernity differently.

This chapter draws on feminist theory and post-colonial approaches to highlight the dynamic social dimensions of capitalist modernity in Asia.

Feminist and post-colonial frameworks analyse capitalism as a cultural practice. Post-colonial theory argues against an image of authentic traditional society that is the opposite of modernity (e.g., Chakrabarty 2000). This framework understands Thai culture as a hybrid, creole formation that incorporates and creates the modern in relation to cross-cultural and transnational processes. From this perspective, Thai modernity can be reduced neither to Asian nor Western influence; instead, both Western and Asian influences have been refracted and recontextualised by actors within the social worlds of Thailand. A feminist lens brings to light the gendered and family labour behind the scenes of corporate capitalism. It reveals the inextricable mix of kinship and business, and informal and formal economies that produced the modern economy. Such an approach also recasts the sexualised image of Western capital 'penetrating' feminised Third World societies (Gibson-Graham 1996) to an image recognising a diversity of economic modes and agents operating within broader structuring contexts of geopolitical or gendered power.

The chapter sketches the emergence of Sino-Thai business families that have been pivotal in economic modernisation in Thailand. It turns to a specific example, the Chirathivat family, which introduced Thailand's first full-fledged department store and created one of the leading corporate empires in Southeast Asia. Bangkok's modern consumer economy illustrates the centrality of Asian agency. The chapter then considers the social and cultural dimensions of modernity in Thailand through an ethnographic, feminist and post-colonial lens. It argues that what appears as modern or Western in Thailand in fact can have multiple sources and is indigenised or interpreted in relation to Thai contexts. As such, the making of modern Thai capitalism provides a case both for what the editors refer to as axiorational behaviour, in that new conventions and norms formed in an incremental manner that then had an impact on the political economy, and also for a form of 'hybridised mimicry', in that Western capitalist discourses were filtered through a Thai cultural lens to produce something altogether new (see Chapter 1). Both of these forms of everyday action informed the Thai case and assisted the transformation of the local, national, regional and, in a smaller way, world economy. The chapter then introduces discussions of gendered labour and ethnic identity to the narrative of capitalist development. The far-reaching effects of Asian-centred modernity, and its inextricability from social processes, is illustrated by a brief discussion of the 1997 Asian economic crisis, which percolated through the creolised worlds of the Chinese diaspora, Thai banking and international finance. In boom and bust, the case of Thailand challenges Eurocentric views of capitalist development, globalisation and modernity as essentially Western projects.

Diasporic agents

Thailand (Siam until the 1940s) was never formally colonised by Europe. Although it was never subject to colonial rule, Siam/Thailand did not escape Europe's imperial and commercial dominance during the period of high colonialism in the region (and was occupied by Japan during the Second World War on the East Asian International Order, see Shogo Suzuki in this volume). In the nineteenth and early twentieth centuries, Europe forced Siam to adopt economic treaties and political arrangements that were favourable to their interests. Europeans dominated the Thai import-export business, Siam's major trade. Colonial-era trade intensified Thai rice production with far-reaching effects in the city and countryside. However, European and later US dominance was limited in time and scope. Europeans' presence was confined to the capital city and their enterprises to import-export businesses. They did not modernise the country. Instead, the deep social transformations associated with modernisation were achieved by the Thai state (which is a separate story) and by the creole Sino-Thai business community, the focus here. Their agency impacted the domestic, regional and ultimately world economy.

One notable representative of Asian agency in both state and commerce is the former prime minister of Thailand, Thaksin Shinawatra. A billionaire tycoon in the information technology field, Thaksin descends from a nineteenth-century immigrant to northern Thailand who began a textile business. The Shinawatra family developed this enterprise into a leading silk manufacturer and expanded into bus lines, real estate, movie theatres and politics. Thaksin and his wife parlayed family money and government connections to create an enormous corporate empire centred on information technology. As the tycoon prime minister, he became the emblem of modern Thailand's possibilities (Wilson 2004: Ch. 4).

The businesses choreographing Thailand's contemporary economy are run by Sino-Thais and have their roots in the 1920s to 1950s. The ancestors of many in this business class came to Thailand from south-central China during the massive emigration of the 1920s, a wave that included far more women and married couples than before. Some began in agricultural businesses, notably rice milling and trading. The Caroen Pokphand (CP) conglomerate, a leading global agribusiness, began as a Bangkok shop selling seed grown on the family farm in China. Others serviced the growing urban population with general stores, brothels, saloons, laundry services and the like: the Chirathivat family I discuss below is one notable example. The Shinawatra family represents one of the few families involved in manufacturing (textiles) before the 1960s.

Migrants and their descendants formed creole Sino-Thai communities, some of which consolidated into the major business and professional
class in Thailand. They raised capital from their small shops, family and
diasporic social networks. They sent money to families in China, producing a huge flow of remittances that caused alarm for the Thai state and
Western observers, but that also enabled diasporic finance entrepreneurs
to develop banking in the region (e.g., the Bangkok Bank). Trans-Asian
capital flows drove Thailand's economy during much of the twentieth
century. With the emergence of banks, local wealth was transformed into
larger sums of capital to expand businesses or start new ventures as new
opportunities arose.

Family enterprises made pragmatic accommodations to various powers:
Europeans, Japanese occupiers, or the Thai state. Even though the Thai
government enacted anti-Chinese policies, Sino-Thai businesses formed
key alliances with government and military figures (Pasuk and Baker
1995). They also exploited possibilities raised by diminished European
influence. This creole Sino-Thai community forged the modern sectors of
the capitalist economy in Bangkok: agribusiness, commerce, real estate,
finance, manufacturing, tourism and telecommunications. They articulated the domestic with transnational economic and cultural flows. To
understand the background to Thailand's modern economy, then, we
require an ethnography and social history to illustrate the everyday nature
of international political economy. In this sense a portrait of a prominent
Sino-Thai business family, the Chirathivats, serves as a basis for an
analysis of how diasporic Asian agents have shaped Thai and transnational capitalist modernity in ways that illustrate both axiorational
behaviour and hybridised mimicry.

From shophouse to department store

The Chirathivat story is well known in Thailand, often recounted in the
business press. The standard version of the story focuses on the patriarch
Tiang (? –1968) and his eldest son Samrit (1925–92). The Chirathivat
family began in villages on the island of Hainan, impoverished from years
of strife with China's regimes. In 1927, Tiang and his first wife, Waan,
and their two-year-old son (later given the Thai name, Samrit) travelled
by junk to Bangkok, where Waan's parents had already settled. They
joined the large flow of mixed-gender migrants from China. In Thailand,
the couple took part in ethnic (Hainanese) and cross-ethnic Chinese
networks that extended into the region.

Borrowing money from Waan's parents, the couple opened a general
store. On the first floor they sold coffee, short-order food and odds and

ends. On the second floor, Waan worked as a seamstress. Shops like the Chirathivats' sold imported canned milk, kerosene, or novelty items, as well as local manufactures like cigarettes, matches and soap. Father and son purchased the retail goods from Sampeng, a crowded lane in 'Chinatown' that was the nation's major wholesale market for consumer goods. The Chirathivats' shop produced enough income to support a growing family: Tiang married two more women and fathered 26 children. The business allowed them to rise in class status and educate their children at top schools in Thailand and later abroad.

During the Second World War, even as the occupation by Japan and violent conflict brought undeniable suffering to the country as a whole, and to the Chirathivat family in particular ways, the retreat of European enterprises during the war provided openings for local Sino-Thai entrepreneurs (Pasuk and Baker 1998). Sino-Thai businesses supplanted Europeans as the brokers for Thailand's intersection with the global economy, serving as polyglot agents crossing national and cultural borders. Families like the Chirathivats were well placed for this role. The eldest sons, well educated and trilingual, had rich social networks through school, family and outside jobs. Samrit had connections that extended into the diaspora communities in the region, for example in Singapore. Using these connections, he became the sole agent for Western brands in Thailand, a role formerly monopolised by Europeans.

In 1947, with capital from his father and friends (guaranteed by his wife's gold necklace), Samrit opened Central Trading Store selling foreign magazines. The new shop was a transitional moment in the transformation from local shophouse to modern retail. It still operated as a family business and the family lived above the store. But in content and organisation, the business was more and more differentiated from the ethnically inflected, small-scale Chinese family shop. These distinctions were not an accident but deliberate strategies that reflected the adoption of new conventions that would become rigorous cultural norms. Samrit emphasised modern marketing techniques, introducing Thailand's first showcase for displaying goods. He advertised the store extensively: fliers announced new 'sweaters', 'neckties' and 'petticoats', using transliterated English terms and Western name brands (Samrit 1992: 141). Samrit saw the need for modern goods that suited the growing cosmopolitanism of the post-war Thai bureaucratic and business classes and their orientation towards Western styles, goods and knowledge.

In 1956, the Chirathivat family opened Central Department Store, the largest and most comprehensive store in Thailand. It was located in Chinatown, which from the 1950s through to the 1970s was the heart of consumption in the city: Central Department Store was *the* department store. It provisioned the transforming and consolidating elite classes of old guard Thai elite, government bureaucrats, business and professional families. The Chirathivats parlayed post-war opportunities, state policies, social networks, family labour and Sino-Thai capital into a profitable enterprise. Over a few decades, Central grew into the largest department store chain in Southeast Asia and reported 'a sales-per-square-foot figure equal to Macy's' (Business in Thailand 1981: 35). By 1993, Central had ten branches in Bangkok and expanded the retail boom to the provinces.

The department store business generated handsome profits that the Chirathivats invested in a diverse range of enterprises. They evolved Central into a conglomerate of thirty interrelated companies involved in retail, hotels, property development, manufacturing and fast foods, with interests in publishing as well. These projects involved collaboration with corporations from the West (e.g., the US, Australia, France and the Netherlands) and Asia (e.g., Hong Kong and Myanmar). Central continues to expand further into the Asian region.

The prevailing business form in Thailand remained a hybrid mode that combined kinship and corporate relations. The Central conglomerate, for example, remained by and large a family affair. Samrit's brothers were leading executives in portions of the diversifying empire; they also sat on the boards of other organisations. Central employed Chirathivat offspring and in-laws, including daughters: one is the president of the Central Department Store company; another is an executive at the chic Zen Department Store. Such elite business families form Thailand's capitalist class, solidifying those ties through intermarriage and joint investments. (Chirathivat offspring have married the children of this class as well as such other notables as a beauty queen and a member of the Thai royalty.)

Asian modernity

Modernity in the Third World is often figured as Western in at least three ways. First, modernity is attributed to Western agents, states, culture and capital: modernisation and capitalist development in the Third World thus represents Western penetration. Second, the *global* in globalisation is often conflated with, or centred on, the West. It is assumed that transnational flows are controlled by Europe or the United States, which are the hubs of globalisation (see also Andrew Herod's chapter in this volume). Third, symbols of modernity – skyscrapers, Western brands, Hollywood – signal Westernisation and global homogenisation: Western styles and elements are assumed to have the same meaning everywhere. A critical, grounded analysis of Thailand's consumer economy challenges these assumptions and the conceptions of Western, modernity, culture and identity that underpin them. In this section, I address the first two over-lapping conceptions of globalised modernity as a Western creation.

Western capital has played a part in modernising Thailand. The United States injected millions of dollars into Thailand during the Indochina conflicts for projects relevant to the agendas of the US and Thai military and the Thai authoritarian state. However significant, the amount and application of this money had less impact on the development of the capitalist economy than is often assumed. Direct foreign investment from the United States remained limited; even into the 1990s, when legal changes gave global finance capital more liberties, most Western capital took the form of short-term investments. Only after the 1997 Asian economic crisis did Western corporations come to claim much power in the Thai economy. The major investments behind the modern economy – that funded gleaming new shopping complexes and bleak industrial parks – were Asian: primarily Sino-Thai and Japanese, followed by newly industrialised countries (NICs) and China.

An examination of Central Department Store and Bangkok's consumer economy challenges the conflation of West and modern that characterises conventional international relations. The example of the Chirathivat family business shows that modern retail in Thailand was the consequence of strategic practices within Asia that reflected hybridised mimicry. Leading Thai and regional corporations emerged from the interplay of ethnic, kin, commercial and state institutions. The key agents were the Sino-Thai entrepreneurs (including their families) who combined Asian and Western capital, technologies and styles. Clearly, the Chirathivats were not merely passive consumers of Western systems, but active innovators, interpreters and agents in economic development. As Samrit Chirathivat writes, 'Our success grew out of our determination to bring Thailand into the modern world' (Central Department Store, 2001).

Asian businesses launched the symbolic and economic dimensions of capitalist modernity in Bangkok. By the 1980s, the Thai economy was growing at one of the fastest rates in the world. Asian investors like the Chirathivat family shifted into new sectors: manufacturing, real estate, hotels and services. They invested in industrial factories producing goods for export. They constructed hotels, which had become trophy investments, but which also provided the rooms for the burgeoning tourism industry, which earned more foreign currency than any other sector. Unfolding developments in state policies, urban space, capital and popular culture created a fertile climate for Bangkok's consumer economy.

Profits from these fields fuelled speculative real estate investments. Downtown rents escalated. Bangkok appeared under construction, as office buildings and commercial venues sprouted across the expanding city. By the mid-1980s, Bangkok had thirty-nine branches of department stores, seven shopping centres, and seventeen more complexes underway. Speculative investments sculpted a new geography of the city oriented to commercial venues, and brought a shopping complex within reach of all Bangkok residents with some cash to spend. Asian development created a modern infrastructure and the modern workers and consumers to fill it.

The consumer economy was encouraged by the Thai state, which saw corporate retail as an important marker of Thailand's progress and encouraged new conventions that supported it (in contrast to disorderly street markets or old-fashioned shophouses). The business press agreed, noting that the opening of an enormous new shopping mall 'sheds new light on the further growth and expansion of Bangkok as a truly modern Asian city' (*Business Review (Thailand)* 1984: 24). With the proliferation of shopping malls, Bangkok's downtown was compared to Singapore, Hong Kong or Kuala Lumpur. These comparisons serve as a reminder that international need not imply Western. Thailand's transnational linkages were not only to the West but also, often more immediately, across Asia. Consider tourism to Thailand, a topic that conjures up images of Western backpackers or sex tourists: more than half of the business travellers and tourists to Thailand come from Asia (Tourist Authority of Thailand 2005). As many have suggested, there are different modes and plural histories of modernity: some of these are centred within Asia. The economic history of Bangkok's consumer economy presented above reveals the regional and domestic nature of development in Thailand. Asian resources installed the architecture and cultivated the subjects that appear as modernity in Asia. These processes point to the ironic nature of Asian modernity, however: Asian actors produced a modernity that obscured its own Asian origins.

Western Asian style

The conventional views of global modernity revolve around conceptions of nations, agents, capitalism and global processes that themselves are predicated on usually unexamined notions of culture, social life, identities and power, notions which have been subject to critical revisions in a number of fields, notably anthropology, social theory, feminist theory and post-colonial scholarship. These critiques suggest that, in order to recognise Asian agency, we need a more social and cultural view of global political economy. The following discussion uses an ethnographic and a social historical lens to illuminate the social and cultural dimensions of capitalist modernity in Asia in a number of ways. I first show that Western elements have particular histories and meanings in Thailand and that signs of the modern derive from within Asia as well. Next, I bring a feminist perspective to show the gendered origins and effects of Thailand's consumer economy. Finally, I show that the identity of Chinese Thais have changed over time in ways that complicate an essentialist understanding of Thai and foreign actors. Revising the concepts of culture, economy and identity, these arguments revise Eurocentric, androcentric and Orientalist understandings of modernity.

Asian consumer culture is chock-full of Western brands, manufactures and designs. Central Trading got its start peddling American magazines, neckties and sports shirts. Western styles in non-Western landscapes suggest a recent borrowing or a wistful mimicry. Imported goods, techniques and terminology reinforce the assumption that modernity came from outside Thailand, specifically from the West. I address this set of assumptions in two ways. First, acknowledging the undeniable popularity of English terms and Western goods, I consider their local meanings. Ethnographic and post-colonial approaches stress that 'foreign' elements are 'indigenised', interpreted and modified in relation to local systems of value (Iwabuchi *et al.* 2004: 2). Second, I point out that another powerful source of influences in Thai society comes from within Asia, trans-Asian flows that are obscured by the assumption that modern consumption is Western. Even seemingly Western influences found in fashions, body ideals, or terminology, may come from global cultures of Japan or Hong Kong, rather than from the United States.

The choice of an English name for the Chirathivat's department store, Central, is an occasion for considering the complexity of Western elements in Thai culture and the use of hybridised mimicry. The preference for an English word confirms its global hegemony as the argot for finance capital and the premier signifier of modernity. In Asia, the ability to speak English confers cultural capital. English was undeniably an indispensable business tool; Samrit was proud of his ability to draft contracts in the lingua franca of commerce. Bangkok's new constructions rely on English place terms like Plaza, Place, Centre or Square. This use of English reflects the orientation of elites, the main consumers of real estate and consumer goods. Their participation in the linguistic hegemony of English reflects not only global power relations but also their navigations of domestic social hierarchies. But the linguistic hegemony of English is incomplete, and it is important to consider how English is used and interpreted.

In fact, the origin of the name Central reflected a synthesis of Western and Chinese influences. According to store history, Samrit derived the name 'Central' from an idea of his father's. Tiang admired a system of the Chinese government called 'Tong Iang', or 'Central' (*klang* in Thai), which managed conflict among political factions. Samrit 'chose the word that had the same meaning in English, "Central", meaning "the heart or the center", to indicate the center of goods and service that best met the wishes of customers' (Samrit 1992: 142; Central Department Store 2001). The choice of an English name illuminates the entrepreneurial pragmatism of Chinese Thais within a context of Western powers and local anti-Chinese sentiments. Yet patently Western images of the modern, like the term central, are woven from multiple strands.

In the 1950s, the name Central indicated modernity not only because it was English, but also because of its connotations, which resonated with post-war visions for a modern economy. Samrit saw a fit between a Chinese political system and the new mode of retail. Centralisation conveyed the economic ideal of the day, which was large-scale, vertically hierarchical and separated into clear functions (compared with later corporate emphases on decentralisation, niche marketing and plurality). Samrit's interpretations of 'modern' retail lay not just with the imported goods or English terms, but also with the infrastructure and operations of the business. His reference points were not only Europe and the United States, but also China and Asia. Significantly, early branches of the store displayed the name in Thai, Chinese and English. In everyday life, English has not supplanted, but supplemented Thai. (The Chirathivat family's real estate enterprise is named Central Pattana, using the Thai word for development, which itself is an indigenised concept.)

The meanings of foreign languages and products are constructed in relation to local systems of interpretation and often combined in new hybrid forms. In this way, English terms can also be seen as design elements in Asian culture, the way overseas Chinese applied European details to the facade of vernacular infrastructure in the homes they built in pre-revolution China, or in the way Thais wear t-shirts bearing English phrases without caring about their meaning.

Attention to Thai interpretations of Western-ness or the English language reveals diverse meanings that are shaped by local social realities. Thailand employs both British and American spellings, sometimes in the same text, as when I worked with a British-educated elite Thai professional producing the program (or programme) guide for Shinawatra's cable television concern. England and British style are favoured by Thai elites. Middle classes are often more oriented to US culture and schools. Tellingly, however, elite Thais are also oriented to Asia, where high-level connections facilitate Asian capital flows and political alliances. These elites are the 'flexible citizens' described by Aihwa Ong (1999): the diasporic entrepreneurs who smoothly operate across national borders and in different economic zones. A cardinal example is Thaksin Shinawatra, who has personal ties to former members of the Khmer Rouge, Chinese businessmen, World Trade Organisation officials, as well as George W. Bush.

Asia is a vital source of technology, culture and models for Thailand. For Thais, many symbols of modernity are Asian. The reference points for Bangkok's downtown are Asian cities – Kuala Lumpur or Hong Kong rather than Los Angeles. Hong Kong epitomises the market society; Japan signifies hip style. In 1964, Daimaru department store, a subsidiary of a two-centuries-old Japanese firm, opened a branch in Bangkok. It introduced the enthralling innovations of escalators and air conditioning. After Daimaru, other Japanese stores entered Bangkok: Jusco, Tokyu, Sogo, and Isetarn, among others. Japanese retail upsets the conventional belief that the US is the source of innovations in consumerism. Since Daimaru's escalators, much of what counts as modern retail is attributed to Japan: avant-garde comfort, leisure centres and an emphasis on convenience (Nakagawa 1987; Samrit 1992: 154). The undeniable popularity of Western brand names can obscure the significant flows of styles, goods and media within Asia.

Koichi Iwabuchi, Stephen Muecke and Mandy Thomas argue that 'intra-Asian cultural traffic of popular and consumer culture ... has produced a new mode of cross-cultural fertilisation and Asian modernities which cannot be a mere copy of Western counterparts' (2004: 2). Thais consume Bollywood films, Hong Kong serials, self-help guides based on Chinese lore, Thai updates on the Ramayana and Filipino jazz bands. This traffic is changing conceptions of identity and aesthetics in Thailand. An emerging pan-Asian body aesthetic draws on Caucasian markers (large breasts, prominent noses) but incorporates Japanese fashions and Chinese features as well. The 'Chinese' type has become esteemed because they are associated with financial success and romanticised notions of Chinese ancestry. A singular focus on Westernisation reflects Western hegemony, which cannot see differentiated and recombined Asian cultural exchanges, as well as static and essentialist conceptions of Asian culture.

Gendered modernity

Recognising Asian agency in forging global modernity calls for different approaches to the characteristics of the global and modern. Taking an ethnographic approach, I interpret capitalism as culturally shaped practices that take place in a social context structured by a larger political economic setting. Informed by feminist and post-colonial theories, this view of capitalism allows us to consider the question of agency differently: to introduce actors who are neglected in conventional theory (notably women) and to recognise that the identity of actors is complex, as their affiliations and positions change over time.

Business and popular accounts of Central Department Store follow the rags-to-riches formula in which individual masculine energy, inspiration and agency result in success. Feminist perspectives challenge such individualist and masculinist narratives by revealing the social and gendered labour behind the corporation (e.g., Yanagisako 2002). As Susan Greenhalgh (1994) notes, 'de-Orientalising the Chinese family firm' entails recognising the place of women, gender and kinship in the economy.

The formal economy of Thailand has been intertwined with, and dependent on, informal realms of kinship, households, gender and ethnicity. This mix was integral to Sino-Thai businesses that developed the modern capitalist economy and once again signals the importance of axiorational behaviour to the creation of Thai capitalism. For example, in the shophouse, which was the predominant business form in Thailand until the 1980s, families and hired hands typically lived and worked together. The Chirathivat clan, for example, lived above their store until the 1950s. Even when they moved to a separate residence, they continued to live together in a large compound. In the Sino-Thai shop, domestic life intimately overlapped with business operations. Shophouses combined production, distribution and consumption. Indeed, as an economic form, the shophouse mode is considered premodern because it combined functions that were ideally separated in a 'modernising' economy (e.g., Polanyi 1944/1957).

Women's labour was crucial to this economy. Family firms like the Chirathivats relied on the work and management skills of wives and daughters (Bao 2004; Basu 1991; Greenhalgh 1994). Some of this work was explicit productive labour: Waan worked as a seamstress and her daughters helped in the stores. But the feminist analysis goes beyond recognising women's neglected participation in the formal economy to argue that 'social reproduction' is central to the operations of political economy (e.g., Bakker and Gill 2003; Mies 1986; Peterson 2003). Tiang's second wife, Bunsri, for example, did less work in the store, but undertook a major share of household labour, which included childrearing, domestic work, charitable activities and spiritual practices. Bunsri took children shopping and taught them about the value of money and goods (Bunsri 1998: 52–9, 74). Both informal and formal education prepared the next generation of family workers. Discussions of the Chirathivat family's success typically remark on the tight-knit family feeling: this was the result of what anthropologist Micaela di Leonardo (1987) describes as 'kinship labour'. Accounts of the family marvel at Bunsri's ability to keep the peace in a large, polygynous, multigenerational household. Kinship labour also includes Bunsri's participation in the broader Chinese community, including her family's name group (the Hantrakul Foundation) and her merit making at Buddhist temples. These efforts were important for family status, legitimacy and connections, as well as their spiritual well being. Thailand's modern economy was underwritten by this hidden gendered labour.

The feminist analysis of capitalist modernity is not confined to a remedial, empirical issue of adding new participants, but represents a transformation to the analysis of processes and systems and addresses the ideological level, explaining how the gendered dimensions of capitalist modernity have been obscured by discourses about modernisation (Gibson-Graham 1996; Mies 1986; Ong 1999; Yanagisako 2002).

Capitalist development in Thailand emerged from family relations and ethnically based business practices grounded in a shophouse economy. In turn, the processes of modernisation transformed these social arrangements. The department store concretely illustrates some of the far-reaching changes wrought by Sino-Thai innovations. The department store enacted 'the radical division of production and consumption; the prominence of standardised merchandise with fixed, marked pricing; ceaseless introduction of new products; the extension of credit; and ubiquitous publicity' (Walkowitz 1992: 47). Even such a minor example as fixed prices, which Central introduced in the 1950s, had manifold consequences. It changed the work involved in selling, supplanting skills at bargaining and knowledge about goods with formal educational credentials. Price tags also changed the codification of value, making goods easily commensurable with international price systems.

The 'modernisation' process that Sino-Thai businesses and the state advanced in the 1950s and 1960s reduced the place of kinship in the formal economy. The rise of wage labour transferred labour away from family businesses (farms, stores or workshops) to commercial agriculture, the state and corporations. The Chirathivat family, for example, transformed their shophouse into a department store and hired non-kin staff: by 1987, Central Department Stores employed 7,000 people. The erosion of family economies altered the relation of kinship to work, consumption to production and public to private. It rationalised economic spheres, the hallmark of modernisation. These transformations were gendered. Disaggregating business and home changed the economic conception of household labour, associating it with consumption and non-economic affective ties. Just as the sensuous displays of the department store obscure the wage labour that enables it, modern retail obscures the social worlds that produced it – kinship, ethnic ties and the shophouse economy. These transformations fostered a vision of Thai femininity that erased women's participation in the labour force at rates among the highest in the world. They also altered the meaning of the Chinese ethnicity, as I show below.

Ethnic modernity: from alien to emblem

Everyday international political economy asks, 'Who acts and how do they enable change over time?' (see Chapter 1). This chapter has shown that Asian families – including wives and daughters – were innovative agents in economic development. Famous within Thailand and even across the region, these actors are considered peripheral only in the West. But the 'who' still invites further consideration. In this case, it revolves around the complex question of Chinese identity in Southeast Asia. As post-colonial and critical theory has shown, ethnic identity is a complex formulation that changes over time. Chineseness in Thailand has a spectrum of meanings, including gendered and sexual dimensions (Bao 2004). The example of Sino-Thai business families shows how Chinese identity has been fraught with economic and political associations and has changed dramatically with modernisation.

For much of the twentieth century (and perhaps continuing to the present), Western and Thai authorities viewed Chinese identity as grounded in timeless culture (e.g., Confucianism). They defined dynamic creole diasporic communities, which incorporated Thai women and spoke Thai, as 'alien', outside of what was considered authentic Thai society. From the late 1930s through to the 1950s, the Thai state attempted to regulate or assimilate 'alien' groups. Resident Chinese were compelled to adopt a Thai surname, follow the Thai version of Buddhism, and place their children in Thai language schools.

Western and Thai authorities recognised Chinese economic activity but credited it to a racial and cultural essence and, for much of the twentieth century, viewed it as a problem, a stranglehold on the 'Thai' economy, and a threat to US, Western and Thai interests. The Thai state accordingly promoted economic nationalism for Thais, using policies like the Alien Business Law to privilege Thai nationals. Given that Thai women have long predominated in local trade, these promotions were specifically intended to incorporate ethnic Thai men into the market economy, a vision of nationalist development that attempted to change the gender and ethnic nature of the formal economy. Western Orientalism and authoritarian Thai nationalism thus reinforced each other.

Drawing on critical theories, the approach of intercivilisational political economy advanced in this volume proposes a different view of ethnicity and culture more akin to ethnographic perspectives. This sees identity and culture as realised in practice, situated in broader contexts, and changing. This view revises the image of Chinese as outsiders to authentic Thai identity. Instead, it examines how Sino-Thais forged creole communities in relation to domestic conditions and to global, particularly trans-Asian, contexts. The Chirathivat family succeeded in part because they complied with expectations for Chinese in Thailand. For example, they adopted the name Chirathivat, a Pali-derived name meaning long-standing grand culture. The blending of Thai, Chinese and other practices represents a hybrid fashion typical of immigrant Chinese families and Sino-Thai descendants. As these accommodations suggest, the identity of Chinese in Thailand has changed over the twentieth century. It has shifted from resident alien to a hyphenated Chinese-Thai identity and even to exemplary Thai. As the power of the market economy increased dramatically in Thai society, Chinese identity and images of Chinese culture and history became more positively valued (and even romanticised). The Chirathivat family, Caroen Pokphand and Shinawatra are now considered successful 'Thai' family dynasties – even as they strengthen their links to China. Their businesses are represented as Thai in contrast with foreign capital from Japan, the United States or Europe. So complete is the shift from 'alien' to 'Thai' that in the 1980s, Samrit attempted to have the government deploy the Alien Business Law, which had been developed to regulate the Chinese, against an influx of foreign retail investments (*Business Review (Thailand)* 1984: 9–10). As Prime Minister, Thaksin Shinawatra styled himself both as the epitome of a cosmopolitan Thai flexible citizen, fluent in the global political economy, and as a populist who understands ordinary Thai people. In 2005 rural Thais – the very figures of authentic Thai society – helped re-elect him by a landslide. The transformation of Sino-Thai identity illustrates the complexity of the identities of actors shaping Asian modernity and the importance of hybridised mimicry as Western capitalist discourses are translated with local Thai meanings.

Conclusion: the Asian economic crisis

This chapter has used the case of Thailand to challenge Eurocentric evaluations of global modernity that ignore non-Western (and non-male) actors and informal, social and cultural processes. The prevailing views conflate modernisation with Western forces, viewing signs of the modern in Asia as the result of mimicry or penetration. Critical theorists have criticised the model of capitalist penetration of traditional societies as an explanation of modernising development, as this volume has shown. Feminists, for example, have shown that the obvious sexualised and gendered geography of the penetration model compromises an effective analysis of the operations of power and resistance (Gibson-Graham 1996; Scott 1995). Emphasising foreign capital penetration reinforces a homogeneous, static view of society; it obscures the dynamic interplay of capitalist and non-capitalist systems; and it ignores the significant role that women, labourers and other marginal actors play in economic development (Gibson-Graham 1996; Wilson 2004). I conclude this chapter with a brief discussion of the 1997 Asian economic crisis that modifies the image of penetration with an emphasis on Asian actors and contexts.

In July 1997, bad loans and currency troubles in Bangkok banks led to a financial crisis in Thailand and a harsh downturn in the East and Southeast Asian economies, the effects of which continue to reverberate across the region today. The Asian economic crisis is partly due to the speed and power of global financial flows, most famously hedge funds. In the 1990s, Thailand was compelled to open its profitable economy to outside investors, resulting in an escalation of capital flows, including more capital from the West. However, most of this escalating flow took the form of short-term investments and was funnelled through the Thai economy through Sino-Thai family firms, such as the Bangkok Bank. A bounty of capital led to hyper-investments in speculative enterprises that created a 'bubble economy'. Thus, the Thai financial crisis was fostered by both global finance and the domestic economy (Wilson 2003). It led to a crisis in economies across the region, a rippling impact still unfolding.

The crisis transformed the Thai economy. Many companies went under. The results of the crisis demonstrated how the official formal economy is intertwined with, and dependent on, other realms that are barely recognised in conventional political and economic theories. Not surprisingly, what sustained people were the devalued yet entrenched practices of social reproduction and the informal economy, both gendered domains that rely on women's labour in particular. Urban migrants returned to their rural homes. Many people began part-time selling, hawking the goods they bought in better times at impromptu bazaars. The well-known centrality of kinship and ethnic networks to Sino-Thai businesses like Central, Caroen Pokphand and Shinawatra, which had helped explain the success of these enterprises, now became seen as a problem labelled 'crony capitalism'. Deeply embedded yet malleable forms of axiorational behaviour that influence Thai capitalism were therefore decried from the outside as illegitimate, such as, for example, the Shinawatras' form of control over their corporate empire. Another example was the close relationship between the Chirathivat family's Central conglomerate and the Sophonpanich family's Bangkok Bank. Central, 'to upgrade its image away from that of a family-run business' (Duangporn 1992: 71), hired more outsiders, generally foreigners from the West and Asia. Even though the economic crisis was caused by the private sector, the International Monetary Fund (IMF) imposed regulations that targeted the public sector, resulting in a fire sale of state enterprises. As a result of the crisis (and responses to it), there are more Western executives in Thai corporations and Western companies have far more of a hold on the Thai economy than they had before. Thais focused their critique on this foreign regulation, and the crisis became known as 'IMF time' (Wilson 2003).

Yet even with such a blatant example of the destructive force of global capital, a contextualised critical understanding of the Asian economic crisis counters the Eurocentric view of Asian modernity as the creation of Western forces. The Asian crisis itself was not simply the result of capital penetration: foreign investments (which were never solely Western) followed upon, and were funnelled through, a speculative economy generated by creolised business elites and trans-Asian flows – by 'non-Western' agents and processes. Asian actors, operating in a broader context shaped by Western hegemonic powers, combined both Western and Asian influences to generate the boom and bust that made Asian modernity. As such, hybridised mimicry was still employed by Asian actors to create new forms that continue to shape everyday practices and in small incremental ways the transformation of the regional and world economies.

10 The agency of subordinate polities: Western hegemony in the East Asian mirror

Shogo Suzuki

At first glance, the political economy of the East Asian international order seems to readily offer a 'home' for regulatory theories of international political economy (IPE), particularly the realist version of hegemonic stability theory, where the order is primarily interpreted as an expression of China's hegemonic interests. East Asia was long dominated by China, and the norms and rules of the regional international order – often (misleadingly) called the 'Chinese world order' – were hegemonic constructs shaped by Confucian philosophy (Fairbank 1968b; Zhang 2001). According to this story, official trade between its member states took the form of 'tributary trade', where goods were presented to the Chinese emperor in the form of tribute, and the emperor dispensed 'official favours' of trading rights and gifts. Furthermore, the order remained remarkably stable; its final collapse only came about in the wake of China's defeat by Japan in 1895, when China's last 'tributary', Korea, was declared an independent, sovereign state in the Treaty of Shimonoseki.

There are two ways of interpreting this international political order. First, it can be interpreted, in similar fashion to Barry Buzan and Richard Little, as a form of a command model of international relations in which 'vassal kingdoms or tribes paid tribute to imperial suzerains or, depending on the balance of power, imperial suzerains paid appeasement bribes to supposed vassals in return for not being attacked by them' (Buzan and Little 2000: 234). The implication here is that states paid tribute to the hegemon whenever the balance of power was in the latter's favour, in a sense 'buying' their security.

Another interpretation is of an international politico-economic order where China played a more benevolent hegemonic role of supplying and enforcing the rules of international economic activity. This view of the Chinese empire as an almost aloof, benign power gains some credibility when we consider the fact that China has often been seen as possessing a self-sufficient economy 'which made supplies unnecessary from abroad' and an ideology that saw 'foreign trade ... an unworthy object for high policy' (Fairbank 1942: 139). Following from this, we can easily picture a hegemon supplying the order necessary for fruitful economic activity (particularly trade with the Chinese empire) within the region. The lesser members of the East Asian international order, then, are quickly relegated to a more passive role; not possessing the material power and riches of China, they have little option but to accept the normative terms set by the hegemon if they wish to benefit from trading with it.

This tale of a largely self-sufficient hegemon providing public goods to the international political economy sounds reminiscent of the United States in the post-1945 period. Indeed, regulatory IPE usually extrapolates from British and American experiences and presents hegemony in an ahistorical manner, arguing that hegemonic domination and the provision of public goods allow 'free-riders' to increase their material capabilities (Gilpin 1987). While there is undoubtedly some truth in this, it is also somewhat simplistic. The biggest reason for this is that it views the agency of weak states as an extension of the hegemon's benevolence. This, in turn, seems to paint a partial picture, as it gives agents very narrow space in which to take *independent* action without the prior sanction of the hegemon. Anything that exceeds this boundary is usually seen as a direct and fundamental challenge to the hegemonic order as a whole. In practice, however, the picture is more complex. Weak actors can indeed act on their own accord and even present some challenges to a hegemon, even though they may not seek to overthrow the hegemonic structures per se. This results in a different depiction from an actor only being able to exercise its agency because the dominant power 'allows' it to, and in order to better capture this more complex picture we are in need of alternative, agent-centred studies.

The main aim of this chapter is to take up this agenda and challenge the 'hegemonic' theoretical focus of conventional IPE by demonstrating how the lesser 'agents' challenged the Chinese hegemon within the social structures of the East Asian international order. Its main focus is on a particular form of contestation by weaker actors which is what the editors call a 'mimetic challenge' (see Chapter 1). In this context a 'mimetic challenge' occurs when a non-hegemonic agent adopts the principles and purposes of the hegemon and constructs an alternative politico-economic order, albeit *within* the overarching hegemonic structures, rather than overthrowing them. By examining this particular form of action, this chapter focuses our attention on the agency of the weak and also on issues of identity and legitimacy. This serves two purposes. First, though not explicitly discussed, nevertheless this chapter's empirical examination of East Asia will generate an alternative account to the Eurocentrism of IPE, which has tended to focus on liberal economic orders maintained under the auspices of Britain and the United States. By examining the different social structures of the East Asian international order, this chapter attempts to problematise conventional rationalist accounts of hegemony. However, while there is a need to move beyond 'Eurocentrism', we must be equally cautious of 'Sinocentrism' and the belief that an understanding of the IPE of East Asia need only be attained through the study of the Chinese empire. The examination of the lesser members – or agents – of this order serves to guard against this fallacy.

The second aim of this chapter is accordingly to focus on the 'weaker' actors within the East Asian international order and explore how they practised their agency in the 'everyday' setting of Chinese hegemony. I do so through a brief case study of Japan's challenge to Chinese moral supremacy in the Tokugawa period (1603–1867). The 'agents' here are the weaker states of the East Asian international order, and in this sense this study does not move beyond the traditional 'statist' predisposition of conventional theories. However, in the context of the East Asian international order, the focus has been overwhelmingly on the central role of the hegemon, China (Fairbank 1968a; Onuma 2000; Zhang 2001), with the examination of its 'junior' members primarily remaining the domain of area specialists. It seems necessary to follow a 'middle path' by examining how 'everyday' agency was demonstrated. Of course, as mentioned above, focus on 'agency' and 'challenges' need not and does not mean an overthrow of the order; as we will see, the members of the East Asian international order worked within the normative framework of their international social environment, and any exertion of power took place within it. Working within this social environment does not undermine the agency of weak actors but instead provides a clear menu of options for ways to transform it. By examining agency within specific social boundaries, potential paths for emancipation may be revealed.

A number of definitions need to be made explicit from the outset. Identity is defined in collective terms in this chapter, and is understood to be formed through membership of an order and interaction with its members. It is, in Alexander Wendt's words, 'sets of meanings that an actor attributes to itself while taking the perspective of others, that is, as a social object' (Wendt 1994: 385). Members' interests are derived from their international social environment, and are shared collectively by members of the order. As elaborated below, the 'moral purpose of the state' within the East Asian international order derived from Confucianism, and aimed for 'the support and maintenance of the moral, social, and cultural order of social peace and harmony' (Schwartz 1964: 10). Accordingly states' fundamental interests within the order became one of enhancing and demonstrating to their peers their ability to maintain the appropriate social hierarchies that would promote cosmic harmony. In Confucian thought, those who stood at the apex of the social hierarchy were charged with the role of maintaining it. This can be understood as a form of noblesse oblige; it was considered a prerogative of the virtuous, and carried substantial prestige. Member states of the East Asian international order thus competed in placing themselves at the highest social position possible. This also reflected the hierarchical 'organising principle of sovereignty' (Reus-Smit 1999) of the East Asian international order.

As mentioned above, the constitutive norms of the East Asian international order were hegemonic constructs that originated from China, and were premised on Confucianism and the assumption of Chinese supremacy. Many states that wished to enter diplomatic relations with China often had little choice but to accept them. The term 'Chinese world order', however, also gives the impression of a monolithic order in which China's pre-eminence was never in doubt. Such Sinocentrism must be avoided. As will become clear in the discussions below, this was hardly the case; a lot more contestation took place within this order than the term 'Chinese world order' implies. At the same time, it is important to keep in mind that these states (Japan, Korea, Ryūkyū, present day Okinawa and Vietnam) never challenged the constitutive norms of the order, indicating that they had to a certain extent internalised the normative stipulations of the Sinocentric international order. All of these states had a long history of cultural borrowing from China, and had internalised Confucian ideology. They shared a 'common image of the world' (Onuma 2000: 11), which formed the basis for the social structures of the East Asian international order, far more than any of China's other neighbours.

The constitutional structures of the East Asian international order

The constitutional structures of the East Asian international order were primarily the extension of universalist Confucian philosophy. Confucian philosophy placed great emphasis on ethical governance, and argued that a 'gentleman' – particularly a ruler – should possess the qualities of 'uprightness or inner integrity ..., righteousness ..., conscientiousness towards others or loyalty ..., altruism or reciprocity ..., and above all, love or human-heartedness' (Fairbank and Reischauer 1989: 20; cf Hsu 1991). But these virtues had to be demonstrated through the appropriate etiquette. Consequently, Confucianism placed great emphasis on the maintenance of hierarchically-defined social relations. This was to be achieved

... by teaching all mortals respect for the five fundamental human relationships: those between man and woman ..., father and son, older and younger friend, friend and friend, sovereign and minister (or subject). When the timeless patterns of these associations were fully understood and realized, peace, order, and happiness were to prevail in the entire community. (Bozeman 1994: 135)

While the degree to which China actually applied 'benevolent' Confucian principles in its international behaviour is highly debatable (Johnston 1995), the normative need to maintain 'proper' social hierarchies did find its expression in the constitutional structures of the East Asian international order.

The organising principle of sovereignty within the tribute system was along hierarchical, familial lines, and provides an interesting contrast with European International Society, where its core 'civilised' members all nominally enjoyed sovereign equality. As Immanuel Hsü has argued, relations within the East Asian international order 'were much like those between members of a family, far more so than the relations between Western nations. It is literally correct to describe them as constituting their own family of nations in East Asia' (Hsü 1960: 3). China assumed (at least theoretically) its superior hierarchical position over all the other polities that surrounded it. The Chinese believed that 'the all-wise example and virtue ... of the Son of Heaven not only reached throughout China proper but continued outward beyond the borders of China to all mankind ... albeit with gradually decreasing efficacy, as parts of a concentric hierarchy' (Fairbank 1968b: 8).

The 'systemic norm of procedural justice' of the tribute system corresponded closely to what Christian Reus-Smit has termed 'ritual justice' (Reus-Smit 1999). The concept of an enforceable, 'international' law was alien to the East Asian international order, and had little role to play (Onuma 2000: 16). Accordingly, diplomacy was carried out primarily in the form of elaborate rituals which extended from Confucian norms and paid particular attention to members' social standing and its maintenance (Fairbank 1968b; Hamashita 1990; Huang 1992). Non-Chinese rulers' envoys would present tribute to the emperor, often in the company of imperial guards and other foreign envoys, which demonstrated both the inclusive character of the Chinese empire and the wide-ranging loyalty the emperor commanded (Hevia 1995: 116–33). They would perform the kowtow to the Chinese emperor, confirming the latter's superior status, and present tribute. The Chinese Son of Heaven (as the emperor was known) would in return present the envoy with gifts, usually of greater value than those which the tributary ruler had presented. Tributary missions were also allowed to take goods out of the country tax-free. This was yet another way of demonstrating a superior position within the order's social hierarchy. Imperial permission to trade 'was intended to be a mark of imperial bounty' to demonstrate China's riches and seeming lack of necessity to trade (Fairbank and Teng 1941: 140), as well as the emperor's benevolence for granting such privileges to the foreigners. In imperial audiences, the emperor would address the foreign envoys in paternalistic language, and this 'embodie[d] aspects of sagely and virtuous kingly rule and, as such, had the power to reorient others' towards Chinese civilisation (Hevia 1995: 120). The tributary states would also be given a seal of investiture and calendar which used the reign title of the Chinese emperor. The Chinese emperor was considered to occupy a unique position between humankind and heaven, and the 'proclamation of the calendar had early become one of the prerogatives of the Son of Heaven' whose job was to 'intermediate between Heaven and Man' (Toby 1991: 90). Foreign rulers' use of the Chinese calendar thus provided the emperor 'with external confirmation of the legitimacy of [his] tenure in the office of cosmic mediator' (Toby 1991: 90). The use of the Chinese calendar thus also denoted hierarchical difference within the East Asian international order.

This hierarchical difference was based on the 'common cornerstone of the ka-i [huayi Middle Kingdom-Barbarian] edifice ... [which] was the logic of difference' (Morris-Suzuki 1996: 51) designed to accentuate the

Table 10.1. *Constitutional structures and fundamental institutions in European international society and the East Asian international order*

Societies of States	International society for European states	East Asian international order
Constitutional structures		
1. Moral purpose of state	Augmentation of individuals' purposes and potentialities	Promoting cosmic and social harmony
2. Organising principle of sovereignty	Sovereign equality, liberal sovereignty	Sovereign hierarchy (civilisational)
3. Systemic norm of procedural justice	Legislative justice (based on positive law)	Ritual justice
Fundamental institutions	Contractual international law Multilateralism	Tribute system

Source: Reus-Smit (1999: 7); Zhang (2001: 57).

differences between the centre of civilisation and peripheral 'barbarians', and reflected the core metanorm of the 'moral purpose of the state' of the East Asian international order. Non-Chinese states were expected to demonstrate their loyalty and filial piety towards the paternal state by offering tribute. The elaborate rituals which governed the presenting of tribute accentuated Chinese hierarchical superiority, and served to reproduce and maintain the Sinocentric world order. Tributary states were usually known to the Chinese as 'vassal states' (*chen* or *shuguo*) or 'suzerains'; while these terms may seem to imply a form of control by the dominant power, the Chinese did not necessarily exert domestic control over the member states of the East Asian international order, and neither did they necessarily control the latter's relations with other non-Chinese states (Nelson 1946: 88; Wang 1997: 28).

The political economy of the East Asian international order

Official economic interaction between member states also served to reinforce the constitutional structures of the East Asian international order. Surprisingly, the symbiotic relationship between international trade and the order's normative structures has not been given the close attention it deserves. This is not to suggest that historians have ignored trade and its connections with the tribute system. However, there exists a tension between a clear recognition of the close connection between trade and the maintenance of the tribute system, and an implicit interpretation of economic activity as a 'rational' realm where rituals and symbols have little part to play. John King Fairbank (1942: 139), for instance, commented:

> it seems anomalous that foreign trade could be considered in Chinese theory to be subordinate to tribute, but so it was. ... In the modern period the Confucian bureaucracy tried to treat the new trading nations of the west as mere tributaries. Naturally they failed, being incapable of changing their immemorial theory to fit a new situation.

The main problem with this statement is that it implicitly assumes that economic activities should take place in a *separate* realm from political relations and do not differ in their nature across geographical space or time; the presentation of tribute thus gets relegated as a form of court ritual or a 'cloak for trade', and its role within the IPE of the East Asian international order gets ignored.

Some historians of the tribute system, however, neglect this dimension, and such interpretations of 'tributary trade' consequently give rise to two further shortcomings. The first is that tributary trade (as opposed to the Western ideological construct of 'free trade') is seen as inherently 'irrational' and intellectually rigid – a view which leads back into Eurocentrism. Secondly, this depiction inadvertently leads to a somewhat narrow, power-politics based view of the East Asian international order. Participation in such 'irrational' economic activities can only make sense if the participants are either equally 'irrational', or the order can supply narrowly defined material benefits (Fairbank 1942). While the latter explanation may be true to non-Chinese states that traded with China, this account again downplays the agency of weaker actors, narrowly focusing on their economic activities as dictated by the hegemon because they had no choice if they wanted to trade with China. This consequently downplays any political power they may have exerted within this relationship.

It is thus more fruitful to conceptualise tributary trade as forming an integral part of the social structures of the East Asian international order. Once this step is taken, official international trade within the order can be reinterpreted as an important 'stage' where its members demonstrated and contested their positions within the social hierarchy. Official international trade was not only a means to make economic gains; it was closely intertwined with the moral purpose of promoting cosmic and social harmony through the maintenance of social hierarchies.

From China's viewpoint, its identity within the East Asian international order was that of the apex of the social hierarchy of the international order, and it assumed itself to have 'the mandate of Heaven to rule *Tianxia* (all-under-heaven)' (Zhang 2001: 53). This meant that it was a given that 'the Chinese world order had to be hierarchical, with the Chinese emperor sitting at the apex of this order with a heavenly mandate' (Zhang 2001: 53). This identity, in turn, informed the fundamental interests of the Chinese empire which centred around the maintenance of appropriate social hierarchies that would reaffirm China's superior moral standing. Tributary trade thus became a sign that 'barbarians' 'could not but appreciate the superiority of Chinese civilization', and was a natural act of 'seek[ing] to "come and be transformed" (*lai-hua*) and so participate in its benefits' (Fairbank 1942: 132), and enhance the social prestige of China. Such international public goods were markers of the emperor's paternalistic benevolence (which again reflected his superior social standing), and were intended to (theoretically at least) keep 'the barbarians in the proper state of submissiveness' and demonstrate imperial virtue (Fairbank and Teng 1941: 140).

The East Asian international order: an agent-centred view

At this point it is necessary to move beyond our Sinocentric focus and examine how the non-Chinese members acted within the East Asian international order. This is for two reasons: a top-down view gives the impression of a social order which is forced upon weaker actors and commands very little legitimacy. To avoid this problem, we need to carry out a more agent-focused investigation. A second reason is that this approach helps us move beyond the 'structural' focus which has been dominant within the broader discipline of IPE. Once we accept that the economic activities of the member states of the East Asian international order had a symbiotic relationship with the latter's socio-political structures, it is possible to generate a more nuanced, agent-centric account of IPE, while avoiding the pitfalls of conceptualising structure and agency in oppositional terms.

Legitimacy of the East Asian international order

The most compelling evidence of the legitimacy the East Asian international order achieved comes from its remarkable longevity. For centuries, the order and its fundamental institution, the tribute system, continued to function well into the nineteenth century. What explains this? There is no doubt that in many instances power relations were an important determining factor. While some scholars (particularly Chinese scholars) have maintained that China's behaviour towards its most Sinified neighbours was generally a peaceful one, this gives an overly Sinocentric impression and ignores the fact that in many historical periods China remained the regional hegemon in East Asia. It was often in a position to enforce its norms on smaller neighbouring polities, and was more than willing to abandon 'benevolent' Confucian norms to impose its will on others (Ōsawa 1975; Inoguchi 1975; Ledyard 1983; Johnston 1995).

It thus comes as no surprise to us to find ample evidence that the norms of the constitutional structure were transmitted to these states. Indeed, it has been argued that sustained contact between actors tends to reproduce the institutions and norms of the hegemonic ideas governing international systems. As states become more integrated into the international system and its constitutive structure, they come 'under a strong compulsion to justify their actions in terms of the system's primary norms of coexistence' (Reus-Smit 1999: 35). The result is a stable pattern of behaviour that strongly reflects the norms of the constitutional structure. The member states of the East Asian international order were no exception. The expansion of the order's constitutional structures which resulted in the formation of a distinctive Sinocentric regional order was primarily a result of extensive contact between China and its East Asian neighbours. States in East Asia engaged in trade and cultural exchanges with the Chinese to facilitate their own development. In their dealings with Imperial China, by far their most powerful neighbour, they had little choice but to participate in the system if they wished to maintain their ties with the Chinese.

This largely power-based explanation, however, only tells half of the story. The problem with this explanation is that is assumes that any international hierarchical structure necessarily lacks legitimacy, and cannot be maintained for a sustained length of time unless the hegemon remains capable of providing public goods or coercing other members of the system. At times, however, the Chinese empire was too weak to effectively enforce the rules, and polities that did not share Confucian culture often ignored the tribute system and its rules. China's pretensions to supremacy thus became a 'myth' that was maintained for domestic purposes (Yang 1968; Krasner 2001: 182–5). Furthermore, the Chinese regularly suffered military defeats at the hands of nomadic tribes from Central Asia, and at times were forced to acknowledge – much to their annoyance and anguish – social equality or even inferiority vis-à-vis the 'barbarian' kings (Rossabi 1983; Zhang 2001: 54).

Despite these limitations of Chinese power, in the case of East Asia the system seems to '[prevail] in times of Imperial China's military weakness precisely because military strength on its own is neither a necessary nor a sufficient condition for the maintenance of this order' (Zhang 2001: 57–8). This suggests that the constitutional structure of the East Asian international system and the tribute system, its fundamental institution, did indeed gain a significant degree of acceptance among the member states in East Asia. As Yongjin Zhang has argued, '[s]o long as the hegemonic belief in the moral purpose of the state and more broadly, of the political community incarnated in Confucianism, prevails, the tribute system as a basic institutional practices [sic] is likely to stay' (Zhang 2001: 57). While China's neighbours may not have ultimately been able to overthrow the tribute system and the East Asian international order, there is no evidence that they sought to do so until Japan did in the late nineteenth century. This is not to imply that the members of the East Asian international order *never* challenged the more Sinocentric norms inherent in the order, as this did indeed take place (as the following discussions will show). 'Mimetic challenges' constituted precisely just such a challenge.

*From 'Barbarian' to 'Middle Kingdom': contestation in the East
Asian international order*

A 'mimetic challenge' within the East Asian international order took the
form of usurping China's social role of 'Middle Kingdom' and establish-
ing an alternative tribute system with the challenger in the centre. Of
course, most members of the East Asian international order did not
possess the military power to pose a fundamental challenge to Chinese
hegemony. Rather, their challenges took the form of contesting the
Chinese empire's Sinocentric assumed supremacy within the East Asian
international order. It would be a mistake to assume that this constituted
an overthrow of the East Asian international order, however; the point is
that while these contestations did take place, they occurred *within* the
order, and did not constitute a challenge to the order itself. By claiming to
be the 'centre' of the social order, the challenger is merely taking over
China's role in 'promoting cosmic and social harmony' (Zhang 2001:
56), while the 'moral purpose of the state' remains the same. Similarly,
the fact that the tribute system continues to be used in the process of
legitimating the claims of the usurper's superior social hierarchy is an
indication that the ritualistic 'systemic norm of procedural justice' has
been left intact.

A challenger would typically take over the responsibility 'for maintaining and harmonizing [the Confucian] social order with the moral examples
it set' (Zhang 2001: 53), even though this 'caused a disjuncture between
reality and cognition' (Hamashita 1999: 38). It would then 'place itself in
the "centre" in relation to its Tributary and non-Tributary states, and
behave like a "Middle Kingdom" in its own right' (Hamashita 1999: 38).
Sakayori Masashi notes that this process of sorting surrounding polities in
a hierarchical order was 'modelled on Sinocentrism and was a necessary
political ideology for legitimating domestic rule and, in the context of
expanding territorial rule, for demonstrating dynastic legitimacy among
the ruling elite' (Sakayori 1993: 53). A challenger would take on the role of
receiving tributary missions. In similar fashion to China, it would place
itself at a higher echelon by requiring its own 'tributaries' to perform
appropriate rituals. The ritual confirmation of the state's 'Middle
Kingdom' status had the effect of demonstrating that the ruler's 'virtue'
had spread far and wide, thus confirming the challenger's superior moral
status, while simultaneously highlighting its capacity to take on the role of
a 'Middle Kingdom' that was able to 'cherish' those at the lower end of the
social order.

But when were the weaker social actors presented with such an opportunity? Was China vulnerable to such contestation? Was the Chinese

empire, even at times of weakness, simply far too powerful to be challenged? One window of opportunity was found in the realm of political
economy, and Japan's 'mimetic challenge' to China's claim to 'Middle
Kingdom' status will be examined in this context.

Japan's challenge to Sinocentrism

Japan had long occupied a position somewhat different from other tributary states in the East Asian international order. It had a long history of
cultural borrowing from China and was a regular participant in the tribute
system, particularly in the eighth century. However, Japan was generally a
peripheral 'tributary state', at least from the Chinese point of view.
Geographical distance meant that missions to China were costly (and at
times dangerous), and Japanese tribute missions were often highly
sporadic as a result. Furthermore, Japan never completely accepted inferior status vis-à-vis China, largely due to Japan's 'self-perception, in large
measure bound up with the mythology of imperial divinity,' which 'made
the acknowledgement of any supervening authority extremely difficult'
(Toby 1991: 172; cf. Wang 1953: 18; Tsukamoto 1979: 3).

The Tokugawa shogunate, which came to power in 1603, was no
exception to this. However, their rejection of Sinocentrism presented
them with a potential problem. In theory, a non-Chinese state had to
seek China's investiture for legitimate statehood in the East Asian international order. As the regional hegemon, China's claims to moral
supremacy were not easily challenged. Seeking Chinese approval for
Tokugawa rule was a risky tactic, however. In the context of the early
Tokugawa period, it would 'require that . . . the representative of Japan . . .
compromise the very independent legitimacy and sovereignty that he
was seeking to establish, by petitioning the Ming emperor in a formal
document . . . in which he called himself a "subject" of Ming, dated in the
Ming calendar' (Toby 1991: 58). Any admission of Chinese supremacy
was sure to hurt Japanese pride and have potentially negative consequences for the Tokugawa shogunate's attempts to legitimate their rule.

The solution to this was found by developing two policies. First, the
Japanese did not seek investiture from China. The resolve to pursue this
policy was strengthened by the rise of the Manchurian Qing dynasty as
the new ruling dynasty of China. The rise of a dynasty ruled by non-Han
Chinese 'barbarians' came as a considerable shock to many in Japanese
elite circles. While feelings towards China remained riddled with contradictions, the emergence of the Qing dynasty did make the Japanese even
more reluctant to seek Chinese investiture (Tsukamoto 1982: 38–56;
Toby 1991: 110–67, 222–5).

Second, following from above, the Japanese now established their own alternative tribute system, which was 'an alternative order of Japanese fantasy, a looking glass which might reflect the reemergent centrality of a newly reunified Japan' (Toby 1991: 173). The centrality (or social superiority) of Japan was demonstrated through elaborate diplomatic rituals and protocol based on the Chinese model. As Ronald P. Toby notes, '[t]he criterion upon which one determined whether a person, or a country, was civilized ... was whether that country knew proper ethics and observed proper ritual' (Toby 1991: 226). Thus, diplomatic correspondence would take place using different forms of language in accordance with the social status of the other party, and visits by foreign envoys were governed by strict rules that would denote the visiting envoy's status within the Japanese tribute system: even banquet and seating arrangements in audiences with the shōgun were minutely specified.

Accordingly, Japan invited tribute missions from Korea and the Ryūkyū kingdom, placing the former on an equal social standing, while the latter was classified as an inferior. China was placed on the lowest rung of the social ladder of the Japan-centric tribute system, with corresponding diplomatic protocol. Correspondence with China was dealt with by Tokugawa authorities of relatively low rank, befitting the former's lowly status. The Chinese were not allowed the 'privilege' of an audience with the shōgun, something granted to the Koreans and the Ryūkyūans. To this end, any references which may have implied Chinese superiority were eliminated in Japanese diplomatic intercourse. The Tokugawa rulers did not use the title 'king' (wang/ō), which implied inferior status to the Chinese emperor. Neither did they use the Chinese calendar in their correspondence.

Although it is tempting to suggest that this constituted a fundamental challenge to the East Asian international order, and indicates a shift in Japan's identity and interest, this was not the case. As noted above, while Japan's actions did contest the norms of the Sinocentric international order, we must be mindful of the fact that this was an 'everyday' form of contestation which did not seek a fundamental challenge of the international politico-economic order, but instead took place *within* the Chinese hegemonic system. This can be seen from the fact that Korea and Ryūkyū continued sending tribute missions to China, while Japan continued to conduct its diplomatic and economic relations within the normative framework of the East Asian international order just as it had done before. The difference now was that Japan assumed the position of the virtuous state, the *ka*, or 'Middle Kingdom'. The assumption of this status entailed labelling other polities as 'barbarians', and its neighbours (including China) readily filled this position (cf. Neumann and Welsh

1991; Neuman 1996, 1999). Tributary missions from Korea and Ryūkyū continued to be an important means by which to enhance Japanese legitimacy, and this is indicative of the fact that the 'constitutional structure of procedural justice' in the Japan-centric tribute system remained one of 'ritual justice' informed by the norms of the Sinocentric tribute system. In similar fashion to the Chinese reception of tributary missions, recognition by fellow member states would serve to show that the Tokugawa's virtuous rule and prestige had emanated far and wide, bolstering the regime's domestic and international legitimacy (Tanaka 1975: 264).

Mimetic challenges and trade

The Tokugawa's refusal to seek Chinese investiture meant that official, 'tributary' relations did not exist between China and Japan throughout the seventeenth century. But this did not mean that the two states ceased contact. While Japan did not seek direct diplomatic relations with both the Ming and Qing, the first shōgun, Tokugawa Ieyasu, was interested in trade with China, and in reality the Tokugawa shogunate could not entirely ignore its powerful neighbour (Tanaka 1975: 265; Toby 1991: 55–61). The eventual solution was to continue trading without compromising Japan's perceived position as the 'Middle Kingdom' of its own tribute system. Chinese traders were permitted to come to Nagasaki to trade, and indirect trade was continued through Korea and the Ryūkyū Kingdom.

The lack of official, diplomatic relations did not deter the Japanese from seizing the opportunity to demonstrate their 'superior' status towards the Chinese, however. The fact that the social norms of the East Asian international order were embedded in international trade meant that Japan's mimetic challenge to Qing China's 'Middle Kingdom' status would become entangled with Sino-Japanese economic relations.

By the eighteenth century, China's hierarchical position within Japan's alternative tribute system was further downgraded. This was spurred on by the fact that 'the rise of the Qing was understood by East Asian intellectuals as a change from a "civilised" Han Chinese state to a "barbarian" Manchu state' (Arano 1988: 37). Japan issued the Chinese with *shinpai*, a form of passport that was to be used by officially sanctioned merchants. While the issuing of the *shinpai* was also a means to prevent the drain of silver and copper out of Japan (Tashiro 1982: 294–296), it also served to establish Japan's 'superior position' in the international hierarchy, as it forced Chinese merchants to accept documents in the *Japanese* calendar. This was a powerful reminder of their 'inferior' status within the Japan-centric tribute system, as well as a clear indication that Japan had taken over the role of mediating between humankind and heaven. In his excellent study of Tokugawa Japan's diplomacy, Toby (1991: 199) explains this particular aspect of the *shinpai* system as follows:

The Chinese were barbarians: the credentials were dated in the Japanese calendar; they called China 'T'ang [Tang, or kara in Japanese],' the vulgar Japanese name for that country, rather than 'ta-Ch'ing [Da Qing],' the formal name usually used in diplomatic discourse ... If Chinese merchants accepted the use of the Japanese calendar, were they not also signalling Chinese acknowledgement of Japan's central role in the world yielding the center to Japan?

Chinese resentment towards the *shinpai* system was strong at the outset, even resulting in merchants petitioning the Qing officials that China was being compelled to enter into subordinate relations with Japan. This issue reached the ears of the Kangxi emperor, but the emperor gave his approval of such Japanese policies. Of course, this had the effect of 'depriving China of the diplomatic symbols of her claims to superiority and centrality . the implication was strengthened by the emperor's acquiescence, Chinese recognition of Japanese superiority and centrality' (Toby 1991: 201).

Why did the Qing accept this blatant defiance to its claims to superiority? One simple reason is that Chinese self-confidence was such that Japanese mimesis – while theoretically constituting a direct challenge to the Qing's superior social status – was not regarded as worth punishing. There were of course practical reasons to be considered – a punitive expedition to Japan would be costly – but the Chinese had also been threatened and even ruled by nomadic tribes they considered barbarians, and were forced to compromise on their claims to hierarchical supremacy (Rossabi 1983). However, Chinese confidence in its *civilisational* (if not military) superiority rarely wavered. Foreigners' lack of respect for Chinese 'superiority' could thus easily be explained and brushed aside as resulting from the former's rudeness (which was to be expected from 'barbarians') and profound ignorance of the benefits Chinese civilisation could offer. Besides, there were enough tributary states to ensure China's superiority complex remained intact, and provided the dynasty's rule was not militarily challenged, recalcitrant barbarians like the Japanese could be easily ignored.

Another answer lies in the peculiar vulnerability the Chinese had developed in their economic relations vis-à-vis Japan. Of course, the same can be said for the Japanese, for their issuing of the *shinpai* was partially (if not exclusively) motivated by their need to protect their copper and silver from haemorrhaging into China. The point is, however, that this vulnerability went both ways. Naturally, the Chinese were not particularly keen on letting their neighbours know of this, and they tried their best to maintain the 'myth' of Chinese superiority through rituals and symbols. In the realm of political economy, the discussion above has argued that the aura of Chinese superiority was transmitted through demonstrating China's abundance of material riches, as well as high-lighting the emperor's generosity of 'granting' trade, despite his lack of need to do so: but China was by no means impervious to economic dependency.

One area of Chinese vulnerability was in the trading of precious metals, namely silver and copper. The cause of China's dependence on silver and copper can be traced back to the decline in the Ming dynasty's paper currency. This led to the growth of a bimetallic monetary system based on silver and copper. By the mid-sixteenth century 'the Ming government introduced the so-called "Single Whip Method" [yitiao bianfa] into its outmoded and appallingly complicated system of taxation ... it essen-tially meant that most land taxes, labour service obligations, and extra levies were commuted into silver payments' (Atwell 1982: 84). The Chinese empire consequently developed a voracious appetite for these minerals.

The repercussions of this development were significant. The high price of silver in China drew in silver throughout the world, encouraging arbitrage trade (Flynn and Giráldez 2002; Hobson 2004: 66). 'There is ample evidence', Dennis O Flynn and Arturo Giráldez write (2002: 400), 'that American silver flowing into India was reexported to China and Southeast Asia'. While this dependence was linked to the world economy, it also presented a window of opportunity for members of the East Asian international order to challenge China's assumed position in the order's social hierarchy and enhance their own status. To be sure, they had been contesting China's 'Middle Kingdom' status regardless of their trade status with China; however, if they could develop extensive trade relations with China and create some dependency, there was less chance of China taking any action to prevent their challenges.

Japan played a crucial role in the Chinese economy in this context. Along with South America, it was one of the key producers of silver and copper in the seventeenth and eighteenth century, and its proximity made it a key supplier for the Chinese market. China, for its part, grew highly dependent on Japanese silver and copper. In addition to its demand for silver, it had exhausted domestic copper ore supplies and 'the use of inefficient refining and casting techniques had produced a chronic lack of coinage' (Tashiro 1982: 295). Until the early eighteenth century (when new mines were discovered) the Qing mints were heavily dependent on Japanese copper (Yang 1952: 38). This gave the Chinese even less reason to punish the Japanese for their lack of respect for the 'Middle Kingdom': the Japanese mimetic challenge, while empowering the Japanese, was certainly not enough for the Chinese to start worrying about the usurpation of their position at the pinnacle of the East Asian international order. Furthermore, if any attempts to punish these ignorant 'barbarians' could spoil an already beneficial trading relationship, then why do so?

Conclusion

What does the East Asian experience suggest to us in the context of 'everyday' challenges? Most importantly, it suggests that weaker actors can demonstrate their agency even under the social normative framework of the Sinocentric hegemonic system. The challenges mounted by the Japanese – such as forcing Chinese merchants to accept the Japanese calendar – were carried out within the normative framework of the East Asian international order. They did not fundamentally shake Chinese confidence in their own superiority, and neither did their 'mimetic challenge' fundamentally overturn the Sinocentric international environment. In this sense, Japan's 'mimetic challenge' undoubtedly constituted a small, 'everyday' form of contestation in this statist story. However, the results that these challenges produced are more significant than meets the eye: the Japanese did succeed in forcing the Chinese to accept a symbolically subordinate social position within their bilateral relations, and this very fact demonstrated that the 'myth' of Chinese superiority – the key theoretical assumption within the East Asian international order – was not impregnable.

The case of the East Asian international order gives us interesting comparisons in our study of hegemony in the context of the contemporary international financial order. This is more than simply a matter of overcoming Eurocentrism, although this is also important. Rather, a comparative examination of hegemonic orders compels us to review our key assumptions which continue to colour our studies. Conventional studies of hegemony and international (financial) order have on the whole tended to assume the primacy of material power and its accumulation, both for hegemons and rising powers. The East Asian case, however, also demonstrates the important role social power plays in international orders. This is not to suggest that material power did not matter at all in the East Asian international order, as the clear link between trade and tributary relations demonstrates quite clearly. The point, however, is that we cannot take for granted that material power is going to assume primacy in hegemonic orders, and the 'markers' of power need to be problematised, rather than assumed. In East Asia, some states would assign greater importance to their social standing within the hierarchy of their international environment. As the Japanese scholar Tanaka Takeo pointed out, in the bilateral relations of Korea and Japan in the seventeenth century, 'the goal was "neither books, nor technology, nor profit," in shogunal diplomacy, "but the establishment of international order"' (Toby 1991: 218–19). Even if many cases were not as clear cut as the Korean-Japanese case, in most instances, the importance attached to material and social power was interrelated to such an extent that it becomes difficult for us to distinguish between the two.

The concept of 'mimetic challenge' also points the way to a more agent-centred research agenda within the literature of IPE. Mainstream debates which focus on hegemonic orders have simplistically framed agents either as faceless 'power-takers' who do not contest the hegemon and its order while structural inequalities exist, or as 'revisionist' powers who seek to launch a fundamental challenge to the very fabric of the international economic order. This, however, obscures many small-scale, 'everyday' contestations which take place within hegemonic orders. The Japanese case suggests to us that weak actors can mount challenges to the economic order while simultaneously adopting the language and symbols of moral authority; they thus frame their contestations as 'legitimate' practices and this in turn socially empowers their challenges. Furthermore, these challenges can, as we have seen in the case of Japan, have some significant effects on weaker actors' perceptions of the hegemonic order's normative structures. In the case of Japan, its 'mimetic challenge' to Chinese 'Middle Kingdom' status could well have relativised its moral authority and paved the way to its quick acceptance of the new, 'superior' European-dominated international order in the nineteenth century, as well as its socialisation into it (Suzuki 2005). 'Mimetic challenges', however, are harder to locate, precisely because they take place within the given politico-economic order and use the very same symbols used by the more powerful actors. An overly top-down theoretical framework, however, will blind us to these 'everyday' activities and their potential to inform political change.

A focus on weaker actors and the exercise of their agency also suggests that a more 'emancipatory' research agenda is possible within IPE. Conventional scholarship has, as suggested in this volume, focused on hegemonic actors and orders, often with the implicit assumption that the hegemon provides a collective good from which all actors can benefit. This particular interpretation, however, results in the production of what

Robert W. Cox famously termed as 'problem-solving' theories, which 'takes the world as it finds it, with the prevailing social and power relationships and the institutions into which they are organized, as the given framework of action' (Cox 1996: 88). It also risks concentrating solely on the 'winners' of the global economic order.

Such theories often obscure the weaker actors, subjected to structural inequalities within the global economic order. The case study of the East Asian international order seems to suggest that greater scholarly attention to these marginalised actors may highlight how marginalised actors try to improve their lives through 'everyday' activities. The Japanese mimetic challenge under the East Asian international order was just one of the many 'everyday' challenges that the Chinese experienced and eventually resulted in them compromising their adherence to Sinocentric superiority. In the context of contemporary IPE, it is by no means inconceivable that everyday politics by weaker, marginalised actors will eventually lead to a weakening in the 'illiberal' propagation of hegemonic neo-liberal economic principles and allow for the emergence of alternative ideologies which may empower marginalised actors. These in turn point the way to potential paths which can be taken up to achieve a more just global economic order.

11   Conclusion: everyday IPE puzzle sets, teaching and policy agendas

John M. Hobson and Leonard Seabrooke

In the introductory chapter we set out the parameters of everyday international political economy (EIPE). In this final, concluding chapter we undertake three tasks. First, we elaborate on the 'puzzle-set' framework set out in the Introduction. The puzzle sets provide us with a way of thinking about new topics that EIPE brings to light, many of which have conventionally been ignored. Second, we present ways in which the teaching of EIPE might be conducted, not least so as to consolidate the arguments made for EIPE. And third, we focus on the policy implications of our approach. In short, this concluding chapter outlines why puzzle sets are of heuristic value; how they provide a coherent teaching program for students to productively blend regulatory IPE (RIPE) and EIPE to new ends, and the insights that the EIPE puzzle set may bring to real-world policy development.

Puzzle sets not research programs

EIPE seeks to channel the many research agendas of heterodox IPE through a focus on everyday actor agency, while also addressing the concerns of RIPE. As established in the Introduction, within orthodox IPE a range of prominent scholars have expressed some dissatisfaction with the narrowness of questions asked within the discipline and have lamented the growing gap between research driven by demonstrations of social scientific rigour within a research program and policy relevance (Katzenstein et al. 1998). The push for increasingly stringent social science methodological standards is not, in our view, necessarily tied to RIPE's obsession with explaining order and economic distribution driven by the top 10 per cent of the population (and affecting only the bottom 10 per cent). Indeed, not only qualitative but also quantitative models are important to the development of EIPE in outlining political and economic trends among a broader population, rather than the 'winners' and 'losers' that RIPE tends to focus on. The advantage of quantitative models is that they are able to reveal the most common forms of behaviour or action (as found typically in regression analyses). Indeed, in our view, quantitative methods are well-suited to revealing how most people live, which can provide keen insights into broader changes in the world economy.

To enhance our capacity to capture how everyday actions are important in the transformation of the world economy we require a good dose of what Peter Katzenstein and others refer to as 'analytical eclecticism' (Katzenstein and Okawara 2001/2; Sil and Katzenstein 2005). Here the analytical tools required depend not on the theory to be tested but the questions to be answered, which inclines away from theoretical reification. It is precisely this aim that our emphasis on puzzle sets seeks to produce: question-driven rather than theory-driven research. This is the way to discover new information about everyday actions, and the best means to start here is to review the main types of everyday action associated with our puzzle sets. These were outlined in the Introduction and were played out in the case studies. Recapping these provides us with an avenue into a discussion on puzzle sets.

In the Introduction we outlined how RIPE commonly explains change in the world economy through three types of action that are all elite-focused – specifically 'coercion', 'mimetic conformity' and 'radical uncertainty'. By contrast we posited three kinds of action that everyday actors use to assert their agency within the political and economic constraints of their environment – 'defiance', 'mimetic challenge' and 'axiorational' behaviour. Defiance provides the most obvious form of action that may be undertaken by everyday actors – overt resistance and protest against those who are dominant. The chapters by Andrew Herod, Adam Morton and Michele Ford and Nicola Piper provide examples of this type of action. The second type of action, mimetic challenge, involves everyday actors intentionally adopting the discourse and structures of the dominant in order to challenge the legitimacy of what they perceive to be an 'unjust' system. The chapters by Shogo Suzuki, Jason Sharman and Ara Wilson illustrate how powerful this subtle form of resistance can be.

On a *prima facie* reading it might be thought that the third form of agential power – axiorationality – is the least effective form of agency. Typically defiance, which is certainly the most dramatic form of agency, is popularly imagined to be the most effective in achieving a certain end (think of the recent French race riots for example, or the violence deployed by Third World anti-colonial movements, or the Bolsheviks in Russia). But axiorationality, which is understood as reason-guided behaviour that is neither purely instrumental nor purely valued-oriented, leads to incremental everyday actions that can have no less an important impact on effecting change in the world economy. And while these actions are not immediately dramatic and are often not 'political' in motive, their political impact can nonetheless be profound (Kerkvliet 2005; Seabrooke 2006a: Ch. 2). Axirational behaviour, as we understand it, is the most common form of behaviour in the world economy, especially since actors cannot *socially* act only upon instrumental goals or value goals all of the time. As such, understanding axirational behaviour requires us to investigate how actors use reason to create incremental change in their everyday lives (see also Seabrooke and Sending 2006). John Hobson, Paul Langley, Leonard Seabrooke and Ara Wilson provide cases of why we should see axirational agency as an important source of change in the world economy, and how differentiating its forms over time provides a more historically sensitive analysis of change.

These three types of action are not restricted to the case studies in this book. Nor are they restricted to the three main themes that this book has used to create an intellectual division of labour ('Regimes as cultural weapons of the weak', 'Global economic change from below' and 'Bringing Eastern agents in'). However, we suggest here that scholars and students alike may consider how our three forms of everyday action and three themes may be combined in various ways to discover new puzzles. The creation of puzzles, in turn, requires us to discover new information about how the world economy works. We encourage the reader to 'mix and match' with the hope of finding new empirical cases and pushing the conceptual boat of EIPE out much further. Such 'analytical eclecticism' provides a fruitful means to discover how everyday actors have the capacity to transform the world economy, as well as to generate new sets of questions and topics that can reveal hitherto masked sites of agency and change. In this sense puzzle sets respond, as discussed in the Introduction, to orthodox IPE's call to bridge the gap between intellectual discussion and real-world policy-making, as well as critical IPE's call for finding avenues to emancipation. The following puzzle-set combinations provide potential avenues for exploration.

Importantly, as we explained in the Introduction, everyday types of action do *not* have to be successful to merit our attention. Such a view would lead us back into the functionalist selection of material for investigation that can be seen in much of the work we identify with RIPE. Moreover, we are also interested in how some forms of action within an everyday strategy fail. For examples of failure point out sources of strength for the dominant, whereas moments of successful resistance can signal their points of weakness. We also noted in the Introduction how RIPE is preoccupied with selecting winners and ignoring losers. This

Table 11.1. *Everyday IPE puzzle sets*

	Defiance	Mimetic challenge	Axiorationality
Regimes as cultural weapons of the weak	1. *Informal networks among migrant workers* 2. **Fair Trade movement** 3. **The new international economic order**	1. *Tax havens and the OECD* 2. **Mixed economies in the former Soviet empire** 3. **Proposal for an Asian Monetary Fund (AMF)**	1. **Hawala currency trading systems** 2. **British work and leisure and the ILO** 3. **Grameen Bank, Bangladesh**
Global economic change from below	1. *Peasant resistance to global neo-liberalism* 2. *Labour challenges to global capital* 3. **Non-collectivist agriculture in Vietnam**	1. **Small-scale piracy of intellectual property** 2. **Creation of tourist zones of comfort** 3. **Environmentalists' pricing of resource rents**	1. *Individual investments in pension schemes* 2. **Workforce casualisation and home work** 3. *Mortgage pools and US financial power*
Bringing Eastern agents in	1. **Red Flag LINUX** 2. **Campaign for indigenous property rights** 3. **Selective use of capital controls**	1. *Japanese challenge to Chinese hegemony* 2. **Indian development of a service economy** 3. **Decolonisation movements**	1. *Diffusion of Asian 'resource portfolios'* 2. *Capitalist modernisation in Thailand* 3. **NGOs and Third World family planning**

Note: We have placed the case studies already provided in this collection in italics within the puzzle set, while new fruitful topics that come to mind are included in bold.

is consistent with the research program predisposition of RIPE and is a function of the concomitant need to defend a theory. By contrast, our concern is to locate sites of agency across the global economy rather than to privilege winners.

Table 11.1 reveals a very wide expanse of topics that can be considered within an EIPE context, though it is in fact only a representative sample of what could be included. Ultimately, we see these topics as important for not just understanding some of the key processes of change that exist today, but because they enable us to explore the origins of the modern global system in novel ways. Indeed it is striking that RIPE has failed to pay serious attention to many of these. Equally, even if some of this might be conceded as important, nevertheless, given the obsession with parsimony in mainstream IPE, the reply might well be that the result is unwieldy and is not conducive for the effective teaching of IPE. Accordingly, in the next section we set out a potential IPE course in order to reply to this potential criticism. But for the moment we need to provide a brief explanation of why we have included the topics situated in Table 11.1. We do not intend to cover all the topics in the table, but instead we focus on one from each box to illustrate our case. We shall consider the three forms of agency as they apply to each of the three themes that are germane to EIPE.

Regimes as cultural weapons of the weak

General questions here include: can everyday actors resist the diktat of international regimes? To whom must formal international regimes be responsible? Does the development of rigorous informal regimes by everyday actors precede formalisation of an international regime for it to be legitimated and sustained? When does mimetic challenge fail and succeed in everyday challenges to international regimes? Are 'bottom-up' axiorational regimes more likely to be integrated and adapted within orthodox regimes because they have changed incrementally and are not viewed as a threat?

Defiance

FAIR TRADE MOVEMENT The Fair Trade movement appeals directly to everyday consumption within Western states (the purchase of Fair Trade coffee, for example), while using a discourse of justice and economic sustenance for the peripheral countries where the products for consumption are produced. As such, the Fair Trade regime's key source of defiance is grounded in tapping into an everyday moral economy that leads to actions that defy a capitalist system based on exploitation (Watson 2006). Given the growing prominence of this regime in the last decade, the Fair Trade movement provides a clear example of defiance to neoclassical economic ideas about supply and demand. Questions remain, however, concerning the political economy of coordination of the Fair Trade movement between Western NGOs and the producers within peripheral countries. Investigation into the management of Fair Trade goods, from everyday producer to everyday consumer, may reveal how the ideal of Fair Trade is distorted in practice. Alternatively, it may reveal how all markets are to some extent moralised, and that the regime's success relies on an appeal to different conceptions of economic and moral value. (On the marketisation of moral goods such as human organs, see Healy 2006.)

Mimetic challenge

PROPOSAL FOR AN ASIAN MONETARY FUND (AMF) The failed AMF proposal deliberately mimicked the rhetoric and institutional design of the IMF to legitimate its claim that post-financial crisis East Asia required a more regionally sensitive fund (Leaver and Seabrooke 2000; Seabrooke 2005a). The proposed institution differed, however, in that it would provide more generous loan conditionality and financing provisions, implicitly on the grounds that Western institutions (read the IMF) are insensitive to cultural traits and impede state sovereignty. While the AMF failed to emerge, the key point here is how peripheral actors can call for regimes that provide a challenge to the governing structures of the day. For example, the AMF proposal, as well as problems with loan conditionality and political 'scapegoating' in the countries worst affected by the financial crisis, led the IMF to question its role and purpose. The IMF's recognition of its legitimacy crisis has led it to enact institutional changes (on voting rights in particular) that give more power to East Asian countries (Seabrooke 2007a). Understanding 'non-starters' such as the AMF is important in revealing the 'pressure points' of dominant institutions and powers in the world economy, especially in exposing legitimacy problems that spur reform.

Axiorationality

BRITISH WORK AND LEISURE AND THE INTERNATIONAL LABOUR ORGANIZATION (ILO) During the 1920s the ILO received lukewarm support from the British government. The Labour government of 1930 opposed the idea of a forty-hour working week supported by the ILO. However, by 1935 the National Government coalition lent its support to the notion (Lowe 1982: 259). While scholars often point to the Keynesian revolution in economy policy (Gourevitch 1986: 142–6), another explanation is that changing attitudes about work time and leisure time among British workers provided strong impulses for the government to reform not only nationally but internationally in order to claim legitimacy (Seabrooke 2007c). Changes here were not necessarily planned, but rather derived from everyday incremental behaviour. Following the experience of the First World War, a desire for housing was widespread, just as there was a clear desire for more leisure time (and expressed through activities such as the cinema and greyhound and motorbike racing). Also during this period was a looser understanding of class politics, with class representing more the family struggle in the world than the rigid labels we typically associate with 'class conflict'. Social change during the 1920s also included changing attitudes towards career development and the unit of measurement for state welfare (the family or the individual?). All of these changes provided strong impulses for policy experimentation since they exposed a clear 'legitimacy gap' between what people in the working and middle classes expected of government, and what government was willing to provide. As such, everyday actions were important in informing what became known as the Keynesian revolution. Understanding historical changes in attitudes among the broader population provides a fruitful basis for learning of the constraints and opportunities for regimes and their legitimation (as recently recognised by Keohane among others; Keohane 2002: Ch. 10).

Global economic change from below

Key questions on 'bottom-up' processes of transformation in the world economy include: can everyday actors work collectively and intentionally to affect real change? Can global change occur in small incremental acts from agents who do not necessarily realise the aggregated consequences of their individual actions?

Defiance

NON-COLLECTIVIST AGRICULTURE IN VIETNAM As Benedict J. Tria Kerkvliet's work has shown (1990, 2005), seemingly disempowered peasants have a capacity to challenge and shape their local political and economic environment through everyday actions. Such actions may then go on to shape national policy and, in doing so, create change in the world economy. For example, in the Vietnamese case national schemes to collectivise agricultural production were slowly undermined by everyday actions by peasants. While much of this action may be understood as axiorational, much can also be understood as defiance. In this case the form of defiance was not the open protests we typically consider. Rather, defiance was demonstrated through deliberate non-compliance, non-performance of assigned work roles and the appropriation of land for purposes other than those intended by the government (using collective land to grow animal fodder, for example). Other forms of active defiance included stealing from rice stocks and reallocating resources to private household food needs like fertilizer (Kerkvliet 2006: 292–3). In this case, a preference for family farming also undermined efforts to collectivise agriculture. As a consequence, and despite national government efforts to reverse the trend, the program failed and land use became increasingly market-driven. Such marketisation of land use was, at first, illegal but, given its widespread nature, was recognised by the government as necessary and became legal. Vietnam's place in the world economy is in part due to these everyday actions that defied the drive to collectivise agriculture (Kerkvliet 2005). Understanding similar cases of everyday actions provides a way into understanding social and institutional change in 'transition' economies, and their capacity for integration into, or to challenge the principles of, the world economy.

Mimetic challenge

SMALL-SCALE PIRACY OF INTELLECTUAL PROPERTY From cases in the Western world, such as that of Napster, to the development of street market sales of pirate CDs, DVDs and software in developing countries, small-scale acts of piracy represent a direct challenge to corporations who have profited from monopoly or oligopoly arrangements to secure higher profits on intellectual property. It also provides a broader challenge to the intellectual property rights regime. Such defiance is now so diffuse that it has created a black market economy that touches our everyday lives. And while large-scale piracy is associated with highly organised interests (such as common tropes about the involvement of the Chinese People's Liberation Army in pirate CDs and DVDs), small-scale piracy provides a case of how infringing intellectual property rights has become everyday behaviour. Undoubtedly those engaged in piracy, whether producers or consumers, have a clear economic incentive to violate intellectual property rights legislation. However, such everyday actions are not taken as active defiance to the World Trade Organization (WTO) or Sony Music (or similar). Rather the distribution of intellectual property through networks is justified on two grounds that are concerned with fairness. The first is a question of access: that the intellectual property should be accessible to a range of people unable to afford official market prices. The second is a question of monopoly rents: that the intellectual property is unfairly priced and places Western states and their corporations in a dominant position to control technology. As the distribution, if not sale, of pirated material occurs in similar ways to legal material (through street markets or via the internet), the spread of piracy represents a form of mimetic challenge.

Axiorationality

WORKFORCE CASUALISATION AND HOME WORK As Louise Amoore's (2002) recent and important work tells us, there are important changes in work practices within Western states that are occurring incrementally. It is likely that those making the changes may not recognise the broader significance of their actions for the world economy. One important and understudied aspect here is the casualisation of jobs in Western economies, especially in the services sector. Such changes come from both top-down processes associated with a shift towards neoliberal flexibilisation among corporations, as well as through bottom-up processes in the form of the choice made by some workers to move away from a nine-to-five format. While there is much work in political economy on skills retraining and other employment concerns (Culpepper 2003; Thelen 2004), as well as the gendered aspects of work regimes (Peterson 2003), the impact of workforce casualisation on the national and world economies remains understudied in IPE. This is perhaps surprising given the implications of workforce casualisation for welfare regimes and the transfer of intergenerational assets within, and across, national political economies. As casualisation has 'crept in' during the past few decades, its worldwide impact on changing economic, social and political attitudes is important to address.

Bringing Eastern agents in

Important questions here include: how are we to consider the significance of cultural-ideational and technological exchanges for change in the world economy? Are discourses of race still important in informing change in the world economy? Are economic systems over time built in opposition to some cultural ideals and identities while holding others as superior? Or, is the global economic system shaped by the interaction of Eastern and Western agents? And finally, to what extent did the origins of the global economy originate in Eastern practices?

Defiance

RED FLAG LINUX It strikes us that an important form of defiance that will transform the East Asian political economy, and with it the world economy, is China's development of 'Reg Flag' LINUX computer operating system software. This operating system software was developed in the late 1990s with the assistance of the Chinese Academy of Science, and acts as the vanguard for developing computing in China. Red Flag Software has since acted with the Chinese government on computing projects, including national standardisation schemes (www.redflag-linux.com). Red Flag Software has also been active in helping American partners to develop its software but remains in competition with Microsoft. This is significant because it provides an alternative to Microsoft's operating system software and a challenge to its commercial practices. In this sense, and unlike the mimetic challenge of piracy, the development of Red Flag Linux represents a fundamental challenge to the world computing industry. The Chinese government has pointed to LINUX as the new operating standard, and the key principles that support LINUX such as 'shareware' and 'freeware' spread the software in a way more closely linked to currently limited Chinese consumer potential for new computing equipment and software at official world market prices. As such, the development of Red Flag LINUX can be seen as a form of resistance against Microsoft's hegemony within the global information technology marketplace (May 2004).

Mimetic challenge

DECOLONISATION MOVEMENTS While it is true that some Third World nationalist movements deployed violent defiance agency against the imperial powers, this was confined to a minority of cases (Abernethy 2000). The major thrust of the nationalist movements was to fight the empire through mimetic challenge or 'rhetorical entrapment' (Schimmelfennig 2001). In essence, the strategy entailed revealing the ways in which colonial policy contradicted the norms of Western discourse. Thus while the West proclaimed to stand for self-determination, the rights of man and democracy, the nationalist movements revealed how colonial policy conformed to none of these ideas (Philpott 2001). Moreover, in marshalling the colonies to fight alongside the imperial allies against Nazism under the banner of anti-racism, so the way was opened for the nationalist movements to rhetorically prosecute the West for its own racist imperial policies. By revealing these inconsistencies, the nationalist movements succeeded in rhetorically entrapping the colonial powers thereby delegitimising colonialism. And in the process the decolonising tidal wave swept rapidly across the world. So successful was this moment of Eastern agency that colonialism is no longer on the menu for any aspiring great power (though this is not to ignore the point that informal neo-imperialism continues). Still, this latter point, though important, should not diminish the significance of the Eastern challenge to formal empire in the first place.

Axiorationality

NON-GOVERNMENTAL ORGANISATIONS (NGOS) AND THIRD WORLD FAMILY PLANNING What has happened to the role of fertility and family planning in our conception of change in the world economy? While debates in the 1950s and 1960s included a strong focus on Malthusian ideas of population growth, the contemporary literature in political economy has a blind spot in how attempts to improve family planning are important for change in the world economy. Sending's (2004) study of the internationalisation of US-led knowledge practices on population control for economic growth in developing states points to the importance of incremental changes in conventions alongside defiance agency. As international NGOs sought to socialise and internalise family planning norms among women in developing countries, the perception that women were treated as objects of regulation did not accord with self-perceptions of the value of family. In particular the notion of 'reproductive health' as a technical issue rather than an emotional and social issue led to policy stumbling and failure. While many women did not wish to become pregnant, they did not use prescribed contraception either. Subsequent studies showed how women viewed fertility and sexuality as separate issues, and that family planning must provide more than a technical fix and must accord with changing social and economic conventions (such as the relationship between nourishing infants and future family planning). As NGOs eventually learnt these lessons from everyday practice they were able to shift the discourse to 'quality of care' and produce more effective policy outcomes. The important reminder about axiorational behaviour here is that norm entrepreneurs working on 'reproductive health' were not able to socialise and internalise these norms in passive recipients in developing states. This failure did not raise mass protest but slid into policy failure. Instead, only through a reverse transfer of knowledge, from everyday practice to policy expert, could policy be furthered, reminding us of the agency of the targets of family planning even if they were unaware of the broader impact that their lack of norm internalisation would produce (Sending 2004: Ch. 9; see also Sending and Neumann 2007).

EIPE teaching frameworks

One could view this collection simply as an assortment of cases in which everyday actions are seen as more important than we would normally recognise. While the puzzle sets outlining the types of everyday action and how they play through the major themes may provide coherence to EIPE, it is not immediately obvious how one might teach EIPE. Moreover, as signalled earlier, RIPE scholars might view our puzzle-set framework as too unwieldy to enable effective teaching of IPE. Here we suggest that the EIPE puzzle set can be used in combination with key themes from RIPE to teach students not only about the institutions and structures of governance of the world economy, but also how everyday actors have agency within them (cf. Amoore and Langley 2001). We also have in mind a particular teaching method that provides students with the macro 'nuts and bolts' of change in the world economy, while also providing a conceptual toolkit which, when coupled with the 'micro' cases, constitutes an effective way of 'putting the nuts and bolts together'. Moreover, the 'pressure points' that everyday actors bring to bear upon the structures of the world economy reveal these structures as far more pliable or malleable than does RIPE. In this way, we concur with Ronnie D. Lipschutz's sentiment that '[b]ecause people matter, global political economy must begin not as something that is ethereal, abstract, and far away, but rooted in the conditions of everyday lives, here and now' (2001: 331).

A number of scholars have noted that RIPE has narrowed in its teaching and research focus. In their authoritative article, Robert Denemark and Robert O'Brien (1997) demonstrated that during the 1990s North American IPE focused almost exclusively on the state and expanded little beyond core concerns of trade, monetary regimes, global financial systems and multinational corporations (though by no means is this to ignore important critical IPE interventions made by numerous critical US scholars (e.g., Tickner 1992, 1997; Murphy 1994; Peterson 2003)). And simultaneously, they noted how the conceptual discussion narrows around the three schools of realism, liberalism and classical structuralism. Issues such as the environment and migration, for example, did not appear on the radar screen. The restricted focus of North American IPE was intended to give it a 'specifically managerial flavour', with special emphasis given over to studying US hegemony (Denemark and O'Brien 1997: 229). This compares with the eclecticism of British IPE, perhaps best epitomised by Susan Strange's *States and Markets* (1988). Still, this latter form of teaching IPE placed greater emphasis on providing a 'critical' reinterpretation of core concerns rather than expanding the number of issues on the table beyond the core issues. And while British, Canadian and Australasian IPE has placed greater emphasis on gender (Whitworth 1994; Waylen 1999, 2005; True 2003), the environment (Helleiner 1996), regionalism (Gamble and Payne 1996; Grugel and Hout 1999a, 1999b) and the political economy of 'territoriality' (Palan 2003), these issues are typically tacked on as 'optional extras' within a standard RIPE teaching framework, usually at the very end of the lecture series.

The narrowing of what is taught within RIPE has occurred at a time when IPE as a field has become more prominent within international relations. Thus we are left with the ironic situation that there are more people studying fewer topics while the range of *potential* questions 'out there' is expanding. Furthermore, some older topics and questions for teaching are fast disappearing: Africa, for example, has blipped off the radar screen (Murphy and Nelson 2001: 397; Breuning *et al.* 2005: 456; Lavelle 2005).

While we argue that RIPE has limitations, we do not wish to throw the proverbial baby out with the bath water. We believe that RIPE performs a valuable and necessary function in educating political economy students

Table 11.2. *Revising international political economy 101*

Week	Issues
1 (RIPE)	Introduction to RIPE
2 (EIPE)	Introduction to EIPE
3 (RIPE)	The rise of global capitalism I: US hegemony
4 (EIPE)	The rise of global capitalism II: Eastern origins
5 (RIPE)	International economic institutions I: the IMF and the OECD
6 (EIPE)	International economic institutions II: resistance in program compliance
7 (RIPE)	The world trading system I: the legalisation of the WTO
8 (EIPE)	The world trading system II: everyday consumer choice and Fair Trade
9 (RIPE)	Globalisation of production I: the rise of the multinational corporation
10 (EIPE)	Globalisation of production II: labour movement resistance
11 (RIPE)	Globalisation of finance I: international financial crises
12 (EIPE)	Globalisation of finance II: the suburbanisation of debt

about the structure, purpose and key economic relationships of the major international economic institutions and great powers of the contemporary period. The purpose of EIPE is to provide us with new information about how the world economy works in addition to the structures and dominant actors discussed by RIPE. EIPE can, therefore, supplement rather than simply supplant RIPE.

A course in EIPE, as we envisage it, would comprise lectures and seminars on the key international economic institutions, great powers and structures of the post-war period. But these would be combined with lectures and seminars that also provide focused case studies that reveal how various everyday actors have transformative capacity to shape these traditional forces. These would also introduce the role of everyday actions in the transformation of the world economy. One possibility among several is offered in Table 11.2.

Table 11.2 provides merely one possible sketch of what an EIPE/RIPE course might look like; one that, of course, speaks directly to the areas of expertise contained in this volume's contributory chapters. In combining RIPE and EIPE we have purposefully presented the relevant topics according to a 'point-counterpoint' logic. Ideally, this would enable students to reflect, argue and, in combination with the puzzle set, explore new avenues of inquiry. To explore this further it helps to scan the course's lectures and seminars, which we present in Table 11.3.

Such a course would also permit students to reflect on how the global economy works in everyday life, to recognise the importance of locating the agency of everyday actors, and to have an awareness and appreciation

Table 11.3. *'Point-counterpoint' issues to be explored in IPE 101*

Week	Issues to be considered
1 – POINT	Powerful states, regimes and elites change and govern the world economy through coercion, mimetic conformity and exploiting radical uncertainty
2 – COUNTERPOINT	But everyday actors can constrain elite power and create change in the world economy through defiance, mimetic challenge and axiorational behaviour
3 – POINT	Our contemporary world order represents the peak of the capitalist world system created and led by US hegemony
4 – COUNTERPOINT	The deeper roots of the contemporary capitalist system come from the globalisation of trade and finance that has significant Eastern origins
5 – POINT	International economic institutions such as the IMF and OECD govern the world economy and encourage the diffusion of transparent neoliberal governance practices
6 – COUNTERPOINT	Compliance in economic reform programs is often weak due to everyday actors' agency, be they individuals in borrowing states or peripheral states who use rhetoric to buck international trends
7 – POINT	The world trading system is being legalised through the creation of the WTO dispute settlement mechanism at the behest of Northern states in order to deepen global free trade
8 – COUNTERPOINT	Resistance to reform within the WTO, especially the clogging of dispute settlement, must be understood in the context of changes in consumer behaviour. The emerging work on the Fair Trade movement stresses how everyday actions are important here
9 – POINT	The rise of multinational corporations has led to the 'flexibilisation' of labour and production that produces a 'race to the bottom' on wages and taxes
10 – COUNTERPOINT	'Flexibilisation' and just-in-time production makes multinationals sensitive to labour demands if trade unions resist across production sites
11 – POINT	Global finance has become delinked from the real economy, and financial crises are the consequence of excessive speculation by financial markets
12 – COUNTERPOINT	Global finance is increasingly embedded in the real economy, as personal individual investment choices and asset securitisation are becoming normal practice within most Western states.

of their different experiences – both contemporary and historical – within the global economy. In short, combining EIPE and RIPE within a teaching program equips students with an understanding of how the world economy functions at the macro level, but also enables a better understanding of how a range of actors beyond the 'winners' can, through everyday actions, transform the international political economy. For us, such a course would stimulate students to be more academically adventurous. It would also ground them by combining their more abstract knowledge of international structures and institutions with concrete on-the-ground change. This brings us to our last point: that EIPE is particularly relevant for understanding the policy challenges of the contemporary world economy.

Policy implications

We believe that EIPE has just as much, if not a greater, capacity for policy relevance than RIPE. After all, what policy-makers want to know is how policies and institutions change 'on the ground'; how policy implementation has occurred within different periods of time and in different social, political and economic contexts; and how policy change has been legitimated to ensure that the changes are enduring rather than simply cosmetic. Within RIPE much of the concentration is on institutional or policy design rather than implementation and, as noted above, the gap between IPE as an intellectual enterprise and actual policy development has been criticised by prominent orthodox scholars. We feel that EIPE provides not only an exciting intellectual enterprise in discovering hitherto unknown or ignored terrain, but also opens up the 'policy imagination' that provides detailed and practical information for policy-makers (see Seabrooke 2007b).

The key to opening up this policy imagination, we believe, lies in abandoning RIPE's search for superior 'research programs' that can subsume all other theories and simultaneously provide a view of the world that is out of touch with how everyday actions transform the world economy. Instead we suggest that EIPE's 'puzzle set' framework provides a coherent agenda for investigation that encourages the development of policy imagination in both an intellectual and practical context. What policy implications may be drawn from EIPE? We suggest that EIPE is highly policy relevant because much of the impulse for policy change in the contemporary world economy comes from below rather than from above. We briefly elaborate upon this by taking three areas of IPE typically held to have high policy relevance: 'policy diffusion', 'global governance' and 'US hegemony'.

First, the growing literature on 'policy diffusion' provides important information on how policies, such as capital account liberalisation, have spread around the world in past decades. This entails the testing of different hypotheses on why this has been the case, such as geography, cultural similarity, external political pressure, domestic political pressure, communication networks among policy-makers and others (Simmons and Elkins 2004). Particularly insightful work in this area has sought to understand under what conditions elites learn that some policies are appropriate and others not (Chwieroth 2007). However, in tracing formal agreement on the international appropriateness of a policy, we know less about how the policies are legitimated within the states that adopt it. If we only consider legitimacy as a form of 'elite proclamation' then we have trouble in comprehending how a process of policy diffusion can lead to effective policy implementation on the ground. For example, we might ask what the root is of Argentina's ongoing financial problems. The Argentinian Treasurer may well agree with the international appropriateness of a policy such as capital account liberalisation as propagated by elite institutions. Nevertheless to place the government on a sure financial footing requires stronger fiscal foundations which, in turn, requires greater social legitimacy. EIPE can provide important policy insight into how everyday actors and their practices assist or hinder policies already formally diffused.

Second, the literature on 'global governance', especially that on transparency and governance, focuses on getting the institutional structures right with the hope that better on-the-ground policies will follow. However, while this literature notes that reform programs regularly fail and seeks to engage 'civil society' to remedy this, its primary aim is to suggest and design 'world's best practice'. As Robert O'Brien (2000) and others have asserted, the literature on global governance is ineffective unless it can tap into how it changes how people conduct their everyday lives while recognising the importance of new social movements on the environment, labour and gender issues (see also Sending and Neumann 2007). Moreover, while the global governance literature focuses on 'getting it right' within the institutions, it has less to say about the agency of peripheral states in rejecting rules dictated to them. Understanding forms of defiance and mimetic challenges from peripheral states and everyday people can provide relevant information for both the international economic institutions and the peripheral states concerned, hopefully with mutual benefit to both.

Third, for all the discussion of hegemony in RIPE, how 'US hegemony' works in practice is less known, primarily because it is typically discussed in terms of the policies supplied. And more often than not, US hegemony is viewed as a blanket structural constraint on those at the receiving end. This conventional view does provide answers to the questions 'who governs?' or 'who benefits?' (as discussed in the introductory chapter), but nevertheless obscures the question of how policies are implemented on the ground for the broader population. Accordingly, we require innovative scholarship to reveal how US hegemony reshapes everyday lives, and how it may provoke different forms of defiance from everyday actors, or how it provides incentives for mimetic challenges.

The three areas of RIPE discussed above are all informed by the regulatory questions – 'who governs?' and 'who benefits?' – in order to understand change in, and governance of, the world economy. However, asking 'who acts?' reveals how individuals and social groups do not blindly follow dictates supplied to them from above, but have their own capacity to resist and, through everyday actions, transform the world economy. In our view, as noted earlier, many real-world policy-makers are more interested in how policy has worked and has been *sustained* rather than whether it is simply accepted by elites. As such, astute policy-makers are interested in the social legitimacy of the institutional changes they are considering, rather than relying on powerful politicians or ideational elites to command or proclaim the legitimacy of a policy. Finally, astute policy-makers also want someone who has policy imagination. That is, someone who can provide critical insight from combining analytical tools within an *open interpretive framework*, which can generate an understanding that expands, rather than restricts, policy choice. Our EIPE puzzle set hopes to foster just such policy imagination.

Conclusion

In sum, the development of EIPE is important for one reason above all others: it can promote an understanding of how the *bulk* of societies – not simply the 10 per cent at the top of the food chain or even the 10 per cent at the bottom – can inform change in the world economy. If we consider how we experience our everyday lives we know that governance structures at the national and international level influence our capacity to buy some goods and not others, to have access to credit in some situations and not others, and the extent to which states and people less fortunate than ourselves are exploited or ignored. This we have some idea about, and RIPE performs an important job in teaching us about the *governing* structures and institutions of the global economy. We do not, however, know so much about how our everyday actions have the capacity to change our own political and economic environment. Nor do we know much about the capacity of peripheral actors outside of the core Western societies to transform their own environment. Understanding how such capacities have developed and how they are changing better informs us about the multiple social sources of change in the world economy. And in so doing, we shall increase our capacity to shape our political and economic environment and to learn how those with power may be tempered or even displaced for the benefit of the majority.

Bibliography

Abdul Rahman, N. 2005: 'Shaping the Migrant Institution: The Agency of Indonesian Domestic Workers in Singapore', in L. Parker (ed.), *The Agency of Women in Asia* (Singapore: Marshall Cavendish): 182–216.

Abdul Rahman, N., B. S. A. Yeoh and S. Huang 2005: ' "Dignity Over Due": Transnational Domestic Workers in Singapore', in Shirlena Huang *et al.* (eds.), *Asian Women as Transnational Domestic Workers* (Singapore: Asian MetaCenter and Marshall Cavendish International): 233–61.

Abernethy, David 2000: *The Dynamics of Global Dominance* (New Haven: Yale University Press).

Abravanel, Martin D. and Mary K. Cunningham 2002: *How Much Do We Know?* (Washington DC: The Urban Institute).

Abu-Lughod, Janet L. 1989: *Before European Hegemony* (Oxford: Oxford University Press).

Ahluwalia, Pal 2001: *Politics and Post-Colonial Theory* (New York: Routledge).

AIFLD (American Institute for Free Labor Development) 1964: 'Country Plan for Mexico', in AIFLD (ed.), *Country Plans for Latin America* (Washington, DC: AIFLD, Social Projects Department).

AIFLD 1967: 'Meany Addresses National Press Club on Work of AIFLD', *AIFLD Report* (August): 1–2.

Aitken, Rob 2002: 'The (Re)Making of Prudential Masculinity: Culture, Discourse and Financial Identity', paper presented at the 43rd International Studies Association Annual Convention, New Orleans.

2003: 'The Democratic Method of Obtaining Capital – Culture, Governmentality and Ethics of Mass Investment', *Consumption, Markets and Culture* 6(4): 293–317.

Aizcorbe, Ana M., Arthur B. Kennickell and Kevin B. Moore 2003: 'Recent Changes in US Family Finances: Evidence from the 1998 and 2001 Survey of Consumer Finances', *Federal Reserve Bulletin* (January) 89: 1–32.

Aldridge, Alan 1998: 'Habitus and Cultural Capital in the Field of Personal Finance', *The Sociological Review* 46(1): 1–23.

AMC (Asian Migration Centre) 2001: *Clearing a Hurried Path* (Hong Kong: AMC).

Amin, Ash, Ronen Palan and Peter Taylor 1994: 'Forum for Heterodox International Political Economy', *Review of International Political Economy* 1(1): 1–12.

Amin, Samir 1973: *Unequal Development* (London: Penguin).
1982: *Dynamics of Global Crisis* (London: Macmillan).
1989: *Eurocentrism* (London: Zed Press).
1993: 'The Ancient World-Systems versus the Modern Capitalist World-System', in A. G. Frank and B. K. Gills (eds.), *The World System* (London: Routledge): 247–77.
Amoore, Louise 2002: *Globalisation Contested* (Manchester: Manchester University Press).
2004: 'Risk, Reward and Discipline at Work', *Economy and Society* 33(2): 174–96.
Amoore, Louise and Paul Langley 2001: 'Experiencing Globalization: Active Teaching and Learning in International Political Economy', *International Studies Perspectives* 2(1): 15–32.
Amoore, Louise, Richard Dodgson, Randall Germain, Barry K. Gills, Paul Langley and Iain Watson 2000: 'Paths to a Historicized International Political Economy', *Review of International Political Economy* 7(1): 53–71.
Andreas, Peter and Thomas Biersteker (eds.) 2003: *The Reordering of North America* (London: Routledge).
Andrews, Edmund L. 2003: 'Bush's Plan for Pensions Is Now Given Low Priority', *New York Times* (26 February).
Anon. 1996: 'A Call for Justice for Malaysian Migrant Workers: An Interview with Irene Fernandez', *Multinational Monitor* (December).
Appadurai, Arjun 1996: *Modernity at Large* (Minneapolis, MN: University of Minnesota Press).
Arano, Yasunori 1988: *Kinsei Nippon to Higashi Ajia* (Tokyo: Tōkyō Daigaku Shuppankai).
Arrifin, R. 1989: 'Women and Trade Unions in West Malaysia', *Journal of Contemporary Asia* 19(1): 78–94.
Atlas, Ron 2004: 'For Mutual Funds, First the Slap. Now Comes the Pinch', *New York Times* (26 August).
Atwell, William S. 1982: 'International Bullion Flows and the Chinese Economy circa 1530–1650', *Past and Present* 95: 68–90.
Augelli, Enrico and Craig N. Murphy 1988: *America's Quest for Supremacy* (London: Pinter).
Avci, G. and C. McDonald 2000: 'Chipping Away at the Fortress: Unions, Immigration and the Transnational Labour Market', *International Migration* 38(2): 191–207.
Avery, Robert B., Raphael W. Bostic, Paul S. Calem and Glenn B. Canner 1999: 'Trends in Home Purchase Lending: Consolidation and the Community Reinvestment Act', *Federal Reserve Bulletin* 85(2): 81–102.
Baker, Tom and Jonathan Simon 2002: 'Embracing Risk', in Tom Baker and Jonathan Simon (eds.), *Embracing Risk* (Chicago: University of Chicago Press): 1–26.
Bakhtin, Mikhail 1985: *Problems of Dostoevsky's Poetics* (Minnesota: University of Minnesota Press).
Bakker, Isabella and Stephen Gill 2003: *Power, Production and Social Reproduction* (Houndmills: Palgrave Macmillan).

Balaam, David N. and Michael Veseth 1996: *Introduction to International Political Economy* (Upper Sadler River, NJ: Prentice-Hall).

Balderston, Theo 1989: 'War Finance and Inflation in England and Germany, 1914–18', *Economic History Review* 42(2): 222–44.

Baldwin, Richard E. and Phillipe Martin 1999: 'Two Waves of Globalisation: Superficial Similarities, Fundamental Differences', NBER Working Paper No. 6904 (Cambridge, MA: National Bureau of Economic Research).

Ball, R. and N. Piper 2005: 'Trading Labour-trading Rights: the Regional Dynamics over Rights Recognition of Migrant Workers in the Asia-Pacific – the Case of the Philippines and Japan', in Kevin Hewison and Ken Young (eds.), *Transnational Migration and Work in Asia* (London: Routledge): 213–34.

Bang, Henrik and Eva Sørensen 2001: 'The Everyday Maker: Building Political rather than Social Capital', in P. Dekker and E. Uslander (eds.), *Social Capital and Participation in Every Day Life* (London: Routledge): 148–61.

Bao, Jiemin 2004: *Marital Acts: Gender, Sexuality, and Identity Among the Chinese Thai Diaspora* (Honolulu: University of Hawaii Press).

Barmeyer, Niels 2003: 'The Guerrilla Movement as a Project: An Assessment of Community Involvement in the EZLN', *Latin American Perspectives* 30(1): 122–38.

Barnett, Michael N. and Martha Finnemore 1999: 'Politics, Power and Pathologies in International Organizations', *International Organization* 53(4): 699–732.

——— 2004: *Rules For the World* (Ithaca: Cornell University Press).

Basu, Ellen Oxfeld 1991: 'The Sexual Division of Labor and the Organization of Family and Firm in an Overseas Chinese Community', *American Ethnologist* 18(4): 700–18.

Battistella, G. and M. M. B. Asis (eds.) 2002: *Unauthorised Migration in Southeast Asia* (Quezon City: Scalabrini Migration Centre).

Beetham, David 1991: *The Legitimation of Power* (London: Macmillan).

Ben-Ami, David 2001: *Cowardly Capitalism* (Chichester: John Wiley).

Bendix, Reinhard 1977: *Nation-Building and Citizenship*, 3rd edition (Berkeley: University of California Press).

——— 1978: *Kings or People?* (Berkeley: University of California Press).

Bentley, Jerry H. 1993: *Old World Encounters* (New York: Oxford University Press).

Bernal, Martin 1991: *Black Athena*, I (New York: Vintage).

Bernstein, George L. 1986: *Liberalism and Liberal Politics in Edwardian England* (Boston: Allen and Unwin).

Bernstein, Harry 2000: ' "The Peasantry" in Global Capitalism: Who, Where and Why?', in Leo Panitch and Colin Leys (eds.), *Socialist Register* (London: Merlin Press).

Bertraut, Carol and Martha Starr-McCluer 1999: 'Household portfolios in the United States', paper presented at the Conference on Household Portfolios, European University Institute, 17–18 December.

Bhabha, Homi K. 1994: *The Location of Culture* (London: Routledge).

Bieler, Andreas and Adam David Morton 2001: 'The Gordian Knot of Agency-Structure in International Relations: A Neo-Gramscian Perspective', *European Journal of International Relations* 7(1): 5–35.

2003: 'Globalisation, the State and Class Struggle: A "Critical Economy" Engagement with Open Marxism', *British Journal of Politics and International Relations* 5(4): 467–99.

2004: ' "Another Europe is Possible?": Labour and Social Movements and the European Social Forum', *Globalizations* 1(2): 303–26.

Biersteker, Thomas J. 1993: 'Evolving Perspectives on International Political Economy', *International Political Science Review* 41(1): 7–33.

Blackburn, Robin 2002: *Banking on Death or Investing in Life* (London: Verso).

Blake, David H. and Robert S. Walters 1976: *The Politics of Global Economic Relations* (Englewood Cliffs, NJ: Prentice-Hall).

Blake Goodman, Susannah 2000: *Girls Just Want to Have Funds* (New York: Hyperion Books).

Blaut, James M. 2000: *Eight Eurocentric Historians* (London: Guilford Press).

Blyth, Mark 2002: *Great Transformations* (Cambridge: Cambridge University Press).

2005: 'Beyond the Usual Suspects: Ideas, Uncertainty, and Building Institutional Orders', mimeo, Department of Political Science, Johns Hopkins University (October).

Bordo, Michael D., Barry Eichengreen and Jongwoo Ki 1998: 'Was there Really an Earlier Period of International Financial Integration Comparable to Today?', NBER Working Paper No. 6738 (Cambridge, MA: National Bureau of Economic Research).

Borgos, Seth 1986: 'Low-Income Homeownership and the ACORN Squatters Campaign', in Rachel G. Bratt, Chester Hartman and Ann Meyerson (eds.), *Critical Perspectives on Housing* (Philadelphia: Temple University Press): 428–46.

Boudon, Raymond 2001: *The Origin of Values* (New Brunswick: Transaction Publishers).

Bowden, Brett and Leonard Seabrooke (eds.) 2006: *Global Standards of Market Civilization* (New York: Routledge).

Bozeman, Adda B. 1994: *Politics and Culture in International History* (New Brunswick: Transaction Publishers).

Brady, Helen and David Collier 2004: *Rethinking Social Inquiry* (Lanham: Rowman & Littlefield).

Braithwaite, John and Peter Drahos 2000: *Global Business Regulation* (Cambridge: Cambridge University Press).

Brass, Tom 2002: 'Latin American Peasants: New Paradigms for Old?', *The Journal of Peasant Studies* 29(3/4): 1–40.

Braudel, Fernand 1992: *Civilization and Capitalism*, III (Berkeley: University of California Press).

Brenner, Robert 1977: 'The Origins of Capitalist Development: A Critique of Neo-Smithian Marxism', *New Left Review* 104: 25–92.

Breuning, Marijke, Joseph Bredehoft and Eugene Walton 2005: 'Promise and Performance: An Evaluation of Journals in International Relations', *International Studies Perspectives* 6(4): 447–61.

Broome, André James 2004: 'Changing Truths about East Asian Industrialisation' (MA dissertation, Victoria University of Wellington).

Broz, J. Lawrence 2005: 'Congressional Politics of International Financial Rescues', *American Journal of Political Science* 49(3): 479–96.

Business in Thailand 1987: 'Department Stores Getting into High Gear' (February): 83–91.

Business Review (Thailand) 1984: 'Fun for All Members of the Family' (March): 18.

Buzan, Barry and Richard Little 2000: *International Systems in World History* (Oxford: Oxford University Press).

Bygrave, Mike 1998: 'From Wall Street to High Street', *The Guardian* (Weekend Supplement, 25 July): 24–9.

Calder, Lendol 1999: *Financing the American Dream* (Princeton: Princeton University Press).

Cameron, Rondo 1967: *Banking in the Early Stages of Industrialization* (New York: Oxford University Press).

Cammack, Paul 2002: 'Attacking the Global Poor', *New Left Review* II(13): 125–34.

Campbell, John L. 1998: 'Institutional Analysis and the Role of Ideas in Political Economy', *Theory and Society* 27(3): 377–409.

    2004: *Institutional Change and Globalization* (Princeton: Princeton University Press).

    2005: 'Where Do We Stand? Common Mechanisms in Organizations and Social Movements Research', in Gerard F. Davis, Doug McAdam, W. Richard Scott and Mayer N. Zald (eds.), *Social Movements and Organization Theory* (Cambridge: Cambridge University Press): 41–68.

Campbell, John L. and Ove K. Pedersen 1996: 'The Evolutionary Nature of Revolutionary Change in Postcommunist Europe', in John L. Campbell and Ove K. Pedersen (eds.), *Legacies of Change* (New York: Aldine de Guyter): 207–51.

Capie, Forrest H. and Michael Collins 1996: 'Industrial Lending by English Commercial Banks: Why Did Banks Refuse Loans?', *Business History* 38(1): 26–44.

Cassis, Youssef 1990: 'British Finance: Success and Controversy' in Jean J. Van Helten and Youssef Cassis (eds.), *Capitalism in a Mature Economy* (Aldershot: Edward Elgar): 1–22.

Castañeda, Jorge G. 1994: *Utopia Unarmed* (New York: Vintage).

    1995: *The Mexican Shock* (New York: The New Press).

Castree, N., N. M. Coe, K. Ward and M. Samers 2004: *Spaces of Work* (London: Sage).

Central Department Store 2001: 'History', <www.central.co.th/web/html/aboutus/history.htm>, accessed 4 November 2001.

Cerny, Philip G. 1994: 'Gridlock and Decline: Financial Internationalization, Banking Politics, and the American Political Process', in Richard Stubbs and Geoffrey Underhill (eds.), *Political Economy and the Changing Global Order* (London: Macmillan): 425–38.

Cerny, Philip G., Susanne Soederberg and Georg Menz (eds.) 2005: *Internalizing Globalization* (London: Palgrave).

Certeau, Michel de 1984: *The Practice of Everyday Life* (Berkeley: University of California Press).

Chakrabarty, Dipesh 2000: *Provincializing Europe* (Princeton: Princeton University Press).

Chan, Gerald 1999: *Chinese Perspectives on International Relations* (New York: Palgrave Macmillan).

Chapman, Stanley 1997: 'Characteristics of English Joint-stock Banking, 1826–1913', in Franz Bobasch and Hans Pohl (eds.), *Das Kreditwesen in der Neuzeit* (Munich: K. G. Saur): 57–67.

Chase-Dunn, Chris and Thomas D. Hall 1991: *Core/Periphery Relations in Pre-Capitalist Worlds* (Boulder, CO: Westview Press).

Chaudhuri, K. N. 1978: *Trade and Civilisation in the Indian Ocean* (Cambridge: Cambridge University Press).

Chen, Jiehua 2001: *Ershiyi Shiji Zhongguo Waijiao Zhanlüe* (Beijing: Shishi Chubanshe).

Chin, C. B. N. 2003: 'Visible Bodies, Invisible Work: State Practices Toward Migrant Women Domestic Workers in Malaysia', *Asian and Pacific Migration Journal* 12(1–2): 49–73.

Chirathivat, Bunsri ('Mae') 1998: *Nangseu Thi Raleuk Ngansob* ['Mother' Bunsri Chirathivat, *Funeral/Cremation Remembrance Book*]. Photocopy of manuscript from Chulalongkorn University, Bangkok, Thailand.

Chirathivat, Samrit 1992: *Nangseu Thi Raleuk Ngansob* [*Funeral/Cremation Remembrance Book*]. Unpaginated photocopy of manuscript from Chulalongkorn Library, Bangkok, Thailand. (Page numbers added by author).

Cholewinski, P. 1997: *Migrant Workers in International Human Rights Law* (Oxford: Clarendon Press).

Christaller, W. 1966: *Central Places in Southern Germany* (Englewood Cliffs: Prentice Hall), originally published in German, 1933.

Chwieroth, Jeffrey M. 2007: 'Neoliberal Economists and Capital Account Liberalization in Emerging Markets,' *International Organization* 61(2): 443–63.

Clapham, John H. 1944: *The Bank of England* (Cambridge: Cambridge University Press).

Clark, Gordon L. 2000: *Pension Fund Capitalism* (Oxford: Oxford University Press).

Clark, Gordon L., Nigel Thrift and Adam Tickell 2004: 'Performing Finance: The Industry, the Media and its Image', *Review of International Political Economy* 11(2): 289–310.

Clayton, James L. 2000: *The Global Debt Bomb* (New York: M.E. Sharpe).

Clowes, Michael J. 2000: *The Money Flood* (New York: John Wiley and Sons).

Cohen, Benjamin J. 1986: *In Whose Interest?* (New Haven: Yale University Press).
1996: 'Phoenix Risen: The Resurrection of Global Finance', *World Politics* 48(1): 268–96.

Cohen, Jillian Clare 2006: 'Civilizing Drugs: Intellectual Property Rights in Global Pharmaceutical Markets', in Brett Bowden and Leonard Seabrooke (eds.), *Global Standards of Market Civilization* (New York: Routledge): 175–187.

Cohn, Theodore H. 2000: *Global Political Economy* (New York: Addison Wesley Longman).

Collier, George A. 1994a: 'Roots of the Rebellion in Chiapas', *Cultural Survival Quarterly* 18(1): 14–18.
1994b: 'The New Politics of Exclusion: Antecedents to the Rebellion in Mexico', *Dialectical Anthropology* 19(1): 1–44.

Collins, Michael 1983: 'Long term growth of the English banking sector and the money stock', *Economic History Review* 36(3): 374–94.

Combs, Ann L. 2004: Remarks of Assistant Secretary Ann L. Combs at the 57th National Conference of the Profit Sharing/401(k) Council, 30 September, www.dol.gov/ebsa/newsroom/sp09004.html, accessed 1 November.

Connolly, William E. 1991: *Identity/Difference* (Ithaca: Cornell University Press).

Constable, N. 1997: *Maid to Order in Hong Kong* (Berkeley: University of California Press).

Cook, Joanne, Jennifer Roberts and Georgina Waylen (eds.) 2000: *Towards a Gendered Political Economy* (Basingstoke: Macmillan).

Cottrell, Philip L. 1991: 'The Domestic Commercial Banks and the City of London, 1870–1939', in Youssef Cassis (ed.), *Finance and Financiers in European History, 1880–1939* (Cambridge: Cambridge University Press): 39–61.

Courville, S. and N. Piper 2004: 'Harnessing Hope through NGO Activism', *The Annals of the American Academy of Political and Social Science* 592: 39–61.

Cox, D. 1997: 'The Vulnerability of Asian Women Migrant Workers to a Lack of Protection and to Violence', *Asian and Pacific Migration Journal* 6(1): 59–75.

Cox, Robert W. 1986: 'Social Forces, States and World Orders: Beyond International Relations Theory', in R. O. Keohane (ed.), *Neorealism and its Critics* (New York: Columbia University Press): 204–54.

　　1987: *Production, Power and World Order* (New York: Columbia University Press).

　　1992: 'Global Perestroika', in L. Panitch and R. Miliband (eds.), *The Socialist Register 1992* (London: Merlin Press): 26–43.

　　1996: *Approaches to World Order* [with Timothy J. Sinclair] (Cambridge: Cambridge University Press).

Crawford, Neta C. 2002: *Argument and Change in World Politics* (Cambridge: Cambridge University Press).

Crawford, Robert A. and Darryl S. L. Jarvis (eds.) 2001: *International Relations – Still an American Social Science?* (Albany, NY: SUNY Press).

Crook, Stephen 1999: 'Ordering Risks', in D. Lupton (ed.), *Risk and Sociocultural Theory* (Cambridge: Cambridge University Press): 160–85.

Culpepper, Pepper D. 2003: *Creating Cooperation* (Ithaca: Cornell University Press).

Cutler, Tony and Barbara Waine 2001: 'Social Insecurity and the Retreat From Social Democracy: Occupational Welfare in the Long Boom and Financialization', *Review of International Political Economy* 8(1): 96–117.

D'Arista, Jane 1999: 'Is a Mortgage Bubble Filling the Treasury Debt Vacuum?', *Flows of Funds: Review and Analysis* (September): 1–4.

Dangerfield, George 1935: *The Strange Death of Liberal England* (New York: Capricorn Books).

Darby, Phillip 2004: 'Pursuing the Political: A Postcolonial Rethinking of Relations International', *Millennium* 33(1): 1–32.

Davies, Matt 2005: 'The Public Spheres of Unprotected Workers?', *Global Society* 19(2): 131–54.

Davies, Matt and Michael Neimann 2002: 'The Everyday Spaces of Global Politics: Work, Leisure, Family', *New Political Science* 24(4): 557–77.

Davis, Gerard F., Doug McAdam, W. Richard Scott and Mayer N. Zald (eds.) 2005: *Social Movements and Organization Theory* (Cambridge: Cambridge University Press).

Davis, Lance E. and Robert E. Gallman 2001: *Evolving Financial Markets and International Capital Flows* (Cambridge: Cambridge University Press).

Daykin, Chris 2002: 'Experience and Trends in Occupational Pensions – Tour d'horizon in OECD Countries', in OECD (ed.), *Regulating Private Pension Schemes*, Private Pensions Series No. 4 (Paris: OECD): 9–26.

Dean, Mitchell 1999a: *Governmentality* (London: Sage).

1999b: 'Risk, Calculable and Incalculable', in D. Lupton (ed.): 131–59.

Denemark, Robert and Robert O'Brien 1997: 'Contesting the Canon: International Political Economy at UK and US Universities', *Review of International Political Economy* 4(1): 214–38.

Denemark, Robert, Jonathan Friedman, Barry K. Gills and George Modelski (eds.) 2000: *World System History* (New York: Routledge).

Deng, Gang 1997: 'The Foreign Staple Trade of China in the Pre-Modern Era', *International History Review* 19(2): 253–85.

Department of Social Security 1998: *A New Contract for Welfare*, Green Paper (London: Department of Social Security).

DeWalt, Billie R. and Martha W. Rees with Arthur D. Murphy 1994: *The End of Agrarian Reform in Mexico* (San Diego: Center for US-Mexican Studies).

di Leonardo, Micaela 1987: 'The Female World of Cards and Holidays: Women, Families, and the Work of Kinship', *Signs* 12: 440–53.

Dodd, Nigel 1994: *The Sociology of Money* (Cambridge: Polity Press)

Drainville, André C. 1994: 'International Political Economy in the Age of Open Marxism', *Review of International Political Economy* 1(1): 105–32.

2004: *Contesting Globalization* (London: Routledge).

Duangporn, Prinyanut 1992: 'Store Wars: The Sequel', *Nation(Thailand)*, Year in Review (December): 71.

Dunn, Kevin C. and Timothy M. Shaw (eds.) 2001: *Africa's Challenge to International Relations Theory* (Basingstoke: Palgrave Macmillan).

The Economist 2000: 'A Fresh Start for Chiapas', (12 August): 53–4.

The Economist 2001: 'Back to Square One in Chiapas', (5 May): 59.

The Economist 2002: 'Time to Grow Up: A Survey of Pensions', (16 February).

Ehrenreich, B. and A. Hochschild Russell (eds.) 2002: *Global Woman: Nannies, Maids and Sex Workers in the New Economy* (New York: Metropolitan Books).

Elman, Colin and Miriam Fendius Elman 2002: 'How Not to Be Lakatos Intolerant: Appraising Progress in IR Research', *International Studies Quarterly* 46(2): 231–62.

Elster, Jon 1989: *Nuts and Bolts for the Social Sciences* (Cambridge: Cambridge University Press).

Emmanuel, Arghiri 1972: *Unequal Exchange* (New York: Monthly Review Press).

Engelen, Ewald 2003: 'The Logic of Funding European Pension Restructuring and the Dangers of Financialisation', *Environment and Planning A* 35(8): 1357–72.

Epstein, Gerard 1985: 'The Triple Debt Crisis', *World Policy Journal* 2(4): 625–57.

Esim, S. and M. Smith (eds.) 2004: *Gender and Migration in Arab States* (Geneva: ILO).

Ewald, François 1991: 'Insurance and Risk', in G. Burchell, C. Gordon and P. Miller (eds.), *The Foucault Effect: Studies in Governmentality* (Hemel Hempstead: Harvester Wheatsheaf): 197–210.

Fairbank, John King 1942: 'Tributary Trade and China's Relations with the West', *Far Eastern Quarterly* 1(2): 129–49.

Fairbank, John King (ed.) 1968a: *The Chinese World Order* (Cambridge, MA: Harvard University Press).

Fairbank, John King 1968b: 'A Preliminary Framework' in John King Fairbank (ed.), *The Chinese World Order* (Cambridge, MA: Harvard University Press).

Fairbank, John King and Edwin O. Reischauer 1989: *China: Tradition and Transformation* (Sydney: Allen and Unwin).

Fairbank, John King and S. Y. Teng 1941: 'On the Ch'ing Tributary System', *Harvard Journal of Asiatic Studies* 6(2): 135–246.

Federal Deposit Insurance Corporation 1998: *History of the Eighties* (Washington, DC: FDIC).

Feldstein, Martin 1997: 'The Case for Privatization', *Foreign Affairs* 76(4): 24–38.

Fernández-Armesto, Felipe 2001: *Civilizations* (London: Pan Books).

Finnemore, Martha 1996: *National Interests in International Society* (Ithaca and London: Cornell University Press).

Finnemore, Martha and Kathryn Sikkink 1998: 'International Norms and Political Change', *International Organization* 52(4): 887–91.

Flynn, Dennis O. and Arturo Giráldez 1994: 'China and the Manila Galleons', in A. J. H. Latham and Heita Kawakatsu (eds.), *Japanese Industrialization and the Asian Economy* (London: Routledge): 71–90.

—— 2002: 'Cycles of Silver: Global Economic Unity through the Mid-Eighteenth Century', *Journal of World History* 13(2): 391–427.

Ford, Michele 2003: 'Beyond the *Femina* Fantasy: The Working-Class Woman in Indonesian Discourses of Women's Work', *Review of Indonesian and Malayan Affairs* 37(2): 83–113.

—— 2004: 'Organizing the Unorganizable: Unions, NGOs and Indonesian Migrant Labour', *International Migration* 42(5): 99–119.

—— 2006: 'After Nunukan: The Regulation of Indonesian Migration to Malaysia' in A. Kaur and I. Metcalf (eds.), *Mobility, Labour Migration and Border Controls in Asia* (Basingstoke: Palgrave Macmillan): 228–47.

Foucault, Michel 1979: 'On Governmentality', *Ideology and Consciousness* 6: 5–22.

Frank, Andre Gunder 1967: *Capitalism and Underdevelopment in Latin America* (London: Monthly Review Press).

—— 1998: *ReOrient* (Berkeley: University of California Press).

Frank, Andre Gunder and Barry K. Gills (eds.) 1996: *The World System* (London: Routledge).

Frey, Bruno 1986: *International Political Economics* (Oxford: Basil Blackwell).

Frieden, Jeffrey and Lisa L. Martin 2002: 'International Political Economy: Global and Domestic Interactions', in Ira Katznelson and Helen V. Milner (eds.), *Political Science* (New York: W.W. Norton & Co.): 118–46.

Fuerbringer, Jonathan 2004: 'Americans Pour Money Into Stock Funds in Near Record Amounts', *New York Times* (13 February).

Fukuyama, Francis 1992: *The End of History* (London: Hamish Hamilton).

Galvao, Gil 2001: 'Countering Money-Laundering: The FATF, the European Union and the Portuguese Experience, Past and Current Developments', paper presented at the United Nations Asia and Far East Institute, Tokyo, (15 January).

Gamble, Andrew and Anthony J. Payne (eds.) 1996: *Regionalism and World Order* (London: Macmillan).

George, Jim 1994: *Discourses of Global Politics* (Boulder: Lynne Rienner).

Germain, Randall D. 1997: *The International Organization of Credit* (Cambridge: Cambridge University Press).

2001: 'Global Financial Governance and the Problem of Inclusion,' *Global Governance* 7(4): 411–26.

Gernet, Jacques 1999: *A History of Chinese Civilization* (Cambridge: Cambridge University Press).

Gibson-Graham, J. K. 1996: *The End of Capitalism (As We Knew It)* (London: Blackwell Publishers).

2002: 'Beyond Global vs. Local: Economic Politics Outside the Binary Frame', in A. Herod and M. W. Wright (eds.), *Geographies of Power* (Oxford: Basil Blackwell): 25–60.

Giddens, Anthony 1976: *New Rules of Sociological Method*, II (Cambridge: Polity Press)

Gijsberts, Merové 2002. 'The Legitimation of Income Inequality in State-Socialist and Market Societies,' *Acta Sociologica* 45(4): 269–85.

Gilbreth, C. and Gerardo Otero 2001; 'Democratisation in Mexico. The Zapatista Uprising and Civil Society', *Latin American Perspectives* 28(4): 7–29.

Gill, Stephen 1990: *American Hegemony and the Trilateral Commission* (Cambridge: Cambridge University Press).

1995: 'Globalisation, Market Civilisation and Disciplinary Neoliberalism', *Millennium* 24(3): 399–423.

Gill, Stephen and David Law 1988: *Global Political Economy* (Baltimore: Johns Hopkins University Press).

Gilligan, George P. 2004: 'Overview: Markets, Offshore Sovereignty and Onshore Legitimacy', in Donato Masciandaro (ed.), *Global Financial Crime* (Aldershot: Ashgate): 7–59.

Gills, Barry K. 2001: 'Re-orienting the New (International) Political Economy, *New Political Economy* 6(2): 233–44.

Gills, D.-S. and N. Piper (eds.) 2002: *Women and Work in Globalising Asia* (London: Routledge).

Gilpin, Robert 1975: *US Power and the Multinational Corporation* (London: Macmillan).

1981: *War and Change in World Politics* (Cambridge: Cambridge University Press).

1987: *The Political Economy of International Relations* (Princeton: Princeton University Press).

2001: *Global Political Economy* (Princeton: Princeton University Press).

Ginsborg, Paul 2005: *The Politics of Everyday Life* (New Haven: Yale University Press).

Goffman, Erving 1959: *The Presentation of Self in Everyday Life* (Garden City, NY: Doubleday).

Goitein, S. D. 1964: *Jews and Arabs* (New York: Schocken Books).

Goody, Jack 2004: *Islam in Europe* (Cambridge: Polity).

Gourevitch, Peter A. 1986: *Politics in Hard Times* (Ithaca, NY: Cornell University Press).

Gramsci, Antonio 1971: *Selections from the Prison Notebooks*, Quintin Hoare and Geoffrey-Nowell Smith (ed. and trans.) (London: Lawrence and Wishart).

1996: *Prison Notebooks*, vol. 2, Joseph A. Buttigieg (ed. and trans.) (New York: Columbia University Press).

Greenhalgh, Susan 1994: 'De-Orientalizing the Chinese Family Firm', *American Ethnologist* 21(4): 746–75.

Greif, Avner 2006: *Institutions and History* (Cambridge: Cambridge University Press).

Gross, Daniel 2000: *Bull Run* (New York: Public Affairs).

Grugel, Jean and Wil Hout 1999a: 'Regions, Regionalism and the South', in J. Grugel and W. Hout (eds.), *Regionalism across the North-South Divide* (London: Routledge): 3–13.

1999b: *Regionalism across the North-South Divide* (London: Routledge).

Haas, Ernst 1959: *The Uniting of Europe* (Berkeley: University of California).

Halbfinger, David M. 2004: 'Campaigning Furiously, With Social Security in Tow', *New York Times* (18 October).

Hall, Peter A. and David Soskice 2001: *Varieties of Capitalism* (Oxford: Oxford University Press).

Hall, Thomas D. 1999: 'World-Systems and Evolution: An Appraisal', in P. N. Kardulias (ed.), *Leadership, Production and Exchange* (Lanham, MD: Rowman and Littlefield).

Hamashita, Takeshi 1990: *Kindai chūgoku no kokusaiteki keiki* (Tokyo: Tōkyō daigaku shuppankai).

1994: 'The Tribute Trade System and Modern Asia', in A. J. H. Latham and Heita Kawakatsu (eds.), *Japanese Industrialization and the Asian Economy* (London: Routledge): 91–107.

1999: 'Higashi ajiashi ni miru kai chitsujo' in Hamashita Takeshi (ed.), *Higashi ajia sekai no chiiki nettowaaku* (Tokyo: Yamakawa shuppansha).

Hardt, Michael and Antonio Negri 2000: *Empire* (Cambridge, MA: Harvard University Press).

Harmes, Adam 2001a: 'Mass Investment Culture', *New Left Review* 9 (May/June): 103–24.

2001b: *Unseen Power* (Toronto: Stoddart Publishing Company).

Harvey, David 1973: *Social Justice and the City* (London: Edward Arnold).

1982: *The Limits to Capital* (Oxford: Basil Blackwell).

Harvey, Neil 1996: 'Rural Reforms and the Zapatista Rebellion: Chiapas, 1988–1995', in Gerardo Otero (ed.), *Neoliberalism Revisited* (Boulder: Westview Press).

1998: *The Chiapas Rebellion* (Durham: Duke University Press).

Hasenclever, Andreas, Peter Mayer and Volker Rittberger 1997: *Theories of International Regimes* (Cambridge: Cambridge University Press).

Havel, Václav 1985: 'The Power of the Powerless', in Václav Havel (ed.), *The Power of the Powerless* (New York: M.E. Sharpe).

Hay, Colin 2004: 'Ideas, Interests and Institutions in the Comparative Political Economy of Great Transformations', *Review of International Political Economy* 11(1): 204–26.

He, Fangchuan 1998: '"Huayi Zhixu" Lun', *Beijing Daxue Xuebao (Zhexue Shehuikexue Ban)* 35(6): 30–45.

Healy, Kieran 2006: *Last Best Gifts* (Chicago: University of Chicago Press).

Hedström, Peter and Richard Swedberg (eds.) 1997: *Social Mechanisms* (Cambridge: Cambridge University Press).

Held, David, Anthony McGrew, David Goldblatt and Jonathon Perraton 1999: *Global Transformations* (Cambridge: Polity).

Helleiner, Eric 1994: *States and the Reemergence of Global Finance* (Ithaca: Cornell University Press).

1996: 'IPE and the Greens', *New Political Economy* 1(1): 59–77.

1999: 'State Power and the Regulation of Illicit Activity in Global Finance', in H. Richard Friman and Peter Andreas (eds.), *The Illicit Global Economy and State Power* (Lanham, MD: Littleman and Rowfield): 53–91.

Hendershott, Patrick H. 1994: 'Housing Finance in the United States', in Yukio Noguchi and James M. Poterba (eds.), *Housing Markets in the United States and Japan* (Chicago: University of Chicago Press): 65–86.

Henderson, David 1999: *The MAI Affair* (London: International Economic Program, Royal Institute of International Affairs).

Hernández Navarro, Luis 1998: 'The Escalation of the War in Chiapas', *NACLA Report on the Americas* 31(5): 7–10.

2004: 'The Global Zapatista Movement', America Program (Silver City: Interhemispheric Resource Centre).

Herod, A. 1995: 'The Practice of International Labor Solidarity and the Geography of the Global Economy', *Economic Geography* 71(4): 341–63.

2000: 'Implications of Just-in-Time Production for Union Strategy: Lessons From the 1998 General Motors-United Auto Workers Dispute', *Annals of the Association of American Geographers* 90(3): 521–47. (Publisher's erratum for figures published *Annals of the Association of American Geographers* (2001) 91(1): 200–2.)

2001: *Labor Geographies* (Guilford Press: New York).

2002: 'Towards a More Productive Engagement: Industrial Relations and Economic Geography Meet', *Labour and Industry* 13(2): 5–17.

2003a: 'Scale: The Local and the Global', in S. Holloway, S. Rice and G. Valentine (eds.), *Key Concepts in Geography* (Sage: London): 229–47.

2003b: 'Geographies of Labor Internationalism', *Social Science History* 27(4): 501–23.

2003c: 'Workers, Space, and Labor Geography', *International Labor and Working-Class History* 64(Fall): 112–38.

Hevia, James L. 1995: *Cherishing Men from Afar* (Durham: Duke University Press).

Hewison, K. and K. Young (eds.) 2006: *Transnational Migration and Work in Asia* (London: Routledge).

Hewitt de Alcántara, Cynthia (ed.) 1994: *Economic Restructuring and Rural Subsistence in Mexico* (San Diego: Centre for US-Mexican Studies).

Higgott, Richard 1991: 'Toward a Nonhegemonic IPE: An Antipodean Perspective', in Craig N. Murphy and Roger Tooze (eds.), *The New International Political Economy* (Boulder, CO: Lynne Rienner): 97–128.

Hildson, A. M. 2000: 'The Contemplacion Fiasco: The Hanging of a Filipino Domestic Worker in Singapore', in A. M. Hilsdon, M. Macintyre, V. Mackie and M. Stivens (eds.), *Human Rights and Gender Politics: Asia-Pacific Perspectives* (London: Routlege), 172–92.

Hinz, Richard 2000: 'Overview of the United States Private Pension System', in OECD (ed.), *Private Pensions Systems and Policy Issues: No. 1* (Paris: OECD): 23–42.

Hobsbawm, Eric 1987: *The Age of Empire, 1875–1914* (London: Weidenfield and Nicolson).

    1994: *Age of Extremes* (London: Penguin).

    1999 [1973]: 'Peasants and Politics', in Eric Hobsbawm (ed.), *Uncommon People: Resistance, Rebellion and Jazz* (London: Abacus).

Hobson, John A. 1906: 'The Taxation of Monopolies', *Independent Review* 9: 20–33.

Hobson, John M. 1997: *The Wealth of States* (Cambridge: Cambridge University Press).

    2000: *The State and International Relations* (Cambridge: Cambridge University Press).

    2002: 'What's at Stake in "Bringing Historical Sociology *Back* into International Relations"? Transcending "Chronofetishism" and "Tempocentrism" in International Relations', in Stephen Hobden and John M. Hobson (eds.), *Historical Sociology of International Relations* (Cambridge: Cambridge University Press): 3–41.

    2004: *The Eastern Origins of Western Civilisation* (Cambridge: Cambridge University Press).

    2007: 'Is Critical Theory Always *For* the White West and *For* Western Imperialism? Beyond Westphilian, Towards A Post-Racist, International Relations', *Review of International Studies* 33(S1): 91–116.

Hodgson, Marshall G. S. 1974: *The Venture of Islam*, 3 vols (Chicago: Chicago University Press).

    1993: *Rethinking World History* (Cambridge: Cambridge University Press).

Holquist, Michael 1990: *Dialogism: Bakhtin and his World* (London: Routledge).

Holsti, K. J. 1985: *The Dividing Discipline* (Boston, MA: Allen & Unwin).

Hopf, Ted 2002: 'Making the Future Inevitable: Legitimizing, Naturalizing, and Stabilizing the Transition in Estonia, Ukraine, and Uzbekistan', *European Journal of International Relations* 8(3): 403–36.

Hourani, Albert F. 1963: *Arab Seafaring in the Indian Ocean in Ancient and Early Medieval Times* (Beirut: Khayats).

Hsu, Cho-yun 1991: 'Applying Confucian Ethics to International Relations', *Ethics and International Affairs* 5: 15–31.

Hsü, Immanuel C. Y. 1960: *China's Entrance into the Family of Nations* (Cambridge, MA: Harvard University Press).

    1995: *The Rise of Modern China* (New York: Oxford University Press).

Huang, S. and B. Yeoh 2003: 'The Difference Gender Makes: State Policy and Contract Migrant Workers in Singapore', *Asian and Pacific Migration Journal* 12(1–2): 75–97.

Huang, Zhilian 1992: *Yazhou de huaxia zhixu* (Beijing: Zhongguo Renmin Daxue Chubanshe).

Hugo, G. 2002: 'Women's International Labour Migration', in K. Robinson and S. Bessell (eds.), *Women in Indonesia: Gender, Equity and Development* (Singapore: Institute of Southeast Asian Studies): 158–78.

Human Rights Watch 2004: 'Help Wanted: Abuses Against Female Migrant Domestic Workers in Indonesia and Malaysia', *Human Rights Watch* 16(9): 1–110.

—— 2005: *Maid to Order* (New York: Human Rights Watch).

Hurd, Ian 2002: 'Legitimacy, Power, and the Symbolic Life of the UN Security Council', *Global Governance* 8(1): 35–51.

Ikenberry, G. John 2001: *After Victory* (Princeton: Princeton University Press).

ILO (International Labour Organization) 2004: *Towards a Fair Deal for Migrant Workers in the Global Economy* (Geneva: ILO).

Ingham, Geoffrey 2004: *The Nature of Money* (Cambridge: Polity Press).

Inoguchi, Takashi 1975 'Dentōteki higashi ajia sekai chitsujo ron', *Kokusaihō gaikō zasshi* 73(5): 36–83.

Iredale, R., N. Piper and A. Ancog (2005), 'Impact of Ratifying the 1990 UN Convention on the Rights of All Migrant Workers and Members of Their Family: Case Studies of the Philippines and Sri Lanka', APMRN Working Paper No. 15, Asia Pacific Migration Research Network, Australian National University.

ITIO (International Tax and Investment Organisation) 2002: *Towards a Level Playing Field* (London: ITIO).

Iwabuchi, Koichi, Stephen Muecke and Mandy Thomas 2004: *Rogue Flows* (Hong Kong: Hong Kong University Press).

Jackson, Robert L. 1993: 'The Weight of Ideas in Decolonization: Normative Change in International Relations', in Judith Goldstein and Robert O. Keohane (eds.) *Ideas and Foreign Policy* (Ithaca: Cornell University Press): 111–38.

Jaffé, Edgar 1905: 'Die Konzentration des Bankwesens in England', *Bank-Archiv: Zeitschrift für Bank- und Bank Börsenwesen* 4(7): 102–6.

James, George G. M. 1954: *Stolen Legacy* (New York: Philosophical Library).

Johnston, Alastair Iain 1995: *Cultural Realism* (Princeton: Princeton University Press).

Jones, Eric L. 1988: *Growth Recurring* (Oxford: Clarendon Press).

Katzenstein, Peter J. 1976: 'International Relations and Domestic Structures: Foreign Economic Policies of Advanced Industrial States', *International Organization* 30(1): 1–45.

—— (ed.) 1978: *Between Power and Plenty* (Madison: University of Wisconsin Press).

—— 1985: *Small States in World Markets* (Ithaca: Cornell University Press).

—— (ed.) 1996a: *The Culture of National Security* (New York: Columbia University Press).

—— 1996b: *Cultural Norms and National Security* (Ithaca: Cornell University Press).

—— 2003: 'Small States and Small States Revisited', *New Political Economy* 8(1): 9–30.

Katzenstein, Peter J., Robert O. Keohane and Stephen D. Krasner 1998: 'International Organization and the Study of World Politics', *International Organization* 52(4): 645–85.

Katzenstein, Peter J. and Nobuo Okawara 2001/2: 'Japan and Asian-Pacific Security: Analytical Eclecticism, not Parsimony', *International Security* 26(2): 153–85.

Keck, Margaret E. and Kathryn Sikkink 1998: *Activists Beyond Borders* (Ithaca: Cornell University Press).

Kemshall, Hazel 2002: *Risk, Social Policy and Welfare* (Buckingham: Open University Press).

Kennickell, Arthur B., Martha Starr-McCluer and Brian J. Surette 2000: 'Recent Changes in US Family Finances: Results from the 1998 Survey of Consumer Finances', *Federal Reserve Bulletin* (January): 1–29.

Keohane, Robert O. 1984: *After Hegemony* (Princeton: Princeton University Press).

1988: 'International Institutions: Two Approaches', *International Studies Quarterly* 32(4): 379–96.

1998: 'Beyond Dichotomy: Conversations between International Relations and Feminist Theory', *International Studies Quarterly* 42(1): 193–8.

2002: *Power and Governance in a Partially Globalized World* (London: Routledge).

Keohane, Robert O. and Lisa L. Martin 2003: 'Institutional Theory as a Research Program', in Colin Elman and Miriam Fendius Elman (eds.), *Progress in International Relations Theory: Appraising the Field* (Cambridge, MA: MIT Press): 71–108.

Kerkvliet, Benedict J. Tria 1977: *The Huk Rebellion* (Berkeley: University of California Press).

1990: *Everyday Politics in the Philippines* (Berkeley: University of California Press).

2005: *The Power of Everyday Politics* (Ithaca: Cornell University Press).

2006: 'Agricultural Land in Vietnam: Markets Tempered by Family, Community and Socialist Practices', *Journal of Agrarian Studies* 6(3): 285–305.

Kindleberger, Charles P. 1973: *The World in Depression, 1929–1939* (Berkeley: University of California Press).

King, Gary, Robert O. Keohane and Sidney Verba 1994: *Designing Social Inquiry* (Princeton: Princeton University Press).

Knights, David 1997: 'Governmentality and Financial Services: Welfare Crises and the Financially Self-Disciplined Subject', in G. Morgan and D. Knights (eds.), *Regulation and Deregulation in European Financial Services* (Basingstoke: Macmillan): 216–36.

Knox, P. L. and S. A. Marston 2004: *Human Geography*, 3rd edition (Upper Saddle River, NJ: Pearson Education, Inc).

Kobata, Atsushi 1993: *Nihon dōkōgyōshi no kenkyū* (Tokyo: Shibunkaku).

Kofman, E. 2004: 'Gendered Migration and Entitlements in the European Union', unpublished background paper, United Nations Research Institute for Social Development, Geneva.

Kovic, Christine 2003: 'The Struggle for Liberation and Reconciliation in Chiapas, Mexico', *Latin American Perspectives* 30(3): 58–79.

Krasner, Stephen D. 1996: 'The Accomplishments of International Political Economy', in Steve Smith, Ken Booth and Marysia Zalewski (eds.), *International Theory: Positivism and Beyond* (Cambridge: Cambridge University Press): 108–27.

2001: 'Organised Hypocrisy in Nineteenth-century East Asia', *International Relations of the Asia-Pacific* 1(2): 173–97.

Kristensen, Peer Hull and Jonathan Zeitlin 2004: *Local Players in Global Games* (Oxford: Oxford University Press).

Lacker, Jeffrey M. 1995: 'Neighborhoods and Banking', *Economic Quarterly* 81(2): 13–38.

Laclau, Ernesto 1977: 'Feudalism and Capitalism in Latin America', *New Left Review* 67: 19–38.

Lairson, Thomas D. and David Skidmore 1993: *International Political Economy* (New York: Holt, Rinehart and Winston).

Lan, P.-C. 2003: 'Political and Social Geography of Marginal Insiders: Migrant Domestic Workers in Taiwan', *Asian and Pacific Migration Journal* 12(1–2): 99–125.

Landes, David S. 1998: *The Wealth and Poverty of Nations* (London: Little, Brown).

Langley, Paul 2002a: 'The Everyday Life of Global Finance', *BISA International Political Economy Group Papers in Global Political Economy*, No. 5.

2002b: *World Financial Orders* (London: Routledge/RIPE Series in Global Political Economy).

2004: 'In the Eye of the "Perfect Storm": The Final Salary Pension Crisis and Financialisation of Anglo-American Capitalism', *New Political Economy* 9(4): 539–58.

Larner, Wendy and Richard Le Heron 2002: 'The Spaces and Subjects of a Globalising Economy: A Situated Exploration of Method', *Environment and Planning D* 20(6): 753–74.

Latour, Bruno 1993: *We Have Never Been Modern*, C. Porter (trans.) (Cambridge, MA: Harvard University Press).

1996: 'On Actor-Network Theory: A Few Clarifications', *Soziale Welt* 47: 369–81.

Lavelle, Kathryn C. 2005: 'Moving in From the Periphery: Africa and the Study of International Political Economy', *Review of International Political Economy* 12(2): 364–79.

Law, L. 2002: 'Sites of Transnational Activism: Filipino Non-Government Organisations in Hong Kong', in B. S. A. Yeoh, P. Teo and S. Huang (eds.), *Gender Politics in the Asia-Pacific Region* (London: Routledge): 205–22.

2003: 'Transnational Cyberpublics: New Political Spaces for Labour Migrants in Asia', *Ethnic and Racial Studies* 26(2): 234–52.

Leaver, Richard 1994: 'International Political Economy and the Changing World Order: Evolution or Involution', in Richard Stubbs and Geoffrey Underhill (eds.), *Political Economy and the Changing Global Order* (London: Macmillan): 130–41.

Leaver, Richard and Leonard Seabrooke 2000: 'Can the IMF be Reformed?' in Walden Bello, Nicola Bullard and Kamal Malhortra (eds.), *Global Finance* (London: Zed Press): 96–113.

Ledyard, Gari 1983: 'Yin and Yang in the China-Manchuria-Korea Triangle' in Morris Rossabi (ed.), *China Among Equals* (Berkeley: University of California Press): 313–53.

Lefebvre, Henri 1976: *The Survival of Capitalism* (London: St. Martin's Press), originally published in French, 1973.

1991a. *The Production of Space* (Oxford: Basil Blackwell), originally published in French, 1974.

1991b: *Critique of Everyday Life*, I (London: Verso).

Lemke, Thomas 2001: ' "The Birth of Bio-politics": Michel Foucault's Lecture at the Collège de France on Neo-liberal Governmentality', *Economy and Society* 30(2): 190–207.

Leonhardt, David 2003: 'House Passes Bill to Loosen 401(k) Rules', *New York Times* (15 May).

Leyshon, Andrew and Nigel Thrift 1997: *Money/Space* (London: Routledge).

Lindio-McGovern, L. 2003: 'Labour Export in the Context of Globalisation: The Experience of Filipino Domestic Workers in Rome', *International Sociology* 18(3): 513–34.

Lipschutz, Ronnie D. 2001: 'Because People Matter: Studying Global Political Economy', *International Studies Perspective* 2(4): 321–39.

Lipson, Charles 1985: *Standing Guard* (Berkeley: University of California Press).

Lösch, A. 1954: *The Economics of Location* (New Haven: Yale University Press).

Loveband, A. 2003: 'Positioning the Product: Indonesian Migrant Women Workers in Contemporary Taiwan', SEARC/CAPSTRANS Working Paper No. 43 (Hong Kong: Southeast Asia Research Centre).

Lowe, R. 1982: 'Hours of Labour: Negotiating Industrial Legislation in Britain, 1919–39', *Economic History Review* 35(2): 254–71.

Lowy, Martin 1991: *High Rollers* (New York: Praeger).

Lyons, L. 2005: 'Transient Workers Count Too? The Intersection of Citizenship and Gender in Singapore's Civil Society', *Sojourn* 20(2): 208–48.

Mancall, Mark 1984: *China at the Centre* (New York: The Free Press).

Mann, Michael 1986: *The Sources of Social Power*, I (Cambridge: Cambridge University Press).

1993: *The Sources of Social Power*, II (Cambridge: Cambridge University Press).

Marchand, Marianne H. and Anne Sisson Runyan (eds.) 2000: *Gender and Global Restructuring* (London: Routledge).

Marcos, Subcommandate 1995: *Shadows of Tender Fury*, Frank Bardacke *et al.* (trans.) (New York: Monthly Review Press).

1997: 'The Fourth World War Has Begun', *Le Monde diplomatique* (September) English print edition, www.monde-diplomatique.fr/en, accessed 16 April 2000.

2000: 'Letter to Vicente Fox' (2 December) www.ezln.org, accessed 30 January 2001.

2001: Carlos Monsiváis and Hermann Belinghausen, 'Interview with Subcomandante Marcos', *La Jornada* [Mexico City] (8 January) www.ezln.org, accessed 30 January 2001.

Marcussen, Martin 2004: 'The Organisation for Economic Co-operation and Development as an Ideation Artist and Arbitrator: Reality or Dream?', in Bob Reinalda and Bertjan Verbeek (eds.), *Decision Making within International Organizations* (London: Routledge): 90–106.

Martin, Randy 2002: *Financialization of Daily Life* (Philadelphia: Temple University Press).

Martin, Ron 1999: 'Selling off the State: Privatisation, the Equity Market and the Geographies of Private Shareholding', in R. Martin (ed.), *Money and the Space Economy* (London: Wiley): 260–83.

Massey, Doreen 1995: *Spatial Divisions of Labour* (London: Macmillan).

May, Christopher 2004: 'Side-stepping TRIPs: The Strategic Deployment of Free and Open Source Software in Developing Countries', IPEG Papers in Global Political Economy, No. 9 (May). See www.bisa.ac.uk

McAdam, Doug, John McCarthy and Mayer N. Zald 1988: 'Social Movements', in Neil Smelser (ed.), *Handbook of Sociology* (Beverly Hills: Sage): 695–737.

McAdam, Doug, John McCarthy and Mayer N. Zald (eds.) 1996: *Comparative Perspectives on Social Movements* (Cambridge: Cambridge University Press).

McAdam, Doug, Sidney Tarrow and Charles Tilly 2001: *Dynamics of Contention* (Cambridge: Cambridge University Press).

McNamara, Kathleen R. 1998: *The Currency of Ideas* (Ithaca: Cornell University Press).

McNeill, William H. 1995: '*The Rise of the West* After Twenty-Five Years', in Stephen K. Sanderson (ed.), *Civilizations and World Systems* (London: Altamira Press): 303–20.

Menocal, María Rosa 2002: *The Ornament of the World* (Boston: Little, Brown).

Meyerson, Ann 1989: 'The Changing Structure of Housing Finance in the United States', in Sarah Rosenberry and Chester Hartman (eds.), *Housing Issues of the 1990s* (New York: Praeger): 155–89.

Mies, Maria 1986: *Patriarchy and Accumulation on a World Scale* (London: Zed Books).

Miller, Peter and Nikolas Rose 1990: 'Governing Economic Life', *Economy and Society* 19(1): 1–31.

Minns, Richard 2001: *The Cold War in Welfare* (London: Verso).

Mitchell, Olivia S. and Sylvester J. Schieber 1998: 'Defined Contribution Pensions: New Opportunities, New Risks', in Olivia S. Mitchell and Sylvester J. Schieber (eds.), *Living with Defined Contribution Pensions* (Philadelphia: University of Pennsylvania Press): 1–13.

Moore, John 1992: 'British Privatization: Taking Capitalism to the People', *Harvard Business Review* 70(1): 115–24.

Moravcsik, Andrew 1998: *The Choice for Europe* (Ithaca: Cornell University Press).

Morris-Suzuki, Tessa 1996: 'The Frontiers of Japanese Identity' in Stein Tønnesson and Hans Antlöv (eds.), *Asian Forms of the Nation* (Richmond: Curzon).

Morton, Adam David 2002: '"La Resurrección del Maíz": Globalisation, Resistance and the Zapatistas', *Millennium* 31(1): 27–54.

2003a: 'Structural Change and Neoliberalism in Mexico: "Passive Revolution" in the Global Political Economy', *Third World Quarterly* 24(4): 631–53.

2003b: 'Historicising Gramsci: Situating Ideas in and Beyond their Context', *Review of International Political Economy* 10(1): 118–46.

2005: 'Change within Continuity: The Political Economy of Democratic Transition in Mexico', *New Political Economy* 10(2): 181–202.

2007: *Unravelling Gramsci* (London: Pluto Press).

Mosley, Layna 2003a: *Global Capital and National Governments* (Cambridge: Cambridge University Press).

2003b: 'Attempting Global Standards: National Governments, International Finance, and the IMF's Data Regime', *Review of International Political Economy* 10(2): 331–62.

Muldrew, Craig 1998: *The Economy of Obligation* (Houndmills: Macmillan).

Munck, Geraldo L. 1995: 'Actor Formation, Social Co-ordination, and Political Strategy: Some Conceptual Problems in the Study of Social Movements,' *Sociology* 29 (November): 667–85.

Munnel, Alicia H. and Annika Sundén 2004: *Coming Up Short* (Washington, DC: Brookings Institution Press).

Murphy, Craig N. 1994: *International Organization and Industrial Change* (Cambridge: Polity).

Murphy, Craig N. and Roger Tooze (eds.) 1991a: *The New International Political Economy* (Boulder, CO: Lynne Rienner).

1991b: 'Introduction', in Craig N. Murphy and Roger Tooze (eds.), *The New International Political Economy* (Boulder, CO: Lynne Rienner): 1–7.

1991c: 'Getting Beyond the "Common Sense" of the IPE Orthodoxy', in Craig N. Murphy and Roger Tooze (eds.), *The New International Political Economy* (Boulder, CO: Lynne Rienner): 11–31.

Murphy, Craig N. and Douglas R. Nelson 2001: 'IPE: A Tale of two heterodoxies', *British Journal of Politics and International Relations* 3(3): 393–412.

Murray, Bruce 1980: *The People's Budget 1909–10* (Oxford: Oxford University Press).

Nakagawa, Takio 1987: 'Asian Retailing Revolution and Japanese Companies: The Thailand Case,' International Economic Conflict Discussion Paper no. 34 (Nagoya: Economic Research Center, University of Nagoya).

Neal, Larry 1998: 'The Financial Crisis of 1825 and the Restructuring of the English Financial System', *Federal Reserve Bank of St. Louis Review* (May/June): 53–76.

Nederveen Pieterse, Jan P. 1990: *Empire and Emancipation* (London: Pluto Press).

Nelson, M. Frederick 1946: *Korea and the Old Orders in Eastern Asia* (Baton Rouge, Louisiana: Louisiana State University Press).

Neuman, Stephanie G. (ed.) 1998: *International Relations Theory and the Third World* (New York: St. Martin's Press).

Neumann, Iver B. 1996: 'Self and Other in International Relations', *European Journal of International Relations* 2(2): 139–74.

1999: *Uses of the Other* (Minneapolis: University of Minnesota Press).

Neumann, Iver B. and Jennifer M. Welsh 1991: 'The Other in European Self-definition: an Addendum to the Literature on International Society', *Review of International Studies* 17(4): 327–48.

Nicholas, Tom 1999: 'Businessmen and Land Ownership in the Late Nineteenth Century', *Economic History Review* 52(1): 27–44.

Nicolaou, L. 1991: *Australian Unions and Immigrant Workers* (St Leonards: Allen & Unwin).

North, Douglass C. 1990: *Institutions, Institutional Change and Economic Performance* (Cambridge: Cambridge University Press).

2004: *Understanding the Process of Economic Change* (Princeton: Princeton University Press).

North, Douglass C. and Robert Thomas 1973: *The Rise of the Western World* (Cambridge: Cambridge University Press).

Nossal, Kim Richard 2001: 'Tales that Textbooks Tell: Ethnocentricity and Diversity in American Introductions to International Relations', in Robert A. Crawford and Darryl S. L. Jarvis (eds.) *International Relations – Still an American Social Science?* (Albany, NY: SUNY Press): 167–86.

NYSE (New York Stock Exchange) 2000: *Shareownership 2000* (New York: NYSE).

O'Brien, Robert 2000: 'Labour and IPE: Rediscovering Human Agency', in Ronen Palan (ed.) *Global Political Economy* (London: Routledge): 89–99.

O'Brien, Robert and Marc Williams 2004: *Global Political Economy* (Basingstoke: Palgrave Macmillan).

O'Brien, Robert, Anne Marie Goetz, Jan Aart Scholte and Marc Williams 2000: *Contesting Global Governance* (Cambridge: Cambridge University Press).

O'Malley, Pat 2000: 'Uncertain Subjects: Risk, Liberalism and Contract', *Economy and Society* 29(4): 460–81.

Oatley, Thomas and Robert Nabors 1998: 'Redistributive Cooperation: Market Failures, Wealth Transfers and the Basle Accord', *International Organization* 52(1): 35–54.

OECD 1998a: *Harmful Tax Competition* (Paris: OECD).

OECD 1998b: *Maintaining Prosperity in an Ageing Society* (Paris: OECD).

OECD 2004: *The 2004 Progress Report* (Paris: OECD).

Offer, Avner 1980: 'Ricardo's Paradox and the Movement of Rents in England, c. 1870–1910', *Economic History Review* 33(2): 236–52.

1981: *Property and Politics, 1870–1914* (Cambridge: Cambridge University Press).

Ogaya, C. 2003: 'Feminisation and Empowerment: Organisational Activities of Filipino Women Workers in Hong Kong and Singapore', in M. Tsuda (ed.), *Filipino Diaspora: Demography, Social Networks, Empowerment and Culture* (Quezon City: Philippine Social Science Council and UNESCO): 67–89.

Olesen, Thomas 2004: 'Globalising the Zapatistas: From Third World Solidarity to Global Solidarity?', *Third World Quarterly* 25(1): 255–67.

Ong, Aihwa 1991: 'The Gender and Labor Politics of Postmodernity', *Annual Review of Anthropology* 20: 279–309.

1999: *Flexible Citizenship* (Durham: Duke University Press).

Onuf, N. 1989: *World of Our Making* (Columbia: University of South Carolina Press).

Onuma, Yasuaki 2000: 'When was the Law of International Society Born? – An Inquiry of the History of International Law from an Intercivilizational Perspective', *Journal of the History of International Law* 2(1): 1–66.

Ōsawa, Kazuo 1975: 'Reichō chūki no min, shin to no kankei (1527–1682)', in Yamamoto Tatsurō (ed.), *Betonamu chūgoku kankei shi* (Tokyo: Yamakawa shuppansha).

Otero, Gerardo 2004: 'Contesting Neoliberal Globalism from Below: The EZLN, Indian Rights, and Citizenship', in Gerardo Otero (ed.), *Mexico in Transition* (London: Zed Books).

Pacey, Arnold 1991: *Technology in World Civilization* (Cambridge, MA: MIT Press).

Pagani, Fabrizio 2002: 'Peer Review: A Tool for Co-operation and Change: An Analysis of the OECD Working Method', General Secretariat, Directorate for Legal Affairs (Paris: OECD).

Palan, Ronen (ed.) 2000: *Global Political Economy* (London: Routledge).

2003: *The Offshore World* (Ithaca: Cornell University Press).

Parsons, Craig 2003: *A Certain Idea of Europe* (Ithaca: Cornell University Press).

Pasuk Phongpaichit and Chris Baker 1995: *Thailand: Economy and Politics* (Singapore: Oxford University Press).

1998: *Thailand's Boom and Bust* (Chiang Mai: Silkwork Books).

Pauly, Louis W. 1997: *Who Elected the Bankers?* (Ithaca: Cornell University Press).

Payne, Anthony 1998: 'The New Political Economy of Area Studies', *Millennium* 27(2): 253–73.

2005: *The Global Politics of Unequal Development* (Houndmills, Basingstoke: Palgrave Macmillan).

Peters, Michael A. 2001: *Poststructuralism, Marxism and Neoliberalism* (Oxford: Rowman & Littlefield).

Peterson, V. Spike 2003: *A Critical Rewriting of Global Political Economy* (London: Routledge).

Petras, James and Henry Veltmeyer 2002: 'The Peasantry and the State in Latin America: A Troubled Past, An Uncertain Future', *The Journal of Peasant Studies* 29(3/4): 41–82.

Phillips, Nicola (ed.) 2005: *Globalizing International Political Economy* (Houndmills: Palgrave Macmillan).

Philpott, Daniel 2001: *Revolutions in Sovereignty* (Princeton: Princeton University Press).

Pijl, Kees Van der 1998: *Transnational Classes and International Relations* (London: Routledge).

Pinches, M. 2001: 'Class and National Identity: The Case of Filipino Migrant Workers', in J. Hutchison and A. Brown (eds.), *Organising Labour in Globalising Asia* (London: Routledge), 187–213.

Piper, Nicola 2003: 'Bridging Gender, Migration and Governance: Theoretical Possibilities in the Asian Context', *Asian and Pacific Migration Journal* 12(1–2): 21–48.

2005: 'Labour Migration, Governance and Transnationalisation of Rights', paper presented at the Conference on Governing International Migration: Current Issues, Challenges and Dilemmas, Ottawa (27–28 May).

Piper, Nicola and Keiko Yamanaka (eds.) 2003: 'Gender, Migration and Governance in Asia', Special Issue, *Asian and Pacific Migration Journal* 12(1–2).

Piper, Nicola and Robyn Iredale 2003: 'Identification of the Obstacles to the Signing and Ratification of the UN Convention on the Protection of the Rights of All Migrant Workers 1990: The Asia Pacific Perspective', APMRN Working Paper No. 14 (Canberra: Australian National University).

Pirenne, Henri 1939: *Mohammed and Charlemagne* (New York: Norton).

Polanyi, Karl 1944/1957: *The Great Transformation* (New York: Beacon Press).

Pollin, Robert 1995: 'Financial Structures and Egalitarian Economic Policy', *New Left Review* 214 (November–December): 26–61.

Pomeranz, Kenneth 2000: *The Great Divergence* (Princeton: Princeton University Press).

Porter, Tony 2001: 'The Democratic Deficit in the Institutional Arrangements for Regulating Global Finance', *Global Governance* 7(4): 427–39.

Porter, Tony and Michael Webb, 2004: 'The Role of the OECD in the Orchestration of Global Knowledge Networks', paper presented to the International Studies Association meeting, Montreal (March).

Prasad, Monica 2006: *The Politics of Free Markets* (Chicago: University of Chicago Press).

Preda, Alex 2001: 'The Rise of the Popular Investor: Financial Knowledge and Investing in England and France, 1840–1880', *The Sociological Quarterly* 42(2): 205–32.

Radaelli, Claudio M. 1999: "Harmful Tax Competition in the European Union: Policy Narratives and Advocacy Coalitions', *Journal of Common Market Studies* 37(4)(December): 661–82.

Raghuram, P. 2000: 'Gendering Skilled Migratory Streams: Implications for Conceptualisations of Migration', *Asian and Pacific Migration Journal* 9(4): 429–57.

Ramamurthy, B. 2003: *International Labour Migrants*, SIDA Studies no. 8 (Stockholm: Swedish International Development Cooperation Agency).

Reus-Smit, Christian 1999: *The Moral Purpose of the State* (Princeton: Princeton University Press).

Reuters 2003: 'For First Time, More Than 50% of US Households Own Stock', *New York Times* (22 January).

Ring, Patrick 2002: 'The Implications of the "New Insurance Contract" for UK Pension Provision: Rights, Responsibilities and Risks', *Critical Social Policy* 22(4): 551–71.

Robinson, William I. 2003: *Transnational Conflicts* (London: Verso).

Rodan, Gary, Kevin Hewison and Richard Robison (eds.) 1997: *The Political Economy of South-East Asia* (Melbourne: Oxford University Press).

Rodinson, Maxime 1974: *Islam and Capitalism* (London: Allen Lane).

Rosamond, Ben 2005: 'The Uniting of Europe and the Foundations of EU Studies: Revisiting the Neofunctionalism of Ernst B. Haas', *Journal of European Public Policy* 12(2): 237–54.

Rosow, Stephen J., Naeem Inayatullah and Mark Rupert (eds.) 1994: *The Global Economy as Political Space* (Boulder, CO: Lynne Rienner).

Ross, John 1995: *Rebellion from the Roots* (Monroe: Common Courage Press).

Rossabi, Morris (ed.) 1983: *China Among Equals* (Berkeley: University of California Press).

Ruggie, John G. 1982: 'International Regimes, Transactions, and Change: Embedded Liberalism in the Postwar Economic Order', *International Organization* 36(2): 379–415.

Said, Edward W. 1978: *Orientalism* (Harmondsworth: Penguin).

Sakayori, Masashi 1993: 'Kai shisō no shosō' in Arano Yasunori, Ishii Masatoshi and Murai Shōsuke (eds.), *Ajia no nakano nihonshi* (vol. 5): *jiishiki to sōgo rikai* (Tokyo: Tōkyō daigaku shuppankai).

Sallaz, Jeffrey J. 2007: *Casino Capitalisms* (Princeton: Princeton University Press).

Santomero, Anthony M. and David L. Eckles 2000: "The Determinants of Success in the New Financial Services Environment: Now That Firms Can Do Everything, What Should They Do, and Why Should Regulators Care?" *Economic Policy Review* (Federal Reserve Bank of New York) 6(4): 11–23.

Scalabrini Migration Center 2004: *Hearts Apart* (Manila: Scalabrini Migration Center).

Schein, Louisa 2001: 'Chinese Consumerism and the Politics of Envy: Cargo in the 1990s?', in Xudong Zhang (ed.), *Whither China?* (Durham: Duke University Press): 285–314.

Schelling, Thomas C. 1997: 'Social Mechanisms and Social Dynamics,' in Peter Hedström and Richard Swedberg (eds.), *Social Mechanisms* (Cambridge: Cambridge University Press): 32–44.

Schimmelfennig, Frank 2001: 'The Community Trap: Liberal Norms, Rhetorical Action, and the Eastern Enlargement of the European Union', *International Organization* 55(1): 47–80.

Schimmelfennig, Frank and Ulrich Sedelmeier (eds.) 2005: *The Europeanization of Eastern Europe* (Ithaca: Cornell University Press).

Schwartz, Benjamin 1964: *In Search of Wealth and Power* (Cambridge: Belknap Press).

Schwartz, Herman M. 1994: *States Versus Markets* (New York: St. Martin's Press).

Scott, Catherine 1995: *Gender and Development* (Boulder: Lynne Rienner).

Scott, James C. 1976: *The Moral Economy of the Peasant* (New Haven: Yale University Press).

  1987: *Weapons of the Weak* (New Haven: Yale University Press).

  1990: *Domination and the Arts of Resistance* (New Haven: Yale University Press).

Seabrooke, Leonard 2001: *US Power in International Finance* (Basingstoke: Palgrave).

  2004: 'The Economic Taproot of US Imperialism: The Bush Rentier Shift', *International Politics* 41(3): 293–318.

  2005a: 'Civilizing Tax Regimes: The International Monetary Fund and Tax Reform in East Asia', paper presented at the International Studies Association annual conference, Hawaii (1–5 March).

  2005b: 'John A. Hobson as an Economic Sociologist', *Economic Sociology* 7(1): 26–35. http://econsoc.mpifg.de.

  2006a: *The Social Sources of Financial Power* (Ithaca: Cornell University Press).

2006b: 'Civilizing Global Capital Markets: Room to Groove?', in Brett Bowden and Leonard Seabrooke (eds.), *Global Standards of Market Civilization* (New York: Routledge): 146–60.

2007a: 'Legitimacy Gaps in the World Economy: Explaining the Sources of the IMF's Legitimacy Crisis', *International Politics* 44(2/3): 250–68.

2007b: 'Why We Need Historical Sociology in Political Economy', *International Politics* 44(4): 390–413.

2007c: 'The Everyday Social Sources of Economic Crises: From "Great Frustrations" to "Great Revelations" in Interwar Britain', *International Studies Quarterly* 51: forthcoming.

Seabrooke, Leonard and Ole Jacob Sending 2006. 'Norms as Doing Things: Cultural Toolkits and Strategic Action in World Politics', mimeo, Norwegian Institute of International Affairs.

Sending, Ole Jacob 2002. 'Constitution, Choice and Change: Some Problems with the "Logic of Appropriateness" and its Use in Constructivist Theory', *European Journal of International Relations* 8(4): 443–70.

2004: 'How Does Knowledge Matter? The Formation, Content, and Change of International Population Policy', Report 86, PhD Dissertation, Department of Administration and Organization Theory, University of Bergen.

Sending, Ole Jacob and Iver B. Neumann 2007: 'Governance to Governmentality: Analyzing NGOs, States, and Power', *International Studies Quarterly* 50(3): 651–72.

Sharman, J. C. 2004: 'The Effective Participation of Small States in International Financial Fora', *Commonwealth Economic Papers* Report No. 60 (London): 59–77.

2006: *Havens In a Storm* (Ithaca: Cornell University Press).

Sheppard, David K. 1971: *The Growth and Role of UK Financial Institutions, 1880–1962* (London: Methuen & Co).

Sidney, Mara S. 2003: *Unfair Housing: How National Policy Shapes Community Action* (Lawrence: University Press of Kansas).

Sil, Rudra and Peter J. Katzenstein 2005: 'What is Analytic Eclecticism and Why Do We Need It? A Pragmatist Perspective on Problems and Mechanisms in the Study of World Politics', Paper presented to the Annual Meeting of the American Political Science Association (1–4 September) Washington, DC.

Silliman, G. S. and L. G. Noble (eds.) 1998: *Organizing for Democracy* (Honolulu: University of Hawaii Press).

Simmons, Beth A. and Zachary Elkins 2004: 'The Globalization of Liberalization: Policy Diffusion in the International Political Economy', *American Political Science Review* 98(1): 171–89.

Sinclair, Timothy J. 2005: *The New Masters of Capital* (Ithaca: Cornell University Press).

Smith, Neil 1990: *Uneven Development* (Oxford: Basil Blackwell).

Snow, David A. and Pamela E. Oliver 1995: 'Social Movements and Collective Behavior: Social Psychological Dimensions and Considerations', in Karen S. Cook, Gary Alan Fine and James S. House (eds.), *Sociological Perspectives on Social Psychology* (Boston: Allyn and Bacon): 571–99.

Soja, Edward W. 1989: *Postmodern Geographies* (London: Verso).

Spero, Joan E. 1992: *The Politics of International Economic Relations* (London: Routledge).

SSA (Social Security Administration) 2004: *The Future of Social Security*, SSA Publication No. 05-10055, www.ssa.gov/pubs/10055.html, accessed 1 November 2004.

Stahl, C. W. 2000: 'Trade in Labour Services and Migrant Worker Protection with Special Reference to East Asia', Centre for Asia Pacific Social Transformation Studies, Universities of Wollongong and Newcastle, www.uow.edu.au/research/centres/capstrans/pubs/stahl.html, accessed July 2001.

Stahl, C. W. and R. T. Appleyard 1992: 'International Manpower Flows in Asia: An Overview', *Asian and Pacific Migration Journal* 3(3–4): 417–76.

Stahler-Stock, Richard 1998: 'The Lessons of Acteal', *NACLA Report on the Americas* 31(5): 11–14.

Steinberg, Marc W. 1998: 'Tilting the Frame: Considerations on Collective Action Framing from a Discursive Turn', *Theory and Society* 27(6): 845–72.

1999: 'The Talk and Back Talk of Collective Action: A Dialogic Analysis of Repertoires of Discourse among Nineteenth-Century English Cotton Spinners', *American Journal of Sociology* 105(3): 736–80.

Steuerle, Eugene 2001: 'Tax Policy From 1990 to 2001', paper presented at the Conference on American Economic Policy in the 1990s, Center for Business and Government, John F. Kennedy School of Government, Harvard University, Cambridge, MA, 27–30.

Stiglitz, Joseph 2003: *The Roaring Nineties* (London: Allen Lane).

Strange, Susan 1987: 'The Persistent Myth of Lost Hegemony', *International Organization* 41(4): 551–74.

1988: *States and Markets* (Oxford: Blackwell).

1996: *The Retreat of the State* (Cambridge: Cambridge University Press).

1998: *Mad Money* (Manchester: Manchester University Press).

Stubbs, Richard and Geoffrey Underhill (eds.) 1994: *Political Economy and the Changing Global Order* (London: Macmillan).

Suzuki, Shogo 2005: 'Japan's Socialization into Janus-Faced European International Society', *European Journal of International Relations* 11(1): 137–64.

Sylvester, Christine 1996: 'The Contributions of Feminist Theory to International Relations', in Steve Smith, Ken Booth and Marysia Zalewski (eds.), *International Theory: Positivism and Beyond* (Cambridge: Cambridge University Press), 254–78.

Tanaka, Takeo 1975: *Chūsei taigai kankeishi* (Tokyo: Tōkyō daigaku shuppankai).

Tarrow, Sidney 1994: *Power in Movement* (Cambridge: Cambridge University Press).

Tashiro, Kazui 1982: 'Foreign Relations during the Edo Period: Sakoku Reexamined', Susan Downing Videen (trans.), *Journal of Japanese Studies* 8(2): 283–306.

Tétreault, Mary Ann 1994: *Women and Revolution in Africa, Asia, and the New World* (Columbia, SC: University of South California Press).

Tétreault, Mary Ann and Ronnie D. Lipschutz 2005: *Global Politics as if People Mattered*, Lanham: Rowman & Littlefield.

Thelen, Kathleen 2004: *How Institutions Evolve* (Cambridge: Cambridge University Press).

Thompson, E. P. 1978: 'Eighteenth-Century English Society: Class Struggle Without Class?', *Social History* 3(2): 133–65.

Tickner, Arlene B. 2002: 'Hearing Latin American Voices in International Relations Studies', *International Studies Perspectives* 4(4): 325–50.

2003: 'Seeing IR Differently: Notes from the Third World', *Millennium* 32(2): 295–324.

Tickner, J. Ann 1992: *Gender in International Relations* (New York: Columbia University Press).

1997: 'You Just Don't Understand: Troubled Engagements between Feminists and International Relations Theorists', *International Studies Quarterly* 41(4): 611–32.

Tilly, Charles 1978: *From Mobilization to Revolution* (Reading: Addison-Wesley).

Toby, Ronald P. 1991: *State and Diplomacy in Early Modern Japan* (Stanford: Stanford University Press).

Tooze, Roger 1988: 'The Unwritten Preface: "International Political Economy" and Epistemology', *Millennium* 17(2): 285–94.

Tourist Authority of Thailand 2005: 'International Tourist Arrivals to Thailand by Country of Residence', www2.tat.or.th/stat/download/1298/nat-1-12.xls, accessed May 2005.

True, Jacqui 2003: *Gender, Globalization, and Postsocialism* (New York: Columbia University Press).

Truong, T.-D. 1996: 'Gender, International Migration, and Social Reproduction. Implications for Theory, Policy, Research and Networking', *Asian and Pacific Migration Journal* 5: 27–52.

Tsukamoto, Manabu 1979: 'Edo jidai ni okeru "i" kannen ni tsuite', *Nihon rekishi* 371: 1–18.

1982: 'Tsunayoshi seiken no rekishiteki ichi o megutte', *Nihonshi kenkyū* 236: 38–56.

Turner, Margarey Austin, Fred Freiberg, Erin B. Godfrey, Carla Herbig, Diane Levy and Robin E. Smith 2002: *All Other Things Being Equal* (Washington, DC: The Urban Institute).

Udovitch, Abraham L. 1970: *Partnership and Profit in Medieval Islam* (Princeton: Princeton University Press).

UN General Assembly 2004: *Women and International Migration* (New York: United Nations).

UNDCCP (United Nations Drug Control and Crime Prevention) 1998: Jack A. Blum, Michael Levi, R. Thomas Naylor and Phil Williams, *Financial Havens, Banking Secrecy and Money Laundering* (New York: United Nations).

United Nations 2003: *Levels and Trends of International Migration to Selected Countries in Asia* (New York: Department of Economic and Social Affairs Population Division, United Nations).

Veltmeyer, Henry 2000: 'The Dynamics of Social Change and Mexico's EZLN', *Latin American Perspectives* 27(5): 88–110.

Vilas, Carlos M. 1996: 'Are There Left Alternatives? A Discussion from Latin America', in Leo Panitch (ed.), *The Socialist Register* (London: Merlin Press): 264–85.

Villalba, M.-A. C. 1997: 'Protecting Migrant Workers' Rights: Government-NGO Conflict and Cooperation', in M. A. Wui and M. G. S. Lopez (eds.), *Philippine Democracy Agenda, Vol. 2: State-Civil Society Relations in Policy-Making* (Quezon City: Third World Studies Centre).

Wade, Robert 1996: 'Globalization and its Limits: Reports of the Death of the National Economy are Greatly Exaggerated', in Suzanne Berger and Ronald Dore (eds.), *National Diversity and Global Capitalism* (Ithaca: Cornell University Press): 60–89.

Wæver, Ole 1998: 'The Sociology of a not so International Discipline: American and European Developments in IR', *International Organization* 52(4): 687–727.

Wagner, Wolfgang and Nicky Hayes 2005: *Everyday Discourse and Common Sense* (Basingstoke: Palgrave Macmillan).

Walkowitz, Judith 1992: *City of Dreadful Delight* (Chicago: University of Chicago Press).

Wallerstein, Immanuel 1974: *The Modern World System*, I (London: Academic Press).

1979: *The Capitalist World Economy* (Cambridge: Cambridge University Press).

1996: 'World System Versus World-Systems: A Critique', in Andre Gunder Frank and Barry K. Gills (eds.), *The World System* (London: Routledge): 292–6.

Waltz, Kenneth N. 1979: *Theory of International Politics* (New York: McGraw Hill).

Wang, Yi-T'ung 1953: *Official Relations between China and Japan 1368–1594*, Harvard-Yenching Institute Studies IX (Cambridge, MA: Harvard University Press).

Wang, Zhenping 1997: *Han tang zhongri guanxi lun* (Taipei: Wenjin chubanshe).

Watson, Matthew 2005: *Foundations of International Political Economy* (Houndmills: Palgrave Macmillan).

2006: 'Civilizing Standards and the Moral Self', in Brett Bowden and Leonard Seabrooke (eds.), *Global Standards of Market Civilization* (New York: Routledge): 45–59.

Watts, J. 2003: 'Mexico-US Migration and Labor Unions: Obstacles to Building Cross-Border Solidarity', Working Paper No. 79 (San Diego: Center for Comparative Immigration Studies, University of California) http://repositories.cdlib.org/ccis/papers/workg79.

Waylen, Georgina 1999: 'IPE, Development and Gender', *Journal of International Relations and Development* 2(4): 435–46.

2006: 'You Still Don't Understand: Why Troubled Engagements Continue Between Feminists and (Critical) IPE', *Review of International Studies* 32(1): 145–64.

Webb, Michael C. 2004: 'Defining the Boundaries of Legitimate State Practice: Norms, Transnational Actors and the OECD's Project on Harmful Tax Competition', *Review of International Political Economy* 11(4): 787–827.

Weber, Adolf 1902: *Depositenbanken und Spekulationsbanken* (Leipzig: Duncker & Humblot).

Weber, Max 1956: *Staatssoziologie* (Berlin: Duncker & Humblot).

1978: *Economy and Society*, I (Berkeley: University of California Press).

1998: *The Agrarian Sociology of Ancient Civilizations* (London: Verso).

Wechsler, William 2001: 'Follow the Money', *Foreign Affairs* 80(4): 40–57.

Wee, V. 2003: 'Whose Problem is it Anyway and Why Does it Matter? Structured Vulnerabilities and Innovative Alliances Among Migrant Women Workers in East and Southeast Asia', Paper presented to the Third International Convention of Asia Scholars, Singapore (19–22 August).

Wee, V. and A. Sim 2005: 'Hong Kong as a Destination for Migrant Domestic Workers', in Shirlena Huang *et al.* (eds.), *Asian Women as Transnational Domestic Workers* (Singapore: Asian MetaCenter and Marshall Cavendish International): 175–209.

Weinberg, Bill 2000: *Homage to Chiapas* (London: Verso).

Weiss, Linda 1999: 'Globalisation and National Governance: Antinomy or Interdependence?', *Review of International Studies* 25(5): 59–88.

Weiss, Meredith 2004: 'Transnational Activism by Malaysians: Foci, Tradeoffs and Implications', in N. Piper and A. Uhlin (eds.), *Transnational Activism in Asia* (London: Routledge): 129–48.

Wendt, Alexander 1994: 'Collective Identity Formation and the International State', *American Political Science Review* 88(2): 384–96.

1999: *Social Theory of International Politics* (Cambridge: Cambridge University Press).

Whitworth, Sandra 1994: *Feminism and International Relations* (London: Macmillan).

Wicksell, Knut 1997: *Nationalekonomiska essäer* (Stockholm: City University Press).

Widmaier, Wesley W., Mark Blyth and Leonard Seabrooke 2007: 'The Social Construction of Wars and Crises as Openings for Change', *International Studies Quarterly*, 51: forthcoming.

Wilson, Ara 2003: 'Bangkok, the Bubble City', in Jane Schneider and Ida Susser (eds.), *Wounded Cities* (Oxford: Berg Press): 203–26.

2004: *The Intimate Economies of Bangkok* (Berkeley: University of California Press).

Wink, André 1990: *Al-Hind: The Making of the Indo-Islamic World*, I (Leiden: E. J. Brill).

Wolf, Eric R. 1982: *Europe and the People Without History* (Berkeley: University of California Press).

World Bank 1994: *Averting the Old Age Crisis* (New York: Oxford University Press).

Yamanaka, K. and N. Piper 2004: 'Gendered Migration, Entitlements and Civil Action in Asia', commissioned background paper for the United Nations Research Institute for Social Development, Geneva.

Yanagisako, Sylvia 2002: *Producing Culture and Capital* (Princeton: Princeton University Press).

Yang, Lien-sheng 1952: *Money and Credit in China* (Cambridge, MA: Harvard University Press).

1968: 'Historical Notes on the Chinese World Order', in John King Fairbank (ed.), *The Chinese World Order* (Cambridge, MA: Harvard University Press): 20–33.

Yeoh, Brenda S. A. and Shirlena Huang 1999: 'Spaces at the Margin: Migrant Domestic Workers and the Development of Civil Society in Singapore', *Environment and Planning A* 31(7): 1147–67.

Yeoh, Brenda, Shirlena Huang and T. Devasahayam 2004: 'Diasporic Subjects in the Nation: Foreign Domestic Workers, the Reach of the Law and Civil Society in Singapore', *Asian Studies Review* 28(1): 7–23.

Zhang, Yongjin 2001: 'System, Empire and State in Chinese International Relations', *Review of International Studies* 27(5): 43–63.

Index

243